CALIFORNIA

TOP SIGHTS, AUTHENTIC EXPERIENCES

Nate Cavalieri, Brett Atkinson, Andrew Bender,
Sara Benson, Alison Bing, Cristian Bonetto, Jade Bremner,
Michael Grosberg, Ashley Harrell, Josephine Quintero,
Andrea Schulte-Peevers, Helena Smith, John A Vlahides,
Clifton Wilkinson

Contents

Welcome to California

From misty Northern California redwood forests to sun-kissed Southern California beaches, the siren call of the Golden State seduces travelers with its heart-aching beauty – not to mention its wildly diverse cultures, fabulous cities and mouthwatering food.

On the edge of a continent, this is a place where it seems like anything can happen – and often does. California's cities pulse with the singular energy of its people, and take on a twinkling magic as the sun sets over the Pacific and lights begin to sparkle across golden hillsides. Lamps illuminate San Diego's Gaslamp Quarter, the Hollywood sign glows as bright as the moon over LA, and Bay Bridge lights welcome San Francisco arrivals with a wink and a shimmy. Consider this your invitation to come out and play, and join the crowds at LA's star-studded nightclubs and movie palaces, San Francisco's historic LGBT hot spots and San Diego's brewpubs. Tomorrow there will be neighborhoods, beaches, spas and boutiques to explore – but tonight is a night on the town like no other.

Far from these cities, California's natural beauty is even more magical. It's no wonder that this is the home of Hollywood; the state's natural features are pure drama themselves, shaped by tectonic upheavals that threaten to shake it right off the continent. After 19th-century mining, logging and oil-drilling threatened the state's natural splendors, California's pioneering environmentalists rescued old-growth trees, reclaimed rivers and cleaned the beaches, ultimately creating national and state parks that continue to astound visitors today.

On the edge of a continent, this is a place where it seems like anything can happen.

A resort in Palm Springs (p182)

Crescent City

Weed ▲ Mt Shasta (14,179ft)

Alturas

Redwood National Park

Arcata
Eureka

Redding

Susan

Red Bluff

Leggett

Chico

Nevada City

Trucke

Mendocino

Coastal Range

Sacramento River

Calistoga

Sacramento

Santa Rosa

Sonoma

Napa

Sutter Creek

San Rafael

Stockton

Sc

Oakland

San Joaquin River

Palo Alto

San Jose

Santa Cruz

Monterey Bay

Monterey

Diablo Range

Cambria

Paso Robles

Morro Bay

San Luis Obispo

PACIFIC OCEAN

Santa Ba.

0
0
200 km
100 miles

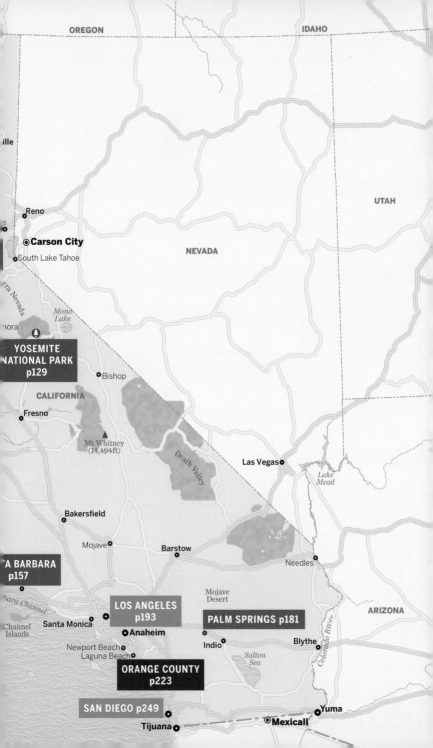

OREGON

IDAHO

ille

Reno

◉ Carson City

South Lake Tahoe

NEVADA

UTAH

Sierra Nevada

Mono Lake

🌲
YOSEMITE
NATIONAL PARK
p129

CALIFORNIA

Bishop

Fresno

Mt Whitney
(14,494ft)

Death Valley

Las Vegas

Lake Mead

Bakersfield

Mojave

Barstow

Needles

A BARBARA
p157

bara Channel

Channel
Islands

Santa Monica

LOS ANGELES
p193

Anaheim

Mojave
Desert

PALM SPRINGS p181

ARIZONA

Colorado River

Newport Beach
Laguna Beach

Indio

Salton
Sea

Blythe

ORANGE COUNTY
p223

SAN DIEGO p249

Tijuana

◉ Mexicali

Yuma

Sunrise at Lake Tahoe (p112)
DON SMITH / GETTY IMAGES ©

Plan Your Trip
California's Top 12

ALEX MENENDEZ / 500PX ©

San Francisco

A wonder of food, culture and beauty

As anyone who has ever clung to the side of a cable car can tell you, this city gives you a heck of a ride, from the Marina's chic waterfront to the edgy (p35) Mission District. And just when you think you have a grasp on the 'Paris of the West,' you turn another corner to find a brightly painted alleyway mural, a filigreed Victorian roofline or a hidden stairway leading up to bay-view panoramas that will entirely change your outlook. Left: Golden Gate Bridge (p38); Right: Downtown

TIMOTHY S ALLEN / SHUTTERSTOCK ©

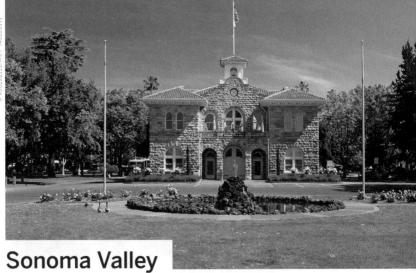

TASFOTONL / SHUTTERSTOCK ©

Sonoma Valley

Sun-drenched hills and vast vineyard landscapes

Locals call it 'Slow-noma,' for unlike fancy Napa, nobody in folksy
Sonoma (p73) cares if you drive a clunker and vote Green. Rolling
grass-covered hills rise alongside pastoral Hwy 12, peppered
by vineyards, family farms and gardens. Amid this bucolic ideal,
charming towns lie in the folds of the valley, waiting to host you for
a meal or overnight on your jumps between wineries. Top: Vineyards,
Sonoma Wine Country (p76); Bottom: Sonoma Plaza (p80)

2

MATT MUNRO / LONELY PLANET ©

Redwood Forests

Wander among awe-inspiring giants

Hugging a tree never came so naturally as it does in California's sun-dappled groves of ancient redwoods (p87), the world's tallest trees. These gentle giants are quintessentially Californian: their roots may be shallow, but they hold each other up and reach dizzying heights. Even a short stroll on the soft forest floor beneath these ancient wonders puts the day-to-day troubles of the rest of the world into perspective. Prairie Creek Redwoods State Park (p90)

3

Coastal Highway 1

An epic drive into California's wild north

Coastal Highway 1 (p99) is a legendary road trip, twisting and turning a thousand feet above the vast blue Pacific, hugging the skirts of mile-high sea cliffs. Along the route you'll pass picture-perfect little towns and eventually come to salt-washed Mendocino. This legendary bohemian outpost is lined with bookstores, natural food shops and fascinating galleries, all swirled in mists carrying fragrant bursts of lavender, jasmine and THC.

Lake Tahoe

A mountain playground for any season

High in the Sierra Nevada Mountains, this all-seasons adventure base camp centers on the USA's second-deepest lake (p111). In summer, startlingly blue waters invite splashing, kayaking and even scuba diving. Meanwhile, mountain bikers careen down single-track runs and hikers follow trails through thick forests to staggering views. After dark, retreat to cozy lakefront cottages and toast s'mores in fire pits. When the lake turns into a winter wonderland, gold-medal ski resorts come alive.

AARON M / 500PX ©

Yosemite National Park

Feeling so small has never felt so grand

Everything is monumental at Yosemite National Park (p129): thunderous waterfalls tumble over sheer cliffs, granite domes tower overhead and the world's biggest trees cluster in mighty groves. Conservationist John Muir considered Yosemite a great temple, and awe is the natural reaction to these vast wildflower-strewn meadows and valleys carved over millennia.

6

Big Sur

Explore the dramatic edge of the continent

Waterfalls splash down bluffs in rainbow mists, and yurt retreats perch at the edge of redwood forests (p145). Beyond purple-sand beaches and coves lined with California jade, pods of migrating whales dot the sparkling Pacific. But don't forget to turn around: hiding behind these coastal bluffs are hot springs and literary retreats, with California condors circling over the cliffs.

7

Santa Barbara

Seaside elegance and culinary decadence

Waving palm trees, powdery beaches, fishing boats clanking in the harbor – it'd be a travel cliché if it wasn't the plain truth. But Santa Barbara (p157) worked hard to stay so idyllic: downtown was rebuilt in signature Spanish Colonial Revival style after a 1925 earthquake and environmentalists lobbied to clean up the beaches in the '60s and '70s. California's 'Queen of the Missions' is a rare beauty, with its signature red-roofed, whitewashed adobe building.

PETER UNGER / GETTY IMAGES ©

Palm Springs
High-class oasis in the desert

A star-studded oasis in the Mojave ever since the heyday of old Blue Eyes and his Rat Pack, Palm Springs (p181) draws LA urbanites in need of a little retro-chic R&R. Follow the lead of A-list stars and hipsters: lounge by the pool at your mid-century-modern hotel, hit the galleries and vintage stores, then refresh with post-sunset cocktails. Too passive? Then explore desert canyons across Native American tribal lands or scramble to a summit in the San Jacinto Mountains, accessed via aerial tramway. Far left: Palm Canyon Dr; Left: Joshua Tree National Park (p184)

Los Angeles

Glitz, grit and endless sunshine

When you're ready for your close-up, there's only one place to go. The stars come out at night for red-carpet premieres at restored movie palaces, and you too can have your Hollywood moment on the pink-starred Walk of Fame. But beyond the streets of Hollywood, Los Angeles (p193) is flourishing, with a thriving art scene, a new-found vibrancy downtown and ultra-hip beach communities. Clockwise from top: Grauman's Chinese Theater (p198); Santa Monica Beach (p219); LA at night

10

TRACEROUDA / GETTY IMAGES ©

Orange County

Classic beaches and a Magic Kingdom

Where orange groves and walnut trees once grew, Walt Disney built his dream world. Since his 'Magic Kingdom' opened in 1955, Disneyland has expanded to neighboring Disney California Adventure to become SoCal's most-visited tourist attraction. For more OC (p223) adventures, hit the world-class beaches; while surfers hang loose in Huntington Beach and yachties mingle in Newport Beach, Laguna Beach lures them all with its natural beauty. Laguna Beach (p234)

11

STEPHEN MOEHLE / 500PX ©

San Diego

Beaches, craft beer and an incredible zoo

San Diego (p249) is known for its golden beaches, but there's another side to this seaside town. Beautiful Balboa Park is the pride of San Diego, with Spanish Colonial and Mission Revival–style architecture along El Prado promenade and more than a dozen art, cultural and science museums. Glimpse exotic wildlife and ride the 'Skyfari' aerial tram at San Diego's world-famous zoo or wander the streets of its historic old town. Panda, San Diego Zoo (p253)

12

Plan Your Trip
Need to Know

When to Go

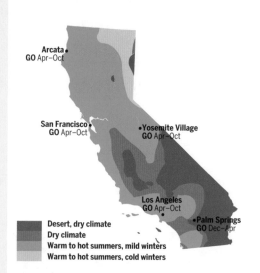

Arcata•
GO Apr–Oct

San Francisco•
GO Apr–Oct

•Yosemite Village
GO Apr–Oct

Los Angeles
GO Apr–Oct
•

•Palm Springs
GO Dec–Apr

- Desert, dry climate
- Dry climate
- Warm to hot summers, mild winters
- Warm to hot summers, cold winters

High Season (Jun–Aug)

o Accommodations prices up 50% to 100% on average; major holidays are even busier and more expensive.

o Summer is low season in the desert, where temperatures exceed 100°F (38°C).

Shoulder (Apr–May & Sep–Oct)

o Crowds and prices drop, especially on the coast and in the mountains.

o Mild temperatures and sunny, cloudless days; typically wetter in spring, drier in autumn.

Low Season (Nov–Mar)

o Accommodations rates lowest along the coast.

o Chilly temperatures, frequent rainstorms and heavy snow in the mountains.

o Winter is peak season in SoCal's desert regions.

Currency
US dollar ($)

Language
English

Visas
Generally not required for stays of 90 days or less for citizens of Visa Waiver Program (VWP) countries with ESTA approval (https://esta.cbp.dhs.gov) – apply online at least 72 hours in advance.

Money
ATMs are widely available. Credit cards are usually required for reservations. Traveler's checks (US dollars) are rarely accepted. Tipping is customary, not optional.

Cell Phones
The only foreign phones that will work in the USA are GSM multiband models. Buy prepaid SIM cards locally. Coverage can be spotty in remote areas.

Time
Pacific Standard Time (UTC minus eight hours). Clocks are set one hour ahead during Daylight Saving Time (DST), from the second Sunday in March until the first Sunday in November.

Daily Costs

Budget: Less than $100

- Hostel dorm beds: $30–55
- Take-out meal: $7–12

Midrange: $100–200

- Motel or hotel double room: $100–150
- Rental car per day, excluding gas and insurance: $50–80

Top End: More than $200

- Upscale hotel or beach resort room: $150–300
- Three-course meal in top restaurant excluding drinks: $80–120

Useful Websites

California Travel & Tourism Commission (www.visitcalifornia.com) Multilingual trip-planning guides.
Lonely Planet (www.lonelyplanet.com/usa/california) Destination information, hotel bookings, traveler forum and more.
LA Times Travel (www.latimes.com/travel) Travel news, deals and blogs.
Sunset (www.sunset.com/travel/california) Local and insider travel tips.
California State Parks (www.parks.ca.gov) Outdoor activities and camping.
CalTrans (www.dot.ca.gov) Current highway conditions.

Opening Hours

Shops and restaurants may close earlier and on additional days during the winter off-season (November to March). Otherwise, standard opening hours are as follows:
Banks 9am–6pm Monday to Friday, some 9am–1pm or later Saturday
Bars 5pm–2am daily
Clubs 10pm–4am Thursday to Saturday
Restaurants 7:30am–10am, 11:30am–2pm and 5pm–9pm daily, some open later Friday and Saturday

Shops 10am–6pm Monday to Saturday, noon–5pm Sunday (malls open later)
Supermarkets 8am–9pm or 10pm daily, some 24 hours

Arriving in California

Los Angeles International Airport Taxis to most destinations ($30 to $50) take 30 minutes to one hour. Door-to-door shuttles ($15 to $20) operate 24 hours. FlyAway bus ($9.75) runs to Downtown LA. Free shuttles connect with LAX City Bus Center and Metro Rail station.
San Francisco International Airport Taxis into the city ($45 to $65) take 25 to 50 minutes. Door-to-door shuttles (from $17) operate 24 hours. BART trains ($8.95, 30 minutes) serve the airport, running from 5:30am (later on weekends) to midnight daily.

Getting Around

Most people drive themselves around California. You can also fly (it's expensive) or take cheaper long-distance buses or scenic trains. In cities, when distances are too far to walk, hop aboard buses, trains, streetcars, cable cars or trolleys, or grab a taxi.

Car Metro-area traffic can be nightmarish, especially during weekday commuter rush hours (roughly 6am to 10am and 3pm to 7pm). City parking is often an expensive hassle.

Train The fastest way to get around the San Francisco Bay Area and LA, but lines don't go everywhere. Pricier regional and long-distance Amtrak trains connect some destinations.

Bus Usually the cheapest and slowest option, but with extensive metro-area networks. Inter-city, regional and long-distance Greyhound routes are limited and more expensive.

For more on **getting around**, see p309

Plan Your Trip
Hot Spots for...

Incredible Food

New cravings have been invented at California's cultural crossroads for 200 years, so get set for the latest trends, from Peking duck empanadas to vegan soul food.

PHOTO.UA / SHUTTERSTOCK ©

San Francisco
From late-night burritos to late-breaking culinary trends, San Francisco is foodie heaven.

Ferry Building
Sustainable food and a farmers market. (p46; pictured)

Sonoma Valley
International acclaim for Sonoma wines in the 1970s bolstered local cheesemakers and restaurateurs.

Cafe La Haye
Only uses produce sourced from within 60 miles. (p82)

Los Angeles
Within LA's famous sprawl is a melting pot of food from around the world.

Mariscos 4 Vientos
Spectacular fried shrimp tacos in East LA. (p212)

National & State Parks

Jagged mountain peaks, high-country meadows, desert sand dunes and wind-tossed offshore islands – California's wild diversity is astonishing.

SIMEONE HUBER / GETTY IMAGES ©

Yosemite National Park
Ascend the Sierra Nevada, where waterfalls tumble into glacier-carved valleys and wildflowers bloom.

Glacier Point
Hike or drive up to this lookout for sunset. (p132)

Redwood Forests
Get lost ambling among ancient groves of the world's tallest trees on the foggy North Coast.

Avenue of the Giants
Drive beneath the boughs of old-growth redwoods. (p92)

Death Valley National Park
Uncover secret pockets of life in this austere desert landscape, peppered with geological oddities (pictured).

Artists Drive
A one-way scenic loop drive. (p177)

Beaches

If your dream vacation involves bronzing on the beach, digging in the sand and paddling in the Pacific, head to Southern California (SoCal).

LOWE LLAGUNO / SHUTTERSTOCK ©

Orange County
When it comes to beautiful beaches (and some excellent surf), OC enjoys a burden of riches.

Huntington City Beach
Some of the best swimming on the coast. (p241)

Santa Barbara
This classy beach town is the perfect destination for beachcombers, sunbathers and surfers alike.

Arroyo Burro Beach
This sandy gem is among the area's best. (p163)

San Diego
California's southern-most beach town has an excellent surf scene and good weather year-round.

Mission & Pacific Beaches
Crowded, but the people watching is great. (p256, pictured)

Museums & Galleries

Who says California only has pop culture? Break up your beach days with top-notch art galleries, science exhibits, planetariums, museums and more.

ALEX MILLAUER / SHUTTERSTOCK ©

San Francisco
Home to a collection of world-class destinations that make for an excellent week of museum hopping.

SFMOMA
Recently renovated and massively expanded. (p53)

Los Angeles
A thriving downtown art and architecture scene has brought tourists and culture back to downtown LA.

LA County Museum of Art
More than 150,000 works of art. (p205, pictured)

San Diego
If you can pull yourself away from the beach, San Diego has a lot of culture on offer.

Balboa Park Museums
Top-notch art, history and science museums. (p254)

Plan Your Trip
Local Life

AN JELIKAGR / SHUTTERSTOCK ©

Activities

California is an all-seasons outdoor playground. Hike among desert wildflowers in spring, dive into the Pacific in summer, mountain bike through fall foliage and ski down wintry mountain slopes. Once California gets your adrenaline pumping, you'll also be ready to hang glide off ocean bluffs, scuba past coastal shipwrecks, scale sheer granite cliffs or white-water raft the rapids. You'll also find that every seaside town has a number of excursions to get you out on and in the water, from guided whale-watching to extended surf tours.

Shopping

It doesn't matter where you go in California, especially along the coast: there's a rack of haute couture, an outlet-mall bargain or a vintage find begging to be stashed in your suitcase. Los Angeles has more star-worthy boutiques than any other place in the state,

while San Francisco is more about eclectic indie flavor. If you want incredible vintage gear, head to Palm Springs, where thrift-store shoppers seek retro 20th-century gems, and there's outlet shopping, too.

Eating

As you graze the Golden State, you'll often want to compliment the chef – and that chef will pass it on to the local farmers, fishers, ranchers, winemakers and artisan food producers that make their menu possible. California cuisine is a team effort that changes with every season – and it's changed the way the world eats. Every region will have its own specialty, but the secret to so many of California's mind-blowing menus is that big swath of green in the middle of the state, the Central Valley. This incredibly fertile area feeds the nation, and brings a constant supply of fresh ingredients to the table.

LEMBI / SHUTTERSTOCK ©

Drinking & Nightlife

Go VIP all the way at California's chic city nightclubs – or skip the velvet ropes and dress codes, and hit the state's come-as-you-are watering holes. LA has glam Hollywood clubs and a thriving scene in WeHo, while San Francisco is all about eclectic lounges, fancy mixology and the chance to party in the famous LGBT enclave of the Castro. If you're out on the town in San Diego, put on your best flip-flops for surfer bars, or your walking shoes for pub crawls through the Gaslamp Quarter, downtown's historic red-light district.

Entertainment

California – perhaps LA specifically – may be the entertainment capital of the world, but that's only the opening act. Aside from world-class venues in thriving music capitals such as San Francisco and LA, every little town you pass is likely to

★ Best California Cuisine

Benu (p62)

In Situ (p61)

Brick & Fire (p97)

Fishetarian Fish Market (p107)

Catch LA (p214)

have a regional playhouse or little indie movie theater. California's great year-round weather also makes it home to some of the nation's most incredible festivals, including Coachella Music & Arts Festival and Burning Man. Then there's live sports: California has more professional sports teams than any other state, and loyalties to NBA basketball, NFL football and major-league baseball teams run deep.

From left: Shopping on Rodeo Dr, Los Angeles (p211); The Castro, San Francisco (p36)

Plan Your Trip
Month by Month

CHRIS NANOSKI / 500PX ©

January

January is the wettest month in California, and a slow time for coastal travel – but this is when mountain ski resorts and Southern California deserts hit their stride.

🎊 Rose Bowl & Parade

The famous New Year's parade held before the Tournament of Roses college football game draws around one million spectators to the LA suburb of Pasadena.

🎊 Lunar New Year

Firecrackers, parades, lion dances and Chinatown night markets usher in the lunar new year, falling in late January or early February. California's biggest parade happens in San Francisco.

February

As California sunshine breaks through the drizzle, skiers hit the slopes in T-shirts and wildflowers burst into bloom.

🏃 Wildlife Watching

February is prime time for spotting whales offshore, seeing thousands of monarch butterflies wintering in California groves, and finding colonies of elephant seals nursing pups in Central Coast dunes.

☆ Academy Awards

Hollywood rolls out the red carpet for movie-star entrances on Oscar night at the Dolby Theatre in late February or early March.

March

As ski season winds down, the beaches warm up, just in time for spring break.

🎊 Mendocino Coast Whale Festivals

Mendocino, Fort Bragg and nearby towns toast the whale migration with wining and dining, art shows and naturalist-guided walks and talks.

CHRISTOPHER POLK / GETTY IMAGES ©

⚘ Festival of the Swallows

After wintering in South America, the swallows return to Mission San Juan Capistrano in Orange County around March 19 – and the historic mission town celebrates its Spanish and Mexican heritage.

April

Wildflower season peaks in the high desert.

☆ Coachella Music & Arts Festival

Headliners, indie rockers, rappers and cult DJs converge outside Palm Springs for a three-day musical extravaganza held over two weekends in mid-April.

☆ San Francisco International Film Festival

The nation's oldest film festival lights up San Francisco nights with star-studded US premieres of 325 films from around the globe.

★ Best Festivals

Rose Bowl & Parade, January

Coachella Music & Arts Festival, April

Pride Month, June

Comic-Con International, July

Monterey Jazz Festival, September

May

Weather starts to heat up statewide. Memorial Day holiday weekend marks the official start of summer.

🏃 Bay to Breakers

On the third Sunday in May, costumed joggers, inebriated idlers and renegade streakers make the annual dash from San Francisco's Embarcadero to Ocean Beach.

From left: Comic books on display at Comic-Con International (July; p24); Coachella Music & Arts Festival

🎯 Kinetic Grand Championship

Artists spend months preparing for this 'triathlon of the art world,' inventing outlandish human-powered and self-propelled sculptural contraptions to cover 42 miles from Arcata to Ferndale.

June

Once school lets out for the summer, everyone heads to California beaches. Mountain resorts offer cool escapes, but the deserts are just too darn hot.

🎊 Pride Month

California celebrates LGBT pride not just for a day but for the entire month of June, with costumed parades, film fests, marches and streets parties. SF Pride sets the global parade standard, with 1.2 million people.

July

California's campgrounds, beaches and theme parks hit peak popularity, especially on the July 4 holiday.

☆ Comic-Con International

Affectionately known as 'Nerd Prom,' the nation's biggest annual convention of comic-book fans, pop-culture collectors, and sci-fi and anime devotees brings out-of-this-world costumed madness to San Diego.

August

School summer vacations may technically be over, but you'd never guess in California – beaches and parks are still packed.

🎊 Old Spanish Days Fiesta

Santa Barbara shows off its early Spanish, Mexican and American *rancho* roots with parades, rodeo events, arts-and-crafts exhibits, and live music and dance shows.

September

Summer's last hurrah is Labor Day holiday weekend, which is busy almost everywhere in California (except hot SoCal deserts).

☆ Monterey Jazz Festival

Old-school jazz cats, cross-cultural sensations and fusion rebels all line up to play the West Coast's legendary jazz festival, held on the Central Coast.

🎊 Tall Ships Festival

The West Coast's biggest gathering of historical tall ships happens at Dana Point in Orange County.

October

Summer arrives at last in Northern California, and Southern Californians take a breather after a long summer of nonstop beach-going.

☆ Hardly Strictly Bluegrass

Over half a million people converge for free outdoor concerts in Golden Gate Park during the first weekend in October.

🍷 Vineyard Festivals

All month long, California's wine countries celebrate bringing in the vineyard harvest with food-and-wine events, harvest fairs, barrel tastings and grape-stomping 'crush' parties.

November

Temperatures drop statewide, the first raindrops fall along the coast, and with any luck, ski season begins in the mountains.

🎊 Día de los Muertos

Mexican communities honor deceased relatives on November 2 with costumed parades, sugar skulls, graveyard picnics, candlelight processions and fabulous altars, including in San Francisco, LA and San Diego.

December

As winter rains reach coastal areas, SoCal's sunny, dry deserts become magnets for travelers.

◎ Parade of Lights

Deck the decks with boughs of holly: boats bedecked with holiday cheer and twinkling lights float through coastal California harbors, including Orange County's Newport Beach and San Diego.

Plan Your Trip
Get Inspired

Read

On the Road (Jack Kerouac; 1957) The epic road trip that inspired free spirits everywhere to come to California.

My California: Journeys by Great Writers (Angel City Press; 2004) Insightful stories by California chroniclers.

Where I Was From (Joan Didion; 2003) California-born essayist shatters palm-fringed fantasies.

If They Come in the Morning (Angela Davis; 1971) Chronicles of the Black Power movement collected by one of its leaders.

Hollywood Babylon (Kenneth Anger; 1959) The tell-all book that exposed the scandals of Hollywood.

Watch

Maltese Falcon (1941) Humphrey Bogart as a San Francisco private eye.

Sunset Boulevard (1950) The classic bonfire of Hollywood vanities.

Vertigo (1958) Alfred Hitchcock's noir thriller, set in San Francisco.

Bladerunner (1982) Ridley Scott's futuristic cyberpunk vision of LA.

LA Confidential (1997) Neo-noir tale of corruption and murder in 1950s LA.

Dogtown and Z-Boys (2001) The stranger-than-fiction story of the teenage SoCal misfits who made skateboarding cool.

Milk (2008) Follow the footsteps of the first openly gay man to hold a major US political office.

Listen

California Girls (Beach Boys; 1965) Early California surf sounds.

California Dreaming (The Mamas & the Papas; 1966) Counterculture folk rock hit.

California (Joni Mitchell; 1971) Haunting ballad.

California Sun (Ramones; 1977) The definitive cover version.

California Love (2Pac; 1996) Comeback single featuring Dr Dre.

Californication (Red Hot Chili Peppers; 1999) Pop-punk portmanteau.

California (Phantom Planet; 2002) Theme song from *The OC*.

California Gurls (Katy Perry; 2010) Pop diva meets rapper Snoop Dogg.

Above: A skateboarder at Venice Beach (p219)

Plan Your Trip
Five-Day Itineraries

Bay Area Escape

Explore the best of Northern California with a romp through San Francisco, a Sonoma Valley stopover and a quick escape up the coast. This is all about great museums and incredible drives, electric nightlife and world-class food and wine.

Mendocino (p102) Detour west through orchards in rural Anderson Valley, and head through redwoods to emerge in Mendocino, a postcard-perfect seaside town.

Sonoma Valley (p73) Cross the Golden Gate bridge and taste world-class wine during a short escape to Sonoma county. 🚗 3 hrs to Mendocino

San Francisco (p35) Jump aboard a cable car and hop on a ferry to infamous Alcatraz prison. Make time for a visit to the Ferry Building. 🚗 2 hrs to Sonoma Valley

SoCal Beaches

All-star attractions, bodacious beaches and fresh seafood are yours to discover on this Southern California sojourn, covering 100 miles of sun, sand and surf. Start here if you've always wanted to live in a Beach Boys song.

Santa Barbara (p157)
This elegant city – known as the 'American Riviera' – has miles of incredible sand. 🚗 2 hrs to Santa Monica

Santa Monica (p196)
Start at the famous pier and cruise past Muscle Beach and LA's beach communities. 🚗 1 hrs to Laguna Beach

Laguna Beach (p234)
Discover the OC's wide sandy beaches, making time to catch a few waves.

FROM LEFT: PAPER CAT / SHUTTERSTOCK ©: ASIF ISLAM / SHUTTERSTOCK ©

Plan Your Trip
10-Day Itinerary

SF to LA

You've got 10 days to settle California's longest-running debate: which is California's better half, north or south? Try not to be distracted by the dazzling ocean views as you navigate the glorious 450-mile coastal drive stretching from the spectacular north to the sunny south.

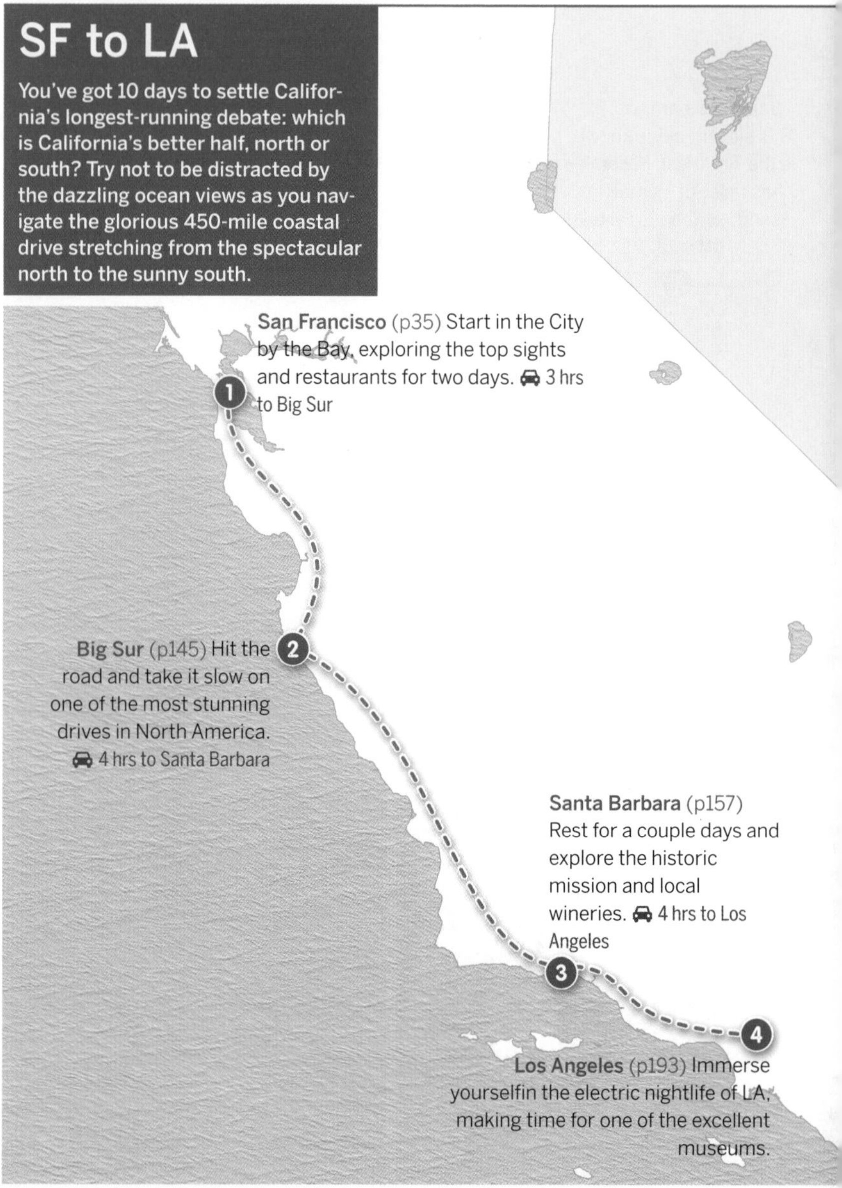

San Francisco (p35) Start in the City by the Bay, exploring the top sights and restaurants for two days. 🚗 3 hrs to Big Sur

1

Big Sur (p145) Hit the road and take it slow on one of the most stunning drives in North America. 🚗 4 hrs to Santa Barbara

2

Santa Barbara (p157) Rest for a couple days and explore the historic mission and local wineries. 🚗 4 hrs to Los Angeles

3

4

Los Angeles (p193) Immerse yourself in the electric nightlife of LA, making time for one of the excellent museums.

Plan Your Trip
Two-Week Itinerary

California Classics

Cover the Golden State's greatest hits on this grand tour. Start amid giant redwoods, seek out the bridge in foggy San Francisco, take in the grand views of Yosemite and get up close and personal with some exotic friends in San Diego.

Redwood National Park (p90) Start with the world-famous giants of California's north woods. 🚗 5 hrs to San Francisco **1**

Lake Tahoe (p111) Hit the slopes or hike around this stunning natural gem. 🚗 3 hrs to Yosemite National **3** Park

San Francisco (p35) **2** Cross the famed Golden Gate and make time for a Chinatown tour. 🚗 4 hrs to Lake Tahoe

4 Yosemite National Park (p129) The most magnificent of all California's national parks, Yosemite will leave you breathless. 🚗 5 hrs to Anaheim

Disneyland (p226) Say hello to Mickey at the world's most famous theme park. 🚗 2 hrs to San Diego

5

San Diego (p249) Lions, tigers, bears and just about every other creature imaginable await at the incredible San Diego Zoo. **6**

Plan Your Trip
Family Travel

SEAN PAVONE / SHUTTERSTOCK ©

The Low-Down

California is a tailor-made destination for family travel. The kids will be begging to go to theme parks, and teens to celebrity hot spots. And, of course, there's the great outdoors – from sunny beaches shaded by palm trees to misty redwood forests to four-seasons mountain playgrounds. Really, there's not too much to worry about when traveling in California with your kids...as long as you keep them covered in sunblock.

Theme Parks

California is theme-park heaven, with **Disneyland Resort** (p226) topping almost every family's must-do list.

Note that at theme parks, some rides may have minimum-height requirements, so let younger kids know about this in advance to avoid disappointment and tears.

National & State Parks

At national and state parks, ask at visitor centers about family-friendly, ranger-led activities and self-guided 'Junior Ranger' programs, in which kids earn themselves a badge after completing an activity booklet.

Accommodations

Rule one: if you're traveling with kids, always mention it when making reservations. At a few places, notably B&Bs, you may have a hard time if you show up with little ones. When booking, be sure to request the specific room type you want, although requests often aren't guaranteed.

Motels and hotels typically have rooms with two beds or an extra sofa bed. They also may have rollaway beds or cots, usually available for a surcharge (request these when making reservations). Some offer 'kids stay free' promotions, which may apply only if no extra bedding is required.

ANTON_IVANOV / SHUTTERSTOCK ©

Dining Out

It's fine to bring kids along to most restaurants, except top-end places. Casual restaurants usually have high chairs and children's menus and break out paper place mats and crayons for drawing. At theme parks, pack a cooler in the car and have a picnic in the parking lot to save money. On the road many supermarkets have wholesome, ready-to-eat takeout dishes.

Need to Know

○ **Baby supplies** Baby food, infant formula, disposable diapers (nappies) and other necessities are widely sold at supermarkets and pharmacies.

○ **Car seats** Any child under age eight who is shorter than 4ft, 9in must be buckled up in the back seat of the car in a child or infant safety seat. Most car-rental agencies offer these for an extra cost, but you must book them in advance.

★ **Best Museums**

Exploratorium (p52)

New Children's Museum (p257)

La Brea Tar Pits & Museum (p207)

California Academy of Sciences (p59)

Griffith Observatory (p200)

○ **Discounts** Children's discounts are available for everything from museum admission and movie tickets to bus fares and motel stays. The definition of a 'child' varies – from 'under 18' to six years old.

○ **Toilets** Many public toilets have a baby-changing table, while private gender-neutral 'family' bathrooms may be available at airports, museums etc.

From left: Griffith Observatory (p200), LA: California Academy of Sciences (p59), San Francisco

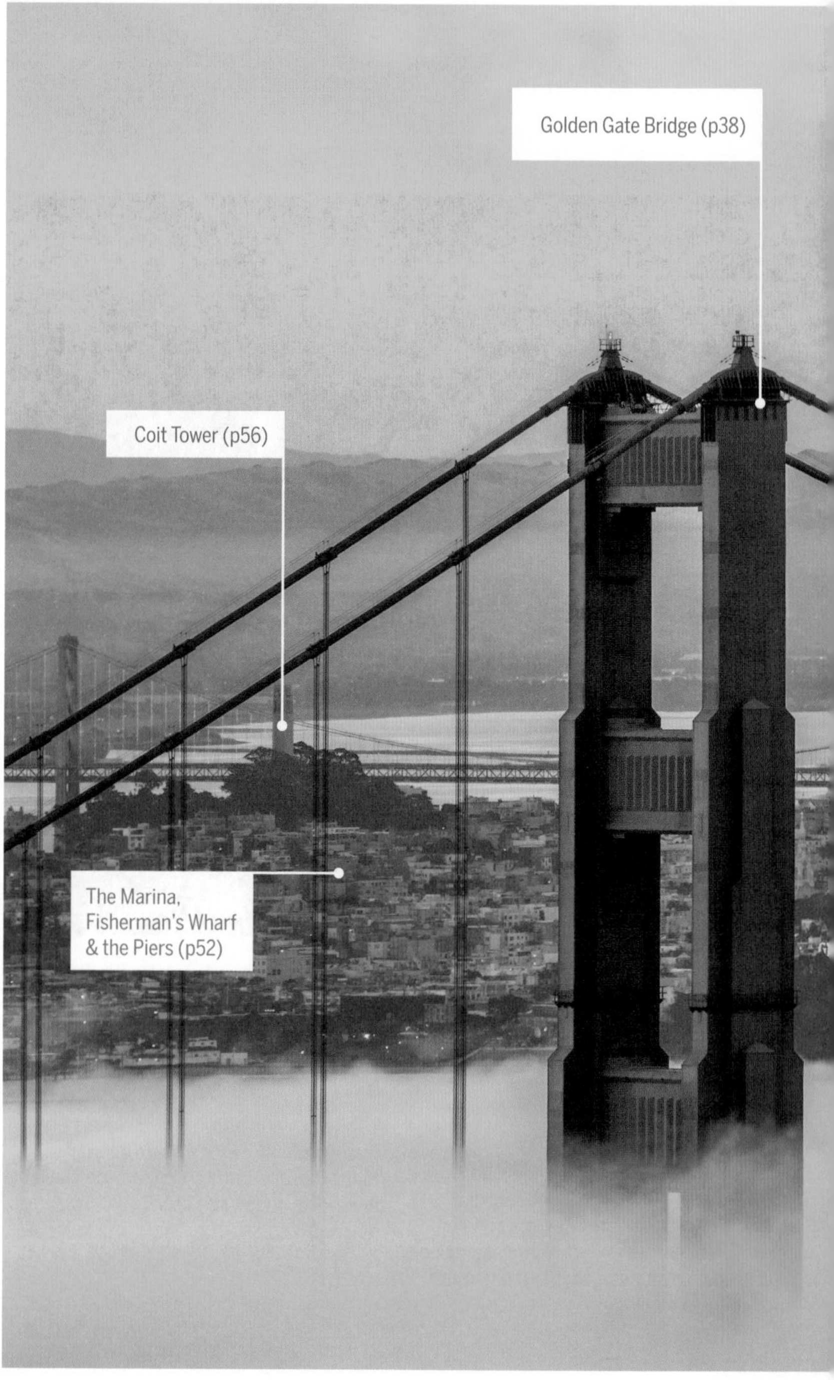

Golden Gate Bridge (p38)
Coit Tower (p56)
The Marina, Fisherman's Wharf & the Piers (p52)

PHITHA TANPAIROJ / SHUTTERSTOCK ©

Sea lions at Fisherman's Wharf (p52)

Arriving in San Francisco

San Francisco Airport (SFO) Fast rides to downtown San Francisco on Bay Area Rapid Transit (BART) cost $8.95; door-to-door shuttle vans cost $17 to $20, plus tip; express bus fare to Temporary Transbay Terminal is $2.50 via SamTrans; taxis cost $40 to $55, plus tip.

Oakland International Airport (OAK) Catch BART from the airport to downtown SF ($10.20); take a shared van to downtown SF for $30 to $40; or pay $60 to $80 for a taxi to SF destinations.

Sleeping

San Francisco hotel rates are among the world's highest. Plan ahead – well ahead – and grab bargains when you see them. Given the choice, San Francisco's boutique properties beat chains for a sense of place – but take what you can get at a price you can afford. For more detailed information, check out Where to Stay (p71).

Golden Gate Bridge

The city's most spectacular icon towers 80 stories above the roiling waters of the Golden Gate, the narrow entrance to San Francisco Bay. When the fog clears it reveals magnificent views.

Great For...

Don't Miss

The cross-section of suspension cable behind Bridge Pavilion Visitor Center.

Other suspension bridges boast impressive engineering, but none can touch the Golden Gate Bridge for showmanship. On sunny days, it transfixes crowds with its radiant glow – thanks to 25 daredevil painters, who reapply 1000 gallons of International Orange paint weekly.

Construction

Nobody thought it could happen. Not until the early 1920s did the City of San Francisco seriously investigate building a bridge over the treacherous, windblown strait. The War Department owned the land on both sides and didn't want to take chances with ships: safety and solidity were its goals, and naval officials preferred a hulking concrete span, painted with caution-yellow stripes, over the soaring art deco design of architects Gertrude and Irving Murrow and engineer Joseph B Strauss.

KAN KANNAVEE / SHUTTERSTOCK ©

❶ Need to Know

📝toll information 877-229-8655; www.golden-gatebridge.org/visitors; Hwy 101; northbound free, southbound $6.50-7.50; 🚌28, all Golden Gate Transit buses

✕ Take a Break

At the **Warming Hut** (📞415-561-3042; www.parksconservancy.org/visit/eat/warming-hut.html; 983 Marine Dr; items $4-9; ⏱9am-5pm; 🅿♿; 🚐PresidiGo shuttle) ✎, kite fliers and wet-suited windsurfers recharge with fair-trade coffee.

★ Top Tip

For on-site info, stop into the **Bridge Pavilion Visitor Center** (📞415-426-5220; www.ggnpc.org; Golden Gate Bridge toll plaza; ⏱9am-7pm Jun-Aug, to 6pm Sep-May).

Luckily, however, the green light was given to the counter-proposal by Strauss and the Murrows for a subtler suspension span, which was economic in form and harmonized with the natural environment. Before the War Department could insist on an eyesore, laborers dove into the treacherous riptides of the bay and got the bridge under way in 1933. Just four years later workers balancing atop swaying cables completed what was then the world's longest suspension bridge – nearly 2 miles long, with 746ft suspension towers, higher than any construction west of New York.

Views of the Bridge

As far as best views go, cinema buffs believe Hitchcock had it right: seen from below at Fort Point, the 1937 bridge induces a thrilling case of *Vertigo*. Fog aficionados prefer the north-end lookout at Marin's Vista Point, to watch gusts billow through bridge cables like dry ice at a Kiss concert.

To see both sides of the debate, hike or bike the 1.7-mile span. Muni bus 28 runs to the parking lot, and pedestrians and cyclists can cross the bridge on sidewalks.

Crossing the Bridge

Pedestrians take the eastern sidewalk. Dress warmly! From the parking area and bus stop (off Lincoln Blvd), a pathway leads past the toll plaza, then it's 1.7 miles across. If the 3.4-mile round-trip seems too much, take a bus to the north side via Golden Gate Transit, then walk back.

By bicycle, from the toll-plaza parking area ride toward the Roundhouse, then follow signs to the western sidewalk, reserved for bikes only.

Cable cars riding along California St

CANADASTOCK / SHUTTERSTOCK ©

Cable Cars

Offering million-dollar vistas and the promise of adventure, cable cars are one of the finest ways to explore San Francisco. These ratcheting wonders bring you lurching into the heart of the city's best neighborhoods.

Today the cable car seems more like a steampunk carnival ride than modern transport, but Andrew Hallidie's 1873 contraptions have held up miraculously well on San Francisco's giddy slopes, and they remain a reliable, low-impact way to conquer San Francisco's highest hills.

Powell-Hyde Cable Car

The ascent up Nob Hill feels like the world's longest roller-coaster climb – but on the Powell-Hyde cable car, the biggest thrills are still ahead. This cable car bobs up and down hills, with the Golden Gate Bridge popping in and out of view on Russian Hill. Hop off the cable car at Lombard St to walk the zigzagging route to North Beach. Otherwise, stop and

Great For...

Don't Miss

The view of twisty Lombard St on the Powell-Hyde line.

Market St cable car

JERRY SHARP / SHUTTERSTOCK ©

Powell St Cable Car Turnaround

Peek through the passenger queue at Powell and Market Sts to spot cable-car operators leaping out, gripping the chassis of each trolley and slowly turning the car atop a revolving wooden platform. Cable cars can't reverse, so they need to be turned around by hand here at the **terminus** (www.sfmta.com; cnr Powell & Market Sts; 🚋Powell-Mason, Mason-Hyde, Ⓜ Powell, Ⓑ Powell) of the Powell St lines. Riders queue up midmorning to early evening here to secure a seat, with raucous street performers and doomsday preachers on the sidelines as entertainment.

smell the roses along stairway walks to shady Macondray Lane and blooming Ina Coolbrith Park.

Powell-Mason Cable Car

The Powell-Hyde line may have multi-million-dollar vistas, but the Powell-Mason line has more culture. Detour atop Nob Hill for tropical cocktails at the vintage tiki Tonga Room (p66), then resume the ride to Chinatown. The route cuts through North Beach at Washington Sq, where you're surrounded by alleyways named after Beat poets. The terminus at Bay and Taylor Sts is handy for visiting two truly riveting attractions: the USS *Pampanito* and the Musée Mécanique.

California St Cable Car

History buffs and crowd-shy visitors prefer San Francisco's oldest cable-car line: the California St cable car, in operation since 1878. This divine ride west heads through Chinatown past Old St Mary's Cathedral and climbs Nob Hill to Grace Cathedral. Hop off at Polk St for Swan Oyster Depot (p62), tempting boutiques and cocktail bars. The Van Ness Ave terminus is a few blocks west of Alta Plaza and Lafayette Parks, which are both ringed by stately Victorians.

Alcatraz

Over the decades Alcatraz has been the nation's first military prison, a forbidding maximum-security penitentiary and disputed territory between Native American activists and the FBI.

Great For...

Don't Miss

The feeling of isolation in the chilling D-Block solitary-confinement cells.

Early History

It all started innocently enough back in 1775, when Spanish lieutenant Juan Manuel de Ayala sailed the *San Carlos* past the 22-acre island that he called Isla de Alcatraces (Isle of the Pelicans). In 1859 a new post on Alcatraz became the first US West Coast fort and it soon proved handy as a holding pen for Civil War deserters, insubordinates and the court-martialed.

By 1902 the four cell blocks of wooden cages were rotting, unsanitary and ill-equipped for the influx of US soldiers convicted of war crimes in the Philippines. The army began building a new concrete military prison in 1909, but upkeep was expensive and the US soon had other things to worry about: WWI, financial ruin and flappers.

FRANK VAN DEN BERGH / GETTY IMAGES ©

⊙ Need to Know

🖉Alcatraz Cruises 415-981-7625; www.nps.
gov/alcatraz; tours adult/child 5-11yr day
$37.25/23, night $44.25/26.50; ⊙call center
8am-7pm, ferries depart Pier 33 half-hourly
8:45am-3:50pm, night tours 5:55pm &
6:30pm; 🚻

✕ Take a Break

Sip a post-Alcatraz drink at **Gold Dust
Lounge** (🖉415-397-1695; www.golddustsf.com;
165 Jefferson St; ⊙9am-2am; 🚌47, 🚋Powell-
Mason, Ⓜ️E, F), a 15-minute walk from Pier 33.

★ Top Tip

Find out if there's a site-specific art installation during your visit, and plan to see it.

Inmates, Escape & Abandonment

In 1934 the Federal Bureau of Prisons took
over Alcatraz as a prominent showcase for
its crime-fighting efforts. The Rock aver-
aged only 264 inmates, but its roster read
like a list of America's Most Wanted. A-list
criminals doing time on Alcatraz included
Chicago crime boss Al 'Scarface' Capone,
dapper kidnapper George 'Machine Gun'
Kelly and hot-headed Harlem mafioso and
sometime poet 'Bumpy' Johnson.

Although Alcatraz was considered
escape-proof, in 1962 the Anglin brothers
and Frank Morris stuffed their beds with
dummies, floated away on a makeshift raft
and were never seen again.

Security and upkeep proved prohibitively
expensive and finally the island prison was
abandoned to the birds in 1963.

Native American Occupation

Native Americans claimed sovereignty over
the island in the 1960s, noting that Alcatraz
had long been used by the Ohlone people
as a spiritual retreat. In 1969, 79 Native
American activists swam to the island and
took it over. During the next 19 months,
some 5600 Native Americans would visit
the occupied island. Public support eventually pressured President Richard Nixon
in 1970 to restore Native territory and
strengthen self-rule for Native nations.

Visiting Alcatraz

The weather changes fast and it's often
windy and much colder on Alcatraz, so
wear extra layers, long pants and a cap.

Visiting Alcatraz means walking – a lot.
The ferry drops you off at the bottom of a
130ft-high hill, which you'll have to ascend
to reach the cell block; wear sturdy shoes.
For people with mobility impairment, there's
a twice-hourly tram from dock to cell house.

Alcatraz

A HALF-DAY TOUR

Book a ferry from Pier 33 and ride 1.5 miles across the bay to explore America's most notorious former prison. The trip itself is worth the money, providing stunning views of the city skyline. Once you've landed at the ❶ **Ferry Dock & Pier**, you begin the 580yd walk to the top of the island and prison; if you need assistance to reach the top, there's a twice-hourly tram.

As you climb toward the ❷ **Guardhouse**, notice the island's steep slope; before it was a prison, Alcatraz was a fort. In the 1850s, the military quarried the rocky shores into near-vertical cliffs. Ships could then only dock at a single port, separated from the main buildings by a sally port (a drawbridge and moat in what became the guardhouse). Inside, peer through floor grates to see Alcatraz's original prison.

Volunteers tend the brilliant ❸ **Officers' Row Gardens**, an orderly counterpoint to the overgrown rose bushes surrounding the burned-out shell of the ❹ **Warden's House**. At the top of the hill, by the front door of the ❺ **Main Cellhouse**, beautiful shots unfurl all around, including a view of the ❻ **Golden Gate Bridge**. Above the main door of the administration building, notice the ❼ **historic signs & graffiti**, before you step inside the dank, cold prison to find the ❽ **Frank Morris cell**, former home to Alcatraz's most notorious jail-breaker.

ADRIEN_G/SHUTTERSTOCK ©

Historic Signs & Graffiti
During their 1969–71 occupation, Native Americans graffitied the water tower: 'Home of the Free Indian Land.' Above the cellhouse door, examine the eagle-and-flag crest to see how the red-and-white stripes were changed to spell 'Free.'

DOPTIS/SHUTTERSTOCK ©

Warden's House
Fires destroyed the warden's house and other structures during the Indian Occupation. The government blamed the Native Americans; the Native Americans blamed agents provocateurs acting on behalf of the Nixon administration to undermine public sympathy.

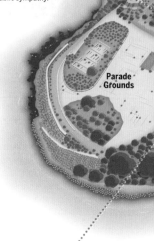

Parade Grounds

Officers' Row Gardens
In the 19th century soldiers imported topsoil to beautify the island with gardens. Well-trusted prisoners later gardened – Elliott Michener said it kept him sane. Historians, ornithologists and archaeologists choose today's plants.

Main Cellhouse

During the mid-20th century, the maximum-security prison housed the day's most notorious troublemakers, including Al Capone and Robert Stroud, the 'Birdman of Alcatraz' (who actually conducted his ornithology studies at Leavenworth).

View of the Golden Gate Bridge

The Golden Gate Bridge stretches wide on the horizon. Best views are from atop the island at Eagle Plaza, near the cellhouse entrance, and at water level along the Agave Trail (September to January only).

Power House

Recreation Yard

Water Tower

Officers' Club

Lighthouse

Guard Tower

Guardhouse

Alcatraz's oldest building dates to 1857 and retains remnants of the original drawbridge and moat. During the Civil War the basement was transformed into a military dungeon – the genesis of Alcatraz as a prison.

Frank Morris Cell

Peer into cell 138 on B-Block to see a recreation of the dummy's head that Frank Morris left in his bed as a decoy to aid his notorious – and successful – 1962 escape from Alcatraz.

Ferry Dock & Pier

A giant wall map helps you get your bearings. Inside nearby Building 64, short films and exhibits provide historical perspective on the prison and details about the Native American Occupation.

TELESNIUK / SHUTTERSTOCK ©

Ferry Building

Global food trends start in San Francisco. To sample tomorrow's menu today, wander through the city's monument to trailblazing, sustainable food. The Ferry Building has the best bites from Northern California.

Other towns have gourmet ghettos, but San Francisco puts its love of food front and center at the Ferry Building. The once-grand port was overshadowed by a 1950s elevated freeway – until the overpass collapsed in 1989's Loma Prieta earthquake. The Ferry Building survived and became a symbol of San Francisco's reinvention, marking your arrival at America's forward-thinking food frontier.

History

The trademark 240ft tower greeted dozens of ferries daily after its 1898 inauguration. But with the opening of the Bay and Golden Gate Bridges, ferry traffic subsided in the 1930s. An overhead freeway was built, obscuring the building's stately facade and turning it black with exhaust fumes. Only after the 1989 earthquake did city planners

Great For...

Don't Miss

Heading out along the Embarcadero waterfront promenade for Bay Bridge views.

MICHAEL WARWICK / SHUTTERSTOCK ©

ℹ Need to Know

📞 415-983-8030; www.ferrybuildingmarket-place.com; cnr Market St & the Embarcadero; ⏰ 10am-7pm Mon-Fri, 8am-6pm Sat, 11am-5pm Sun; 👪; 🚌 2, 6, 9, 14, 21, 31, Ⓜ Embarcadero, Ⓑ Embarcadero

✕ Take a Break

Slurp the bounty of the North Bay at **Hog Island Oyster Company** (📞 415-391-7117; www.hogislandoysters.com; 1 Ferry Bldg, cnr Market St & the Embarcadero; 4 oysters $14; ⏰ 11am-9pm; 🚌 2, 6, 9, 14, 21, 31, Ⓜ Embarcadero, Ⓑ Embarcadero) ♿.

★ Top Tip

You can still catch ferries at the Ferry Building and, on sunny days, crossing the sparkling bay is a great escape.

realize what they'd been missing: with its grand halls and bay views, this was the perfect place for a new public commons.

Foodie Hot Spot

Today the grand arrivals hall tempts commuters to miss the boat and get on board with San Francisco's latest culinary trends instead. Indoor kiosks sell locally roasted espresso, artisan cheese and cured meats, plus organic ice-cream flavors to match – that's right, Vietnamese coffee, cheese and prosciutto. People-watching wine bars and award-winning restaurants are further enticements to stick around.

Ferry Plaza Farmers Market

Even before Ferry Building renovations were completed in 2003, the **Ferry Plaza Farmers Market** (📞 415-291-3276; www.cuesa.org; cnr Market St & the Embarcadero; street food $3-12; ⏰ 10am-2pm Tue & Thu, from 8am Sat; 🚼👪; 🚌 2, 6, 9, 14, 21, 31, Ⓜ Embarcadero, Ⓑ Embarcadero) ♿ began operating out front on the sidewalk. Soon the foodie action spread to the bayfront plaza, with 50 to 100 local food purveyors catering to hometown crowds three times a week. While locals sometimes grumble that the prices are higher here than at other markets, there's no denying that the Ferry Plaza market offers seasonal, sustainable, handmade gourmet treats and specialty produce not found elsewhere.

Join San Francisco's legions of professional chefs and semiprofessional eaters, and taste-test the artisan goat cheese, fresh-pressed California olive oil, wild boar and organic pluots for yourself. The Saturday morning farmers market offers the best people-watching – it's not uncommon to spot celebrities – but arrive early if you're shopping.

JON CHICA / SHUTTERSTOCK ©

Chinatown

The 41 historic alleyways packed into Chinatown's 22 blocks have seen it all since 1849: gold rushes and revolution, incense and opium, fire and icy receptions.

Great For...

Don't Miss

Hearing mah-jongg tiles, temple gongs and Chinese orchestras as you wander Chinatown's alleyways.

In clinker-brick buildings lining Chinatown's narrow backstreets, temple balconies jut out over bakeries, laundries and barbers – there was nowhere to go but up in Chinatown after 1870, when laws limited Chinese immigration, employment and housing.

Grant Avenue

Enter Chinatown through the Dragon's Gate, donated by Taiwan in 1970, and you'll find yourself on the street formerly known as Dupont in its notorious red-light heyday. The pagoda-topped 'Chinatown deco' architecture beyond this gate was innovated by Chinatown merchants, led by Look Tin Ely, in the 1920s – a pioneering initiative to lure tourists with a distinctive modern look.

It's hard to believe this souvenir-shopping strip was once notorious and brothel-lined – at least until you see

ℹ️ Need to Know

btwn Grant Ave, Stockton St, California St & Broadway; 🚌1, 30, 45, 🚋Powell-Hyde, Powell-Mason, California

✖️ Take a Break

Pick up where Jack Kerouac left off at Li Po (p66), a historical Beat hangout.

★ Top Tip

Parking is tough. There's public parking underneath Portsmouth Sq and at the Good Luck Parking Garage.

the fascinating displays at the **Chinese Historical Society of America** (CHSA; 📞415-391-1188; www.chsa.org; 965 Clay St; adult/student/child $15/10/free; ⏱️11am-4pm Wed-Sun; ♿; 🚌1, 8, 30, 45, 🚋California, Powell-Mason, Powell-Hyde) FREE.

Waverly Place

Grant Ave may be the economic heart of Chinatown, but its soul is Waverly Pl, lined with flag-festooned temple balconies. Due to the 19th-century race-based restrictions, family associations and temples were built right on top of the barber shops, laundries and restaurants lining these two city blocks. Through good times and bad, Waverly Pl stood its ground, and temple services have been held here since 1852 – even after San Francisco's 1906 earthquake and fire, when altars were still smoldering.

Spofford Alley

Sun Yat-sen once plotted the overthrow of China's Manchu dynasty here at No 36, and, during Prohibition, this was the site of turf battles over local bootlegging and protection rackets. Spofford has mellowed with age: it's now lined with seniors community centers. But the action still starts around sundown, when a Chinese orchestra strikes up a tune and the clicking of a mah-jongg game begins.

Chinatown Tours

On two-hour **Chinatown Alleyway Tours** (www.chinatownalleywaytours.org), teenage Chinatown residents guide you through backstreets that have seen it all.

Local-led, kid-friendly **Chinatown Heritage Walking Tours** (www.cccsf. us) take a themed approach and visit key historic sights (including the Golden Gate Fortune Cookie Company and Tin How Temple).

North Beach Beat

Hit North Beach literary hot spots and walk in the footsteps of San Francisco's Beat poets.

Start City Lights Books
Distance 1.5 Miles
Duration Two Hours

4 Peaceful **Bob Kaufman Alley** is named after the legendary street-corner poet who endured a 12-year vow of silence.

3 Look for parrots in the treetops and octogenarians in tai chi stances on the lawn of **Washington Sq**.

Classic Photo Browsing the shelves at City Lights

1 Pick up a copy of Ferlinghetti's *San Francisco Poems* from **City Lights Books** (p57), home of Beat poetry and free speech.

N 0 ———— 400 m
0 ———— 0.2 miles

2 With opera on the jukebox and potent espresso, **Caffe Trieste** (p66) is where Coppola allegedly drafted *The Godfather*.

Filbert St

Union St

Kearny St

Green St

Grant Ave

Vallejo St

Broadway

5 The **Beat Museum** (☏800-537-6822; www.kerouac.com; 540 Broadway; adult/student $8/5, walking tours $25; ☺museum 10am-7pm, walking tours 2-4pm Sat; ☒ Powell-Mason, ☒ 8, 10, 12, 30, 41, 45) is the closest you can get to the complete Beat experience without breaking the law.

START

FINISH

Pacific Ave

Columbus Ave

6 Finish your tour, but start your evening, at memorabilia-heavy **Specs** (p65), the perfect jumping-off point for a literary bar crawl.

Washington St

Grant Ave

Take a Break
Pop into **Comstock Saloon** (p65) for pisco punch.

1 RANDY ANDY / SHUTTERSTOCK © 3 MANAKIN / GETTY IMAGES © 5 KRIS DAVIDSON / LONELY PLANET ©

◎ SIGHTS

Most major museums are downtown, though Golden Gate Park is home to the de Young Museum and the California Academy of Sciences. The city's most historic districts are the Mission, Chinatown, North Beach and the Haight. Galleries are clustered downtown and in North Beach, the Mission, Potrero Flats and Dogpatch. You'll find hilltop parks citywide, but Russian, Nob and Telegraph Hills are the highest and most panoramic.

◎ The Marina, Fisherman's Wharf & the Piers

Sights along **Fisherman's Wharf** (www.fishermanswharf.org; 🚻; 🚌19, 30, 47, 49, 🚋Powell-Mason, Powell-Hyde, Ⓜ️F) **FREE** – the Embarcadero and Jefferson St waterfront running from Pier 29 to Van Ness Ave – are geared entirely to tourists, particularly families, and it's easy to get stuck with so much vying for your attention. Stick to the waterside and keep moving.

Maritime National Historical Park   Historic Site

(📞415-447-5000; www.nps.gov/safr; 499 Jefferson St, Hyde St Pier; 7-day ticket adult/child $10/free; ⏱9:30am-5pm Oct-May, to 5:30pm Jun-Sep; 🚻; 🚌19, 30, 47, 🚋Powell-Hyde, Ⓜ️F) Four historic ships are floating museums at this maritime park, Fisherman's Wharf's most authentic attraction. Standouts moored along Hyde Street Pier include the 1891 schooner *Alma*, which hosts guided sailing trips in summer; 1890 steamboat *Eureka*; paddlewheel tugboat *Eppleton Hall*; and iron-hulled *Balclutha*, which brought coal to San Francisco. It's free to walk the pier; pay only to board ships.

Exploratorium   Museum

(📞415-528-4444; www.exploratorium.edu; Pier 15; adult/child $30/20, 6-10pm Thu $15; ⏱10am-5pm Tue-Sun, over 18yr only 6-10pm Thu; 🅿️🚻; Ⓜ️E, F) 🖋 Is there a science to skateboarding? Do toilets really flush counterclockwise in Australia? Find out things you'll wish you learned in school at San Francisco's thrilling hands-on science museum. Combining

Fisherman's Wharf

science with art and investigating human perception, the Exploratorium nudges you to question how you perceive the world around you. The setting is thrilling: a 9-acre, glass-walled pier jutting straight into San Francisco Bay, with large outdoor portions you can explore free of charge, 24 hours a day.

◎ Downtown & Civic Center

Asian Art Museum   Museum

(🖉415-581-3500; www.asianart.org; 200 Larkin St; adult/student/child $15/10/free, 1st Sun of month free; ⊘10am-5pm Tue, Wed & Fri-Sun, to 9pm Thu; 👫; ⓂCivic Center, ⒷCivic Center) Imaginations race from ancient Persian miniatures to cutting-edge Japanese minimalism through three floors spanning 6000 years of Asian art. Besides the largest collection outside Asia – 18,000 works – the museum offers excellent programs for all ages, from shadow-puppet shows and tea tastings with star chefs to mixers with cross-cultural DJ mash-ups.

Contemporary
Jewish Museum   Museum

(🖉415-344-8800; www.thecjm.org; 736 Mission St; adult/student/child $14/12/free; after 5pm Thu $5; ⊘11am-5pm Mon, Tue & Fri-Sun, to 8pm Thu; 👫; 🚊14, 30, 45, ⒷMontgomery, ⓂMontgomery) That upended blue-steel box miraculously balancing on one corner isn't sculpture; it's the Yerba Buena Lane entry to the Contemporary Jewish Museum – an institution that upends conventional ideas about art and religion. Exhibits here are compelling explorations of Jewish ideals and visionaries, including writer Gertrude Stein, rock promoter Bill Graham, cartoonist Roz Chast and filmmaker Stanley Kubrick.

San Francisco Museum
of Modern Art   Museum

(SFMOMA; 🖉415-357-4000; www.sfmoma.org; 151 3rd St; adult/child under 18yr/student $25/ free/$19; ⊘10am-5pm Fri-Tue, to 9pm Thu, public spaces from 9am; 👫; 🚊5, 6, 7, 14, 19, 21, 31, 38, ⓂMontgomery, ⒷMontgomery) The expanded SFMOMA is a mind-boggling feat, tripled in

 San Francisco for Children

San Francisco is packed with family-friendly attractions, including the **California Academy of Sciences** (p59) in Golden Gate Park and the waterfront **Exploratorium** (p52).

Prison tours of **Alcatraz** (p42) fascinate kids and give them an interesting, safe place to run around, while in SoMa the **Children's Creativity Museum** (🖉415-820-3320; http://creativity.org/; 221 4th St; $12; ⊘10am-4pm Wed-Sun; 👫; 🚊14, ⓂPowell, ⒷPowell) has technology that's too cool for school: robots, live-action video games and 3D animation workshops.

Plus there's always an old-school cable-car ride – a joy for the whole family.

California Academy of Sciences
ANTON_IVANOV / SHUTTERSTOCK ©

size to accommodate a sprawling collection of modern masterworks and 19 concurrent exhibitions over 10 floors – but, then again, SFMOMA has defied limits ever since its 1935 founding. SFMOMA was a visionary early investor in then-emerging art forms, including photography, installations, video, performance art, and (as befits a global technology hub) digital art and industrial design. Even during the Depression, the museum envisioned a world of vivid possibilities, starting in San Francisco.

SF Camerawork   Gallery

(🖉415-487-1011; www.sfcamerawork.org; 1011 Market St, 2nd fl; ⊘noon-6pm Tue-Sat; 🚊6, 7, 9, 21, ⒷCivic Center, ⓂCivic Center) **FREE** Since 1974, this nonprofit art organization has

San Francisco

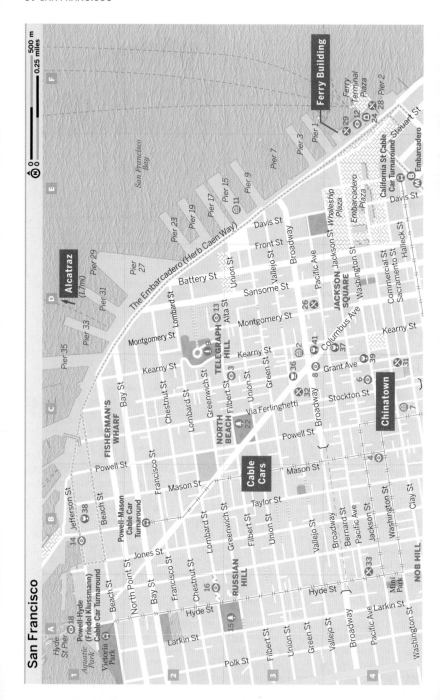

Alcatraz
(1.7mi)

Ferry Building

Cable Cars

Chinatown

FISHERMAN'S WHARF

NORTH BEACH

TELEGRAPH HILL

RUSSIAN HILL

JACKSON SQUARE

NOB HILL

San Francisco Bay

Aquatic Park

Victoria Park

Mini Park

Powell-Hyde (Friedel Klussmann) Cable Car Turnaround

Powell-Mason Cable Car Turnaround

California St Cable Car Turnaround

Embarcadero Plaza

Ferry Terminal Plaza

Jackson St Whaleship Plaza

Hyde St Pier

The Embarcadero (Herb Caen Way)

Pier 2
Pier 1
Pier 3
Pier 7
Pier 9
Pier 11
Pier 15
Pier 17
Pier 19
Pier 23
Pier 27
Pier 29
Pier 31
Pier 33
Pier 35

Jefferson St
Beach St
North Point St
Bay St
Francisco St
Chestnut St
Lombard St
Greenwich St
Filbert St
Union St
Green St
Vallejo St
Broadway
Pacific Ave
Jackson St
Washington St
Clay St
Sacramento St
California St
Davis St
Front St
Battery St
Sansome St
Montgomery St
Kearny St
Grant Ave
Stockton St
Powell St
Mason St
Taylor St
Jones St
Leavenworth St
Hyde St
Larkin St
Polk St

Columbus Ave
Via Ferlinghetti
Alta St
Bernard St
Commercial St
Halleck St
Steuart St
Spear St

500 m
0.25 miles

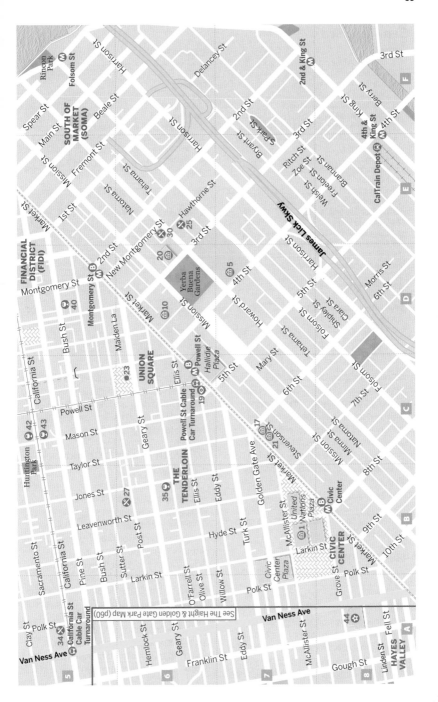

San Francisco

championed experimental photo-based imagery beyond classic B&W prints and casual digital snapshots. Since moving into this spacious new Market St gallery, Camerawork's far-reaching exhibitions have examined memories of love and war in Southeast Asia, taken imaginary holidays with slide shows of vacation snapshots scavenged from the San Francisco Dump and showcased San Francisco–based Iranian American artist Sanaz Mazinani's mesmerizing Islamic-inspired photo montages made of tiny Trumps.

Luggage Store Gallery　　Gallery
(📞415-255-5971; www.luggagestoregallery.org; 1007 Market St; ⊙noon-5pm Wed-Sat; 🚍5, 6, 7, 21, 31, Ⓜ Civic Center, Ⓑ Civic Center) Like a dandelion pushing through sidewalk cracks, this plucky nonprofit gallery has brought signs of life to one of the Tenderloin's toughest blocks for two decades. By giving San Francisco street artists a gallery platform, the Luggage Store helped launch

graffiti-art star Barry McGee, muralist Rigo and street photographer Cheryl Dunn. Find the graffitied door and climb to the 2nd-floor gallery, which rises above the street without losing sight of it.

◎ North Beach & Chinatown

Coit Tower　　Public Art
(📞415-249-0995; www.sfrecpark.org; Telegraph Hill Blvd; nonresident elevator fee adult/child $8/5; ⊙10am-6pm Apr-Oct, to 5pm Nov-Mar; 🚍39) The exclamation mark on San Francisco's skyline is Coit Tower, with 360-degree views of downtown and wraparound 1930s Works Progress Administration murals glorifying SF workers. Initially denounced as Communist, the murals are now a national landmark. For a wild-parrot's panoramic view of San Francisco, 210ft above the city, take the elevator to the tower's open-air platform. To glimpse seven recently restored murals up a hidden stairwell on the 2nd floor, join the 11am tour

Wednesday or Saturday (free; donations welcome).

City Lights Books   Cultural Center

(📞415-362-8193; www.citylights.com; 261 Columbus Ave; ⏰10am-midnight; 👶; 🚌8, 10, 12, 30, 41, 45, 🚋Powell-Mason, Powell-Hyde) Free speech and free spirits have flourished here since 1957, when City Lights founder and poet Lawrence Ferlinghetti and manager Shigeyoshi Murao won a landmark ruling defending their right to publish Allen Ginsberg's magnificent epic poem *Howl*. Celebrate your freedom to read freely in the designated Poet's Chair upstairs overlooking Jack Kerouac Alley, load up on zines on the mezzanine and entertain radical ideas downstairs in the new Pedagogies of Resistance section.

Filbert Street Steps   Architecture

(🚌39) Halfway through the steep climb up the Filbert Street Steps to Coit Tower, you might wonder if it's all worth the trouble. Take a breather and notice what you're passing: hidden cottages along Napier Lane's wooden boardwalk, sculpture-dotted gardens in bloom year-round and sweeping Bay Bridge vistas. If you need further encouragement, the wild parrots in the trees have been known to interject a few choice words your gym trainer would probably get sued for using.

◉ Nob Hill & Russian Hill

Lombard Street   Street

(🚋Powell-Hyde) You've seen the eight switch-backs of Lombard St's 900 block in a thousand photographs. The tourist board has dubbed it 'the world's crookedest street,' which is factually incorrect: Vermont St in Potrero Hill deserves that award, but Lombard is much more scenic, with its redbrick pavement and lovingly tended flowerbeds. It wasn't always so bent; before the arrival of the car it lunged straight down the hill.

Cable Car Museum   Historic Site

(📞415-474-1887; www.cablecarmuseum.org; 1201 Mason St; donations appreciated; ⏰10am-6pm Apr-Sep, to 5pm Oct-Mar; 👶; 🚋Powell-Mason, Powell-Hyde) 【FREE】 Hear that whirring beneath the cable-car tracks? That's the sound of the cables that pull the cars, and they all connect inside the city's long-functioning cable-car barn. Grips, engines, braking mechanisms...if these warm your gearhead heart, you'll be besotted with the Cable Car Museum.

◉ The Mission

Balmy Alley   Public Art

(📞415-285-2287; www.precitaeyes.org; btwn 24th & 25th Sts; 🚌10, 12, 14, 27, 48, Ⓑ24th St Mission) Inspired by Diego Rivera's 1930s San Francisco murals and provoked by US foreign policy in Central America, 1970s Mission *muralistas* (muralists) led by Mia Gonzalez set out to transform the political landscape, one mural-covered garage door at a time. Today, Balmy Alley murals span three decades, from an early memorial for El Salvador activist Archbishop Óscar Romero to a homage to Frida Kahlo, Georgia O'Keeffe and other trailblazing female modern artists.

Dolores Park   Park

(http://sfrecpark.org/destination/mission-dolores-park; Dolores St, btwn 18th & 20th Sts; ⏰6am-10pm; 👶🐕; 🚌14, 33, 49, Ⓑ16th St Mission, ⓂJ) Semiprofessional tanning and taco picnics: welcome to San Francisco's sunny side. Dolores Park has something for everyone, from street ball and tennis to the Mayan-pyramid playground (sorry, kids: no blood sacrifices allowed). Political protests and other favorite local sports happen year-round, and there are free movie nights and mime troupe performances in summer. Climb to the upper southwestern corner for superb views of downtown, framed by palm trees.

◉ The Haight

Haight & Ashbury   Landmark

(🚌6, 7, 33, 37, 43) This legendary intersection was the epicenter of the psychedelic '60s, and 'Hashbury' remains a counter-culture magnet. On average Saturdays here you can sign Green Party petitions,

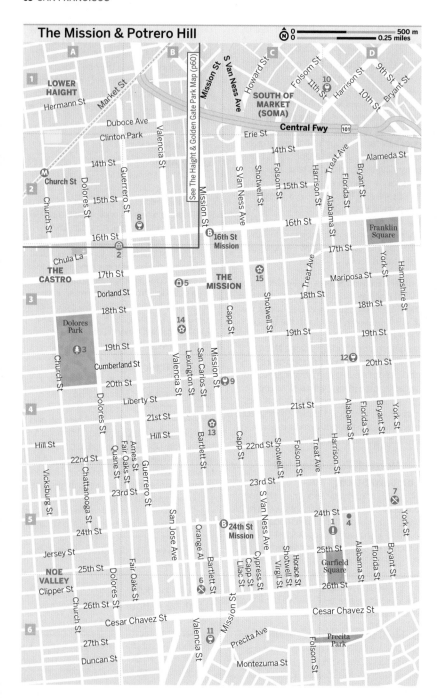

The Mission & Potrero Hill

N

0 — 500 m
0 — 0.25 miles

LOWER HAIGHT

Hermann St

Market St

Duboce Ave

Clinton Park

Valencia St

14th St

Church St

Dolores St

Guerrero St

15th St

Church St

8

16th St

Chula La

THE CASTRO

17th St

Dorland St

18th St

Dolores Park

3

19th St

Church St

Cumberland St

20th St

Liberty St

21st St

Hill St

Hill St

22nd St

Vicksburg St

Chattanooga St

Dolores St

Fair Oaks St

Quane St

Ames St

Guerrero St

23rd St

24th St

Jersey St

NOE VALLEY

Clipper St

25th St

Church St

Dolores St

Fair Oaks St

26th St

Cesar Chavez St

27th St

Duncan St

See The Haight & Golden Gate Park Map (p90)

Mission St

S Van Ness Ave

Howard St

Folsom St

11th St

10

Harrison St

10th St

9th St

Bryant St

SOUTH OF MARKET (SOMA)

Erie St

Central Fwy 101

14th St

Shotwell St

Folsom St

15th St

Harrison St

Treat Ave

Alameda St

Bryant St

Florida St

Alabama St

16th St

Mission St

16th St Mission

17th St

Franklin Square

York St

Hampshire St

5

THE MISSION

15

Treat Ave

Mariposa St

18th St

18th St

Capp St

Shotwell St

19th St

19th St

14

San Carlos St

Lexington St

Valencia St

Mission St

9

12

20th St

Cumberland St

Liberty St

21st St

Alabama St

Florida St

Bryant St

York St

Bartlett St

13

Capp St

22nd St

Shotwell St

Folsom St

Treat Ave

Harrison St

23rd St

S Van Ness Ave

7

24th St

San Jose Ave

Orange Al

24th St Mission

Bartlett St

Cypress St

Capp St

Shotwell St

Virgil St

Horace St

Folsom St

Alabama St

Florida St

Bryant St

York St

1

4

25th St

Garfield Square

Lilac St

26th St

6

Cesar Chavez St

11

Valencia St

Mission St

Precita Ave

Precita Park

Folsom St

Montezuma St

The Mission & Potrero Hill

commission a poem and hear Hare Krishna on keyboards and Bob Dylan on banjo. The clock overhead always reads 4:20 – better known in herbal circles as International Bong-Hit Time. A local clockmaker recently fixed the clock; within a week it was stuck again at 4:20.

◎ Golden Gate Park

When San Franciscans refer to 'the park,' there's only one that gets the definite article: Golden Gate Park. Everything San Franciscans hold dear is here: free spirits, free music, redwoods, Frisbee, protests, fine art, bonsai and buffalo.

California Academy of Sciences   Museum

(☎415-379-8000; www.calacademy.org; 55 Music Concourse Dr; adult/student/child $35/30/25; ⊙9:30am-5pm Mon-Sat, from 11am Sun; ℗🏛; 🚌5, 6, 7, 21, 31, 33, 44, ⓂN) 🖈 Architect Renzo Piano's 2008 landmark Leadership in Energy and Environmental Design–certified green building houses 40,000 weird and wonderful animals in a four-story rainforest, split-level aquarium and planetarium all under a 'Living Roof' of California wildflowers.

de Young Museum   Museum

(☎415-750-3600; http://deyoung.famsf.org; 50 Hagiwara Tea Garden Dr; adult/child $15/free, 1st Tue of month free; ⊙9:30am-5:15pm Tue-Sun, to 8:45pm Fri Apr-Nov; 🏛; 🚌5, 7, 44, ⓂN) Follow sculptor Andy Goldsworthy's artificial

fault line in the sidewalk into Herzog & de Meuron's sleek, copper-clad building that's oxidizing green to blend into the park. Don't be fooled by the de Young's camouflaged exterior: shows here boldly broaden artistic horizons, from Oceanic ceremonial masks and trippy hippie handmade fashion to James Turrell's domed 'Skyspace' installation, built into a hill in the sculpture garden. Your ticket includes free same-day entry to the **Legion of Honor** (☎415-750-3600; http://legionofhonor.famsf.org; 100 34th Ave; adult/child $15/free, discount with Muni ticket $2, 1st Tue of month free; ⊙9:30am-5:15pm Tue-Sun; 🏛; 🚌1, 2, 18, 38).

🏪 SHOPPING

Park Life   Gifts & Souvenirs

(☎415-386-7275; www.parklifestore.com; 220 Clement St; ⊙11am-8pm Mon-Sat, to 6pm Sun; 🚌1, 2, 33, 38, 44) The Swiss Army knife of hip San Francisco emporiums, Park Life is a design store, indie publisher and art gallery all in one. Browse presents too clever to give away, including toy soldiers in yoga poses, Tauba Auerbach's reprogrammed Casio watches, Park Life catalogs of Shaun O'Dell paintings of natural disorder and sinister Todd Hido photos of shaggy cats on shag rugs.

Community Thrift   Clothing, Vintage

(☎415-861-4910; www.communitythriftsf.org; 623 Valencia St; ⊙10am-6:30pm; 🚌14, 22, 33, 49, 🅱16th St Mission) 🖈 When local collectors and retailers have too much of a good

The Haight & Golden Gate Park

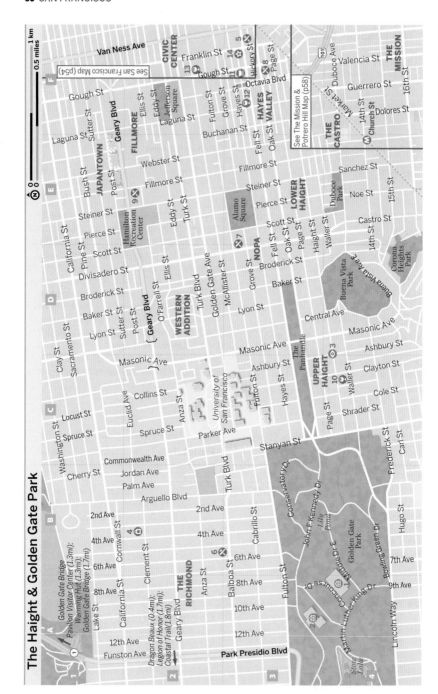

The Haight & Golden Gate Park

thing, they donate it to nonprofit Community Thrift, where proceeds go to 200-plus local charities – all the more reason to gloat over your $5 totem-pole teacup, $10 vintage windbreaker and $14 disco-era glitter romper. Donate your cast-offs (until 5pm daily) and show some love to the Community.

Recchiuti Chocolates Food & Drinks
(🖉415-834-9494; www.recchiuticonfections. com; 1 Ferry Bldg, cnr Market St & the Embarcadero; ☺10am-7pm Mon-Fri, 8am-6pm Sat, 10am-5pm Sun; Ⓜ️Embarcadero, ⒷEmbarcadero) No San Franciscan can resist award-winning Recchiuti: Pacific Heights parts with old money for its *fleur de sel* caramels; Noe Valley's foodie kids prefer S'more Bites to the campground variety; North Beach toasts to the red-wine-pairing chocolate box; and the Mission approves San Francisco–landmark chocolates designed by Creativity Explored – proceeds benefit the Mission arts-education nonprofit for artists with developmental disabilities.

✸ EATING

✸ Downtown & Civic Center

farm:table American $
(🖉415-292-7089; www.farmtablesf.com; 754 Post St; dishes $6-9; ☺7:30am-2pm Tue-Fri, 8am-3pm Sat & Sun; 🖉; 🚌2, 3, 27, 38) A ray of sunshine in the concrete heart of the city, this plucky little storefront showcases seasonal California organics in just-baked breakfasts and farmstead-fresh lunches.

Check the menu on Twitter (@farmtable) for today's homemade cereals, savory tarts and game-changing toast, such as ginger peach and mascarpone on whole-wheat sourdough. Tiny space, but immaculate kitchen and great coffee. Cash only.

Cotogna Italian $$
(🖉415-775-8508; www.cotognasf.com; 490 Pacific Ave; mains $19-35; ☺11:30am-10:30pm Mon-Thu, to 11pm Fri & Sat, 5-9:30pm Sun; 🖉; 🚌10, 12) Chef-owner Michael Tusk racks up James Beard Awards for a quintessentially Italian culinary balancing act: he strikes ideal proportions among a few pristine flavors in rustic pastas, wood-fired pizzas and salt-crusted branzino. Reserve, especially for bargain $55 four-course Sunday suppers with $35 wine pairings – or plan a walk-in late lunch or early dinner.

In Situ Californian, International $$
(🖉415-941-6050; http://insitu.sfmoma.org; SFMOMA, 151 3rd St; mains $14-34; ☺11am-3:30pm Mon & Tue, 11am-3:30pm & 5-9pm Thu-Sun; 🚌5, 6, 7, 14, 19, 21, 31, 38, ⒷMontgomery, Ⓜ️Montgomery) The landmark gallery of modern cuisine attached to SFMOMA also showcases avant-garde masterpieces – but these ones you'll lick clean. Chef Corey Lee collaborates with star chefs worldwide, scrupulously recreating their signature dishes with California-grown ingredients so that you can enjoy Harald Wohlfahrt's impeccable anis-marinated salmon, Hiroshi Sasaki's decadent chicken thighs and Albert Adrìa's gravity-defying cocoa-bubble cake in one unforgettable sitting.

Mission Mural Tours

Muralists from Precita Eyes lead weekend walking **tours** (☎415-285-2287; www.precitaeyes.org; 2981 24th St; adult $15-20, child $3; 🚇; 🚌12, 14, 48, 49, 🅱24th St Mission) covering 60 to 70 Mission murals within a six- to 10-block radius of mural-bedecked Balmy Alley (p57). Tours last 90 minutes to 2¼ hours (for the more in-depth Classic Mural Walk). Proceeds fund mural upkeep at this community-arts nonprofit.

'Un Pasado Que Aún Vive', 2004 Joel Bergner
LONELY PLANET / GETTY IMAGES ©

Benu Californian, Fusion $$$

(☎415-685-4860; www.benusf.com; 22 Hawthorne St; tasting menu $285; ⏱6-9pm seatings Tue-Sat; 🚌10, 12, 14, 30, 45) San Francisco has pioneered Asian fusion cuisine for 150 years, but the pan-Pacific innovation of chef-owner Corey Lee brings to the plate is gasp-inducing: foie-gras soup dumplings – what?! Dungeness crab and truffle custard pack such outsize flavor into Lee's faux-shark-fin soup, you'll swear Jaws is in there. Benu dinners are investments, but don't miss star sommelier Yoon Ha's ingenious pairings ($185).

✖ North Beach & Chinatown

Molinari Deli $

(☎415-421-2337; www.molinarisalame.com; 373 Columbus Ave; sandwiches $10-13.50; ⏱9am-6pm Mon-Fri, to 5:30pm Sat; 🚌8, 10, 12, 30, 39, 41, 45, 🚋Powell-Mason) Observe quasi-religious North Beach noontime rituals: enter Molinari, and grab a number and a crusty roll. When your number's called, wisecracking staff pile your roll with heavenly fixings: milky buffalo mozzarella, tangy sun-dried tomatoes, translucent sheets of prosciutto di Parma, slabs of legendary house-cured salami, drizzles of olive oil and balsamic. Enjoy hot from the panini press at sidewalk tables.

Mister Jiu's Chinese $$

(☎415-857-9688; http://misterjius.com; 28 Waverly Pl; mains $14-45; ⏱5:30-10:30pm Tue-Sat; 🚌30, 🚋California) Ever since the gold rush, San Francisco has craved Chinese food, powerful cocktails and hyperlocal specialties – and Mister Jiu's satisfies on all counts. Build your own banquet of Chinese classics with California twists: chanterelle chow mein, Dungeness-crab rice noodles, quail and Mission-fig sticky rice. Cocktail pairings are equally inspired – try jasmine-infused-gin Happiness ($13) with tea-smoked Sonoma-duck confit.

✖ Nob Hill & Russian Hill

Swan Oyster Depot Seafood $$

(☎415-673-1101; 1517 Polk St; dishes $10-25; ⏱10:30am-5:30pm Mon-Sat; 🚌1, 19, 47, 49, 🚋California) Superior flavor without the superior attitude of typical seafood restaurants – Swan's downside is an inevitable wait for the few stools at its vintage lunch counter, but the upside of high turnover is incredibly fresh seafood.

Seven Hills Italian $$$

(☎415-775-1550; www.sevenhillssf.com; 1550 Hyde St; mains $19-31; ⏱5:30-9:30pm Sun-Thu, to 10pm Fri & Sat; 🚌10, 12, 🚋Powell-Hyde) Anthony Florian has studied with some of the great chefs of California and Italy, and he's an expert at taking several seasonal ingredients and making them shine. His short, market-driven menu features house-made pastas with elements such as rabbit and house-cured pancetta. The four mains showcase quality California meats. Tables are close in the elegant little storefront, but brilliant sound-canceling technology eliminates noise. Stellar service, too.

The Mission

La Palma Mexicatessen Mexican $

(📞415-647-1500; www.lapalmasf.com; 2884 24th St; tamales, tacos & huarache $3-5; ⏰8am-6pm Mon-Sat, to 5pm Sun; 🅿️🚼; 🚌12, 14, 27, 48, 🚇24th St Mission) ✦ Follow the applause: that's the sound of organic tortilla-making in progress at La Palma. You've found the Mission mother lode of handmade tamales, *pupusas* (tortilla pockets) with potato and *chicharones* (pork crackling), *carnitas* (slow-roasted pork), *cotija* (Oaxacan cheese) and La Palma's own tangy tomatillo sauce. Get takeout, or bring a small army to finish that massive meal at sunny sidewalk tables.

Al's Place California $$

(📞415-416-6136; www.alsplacesf.com; 1499 Valencia St; share plates $15-19; ⏰5:30-10pm Wed-Sun; 🅿️; 🚌12, 14, 49, 🚇J, 🚇24th St Mission) ✦ The Golden State dazzles on Al's plates, featuring homegrown heirloom ingredients, pristine Pacific seafood, and grass-fed meat on the side. Painstaking preparation yields sun-drenched flavors and exquisite textures: crispy-skin cod with frothy preserved-lime dip, grilled peach melting into velvety foie gras. Dishes are half the size but thrice the flavor of mains elsewhere – get two or three, and you'll be California dreaming.

The Haight & Hayes Valley

Mill Bakery $

(📞415-345-1953; www.themillsf.com; 736 Divisadero St; toast $4-7; ⏰7am-7pm Tue-Thu, to 8pm Fri-Sun, to 9pm Mon; 🅿️🚼; 🚌5, 21, 24, 38) Baked with organic whole grain stone-ground on-site, hearty Josey Baker Bread sustains Haight skaters and start-uppers alike. You might think San Francisco hipsters are gullible for queuing for pricey toast, until you taste the truth: slathered in housemade hazelnut spread or California-grown almond butter, it's a meal. Monday is pizza night, and any time's right for made-in-house granola with Sonoma yogurt.

Rich Table California $$

(📞415-355-9085; http://richtablesf.com; 199 Gough St; mains $17-36; ⏰5:30-10pm Sun-Thu, to 10:30pm Fri & Sat; 🚌5, 6, 7, 21, 47, 49, 🚇Van Ness) ✦ Impossible cravings begin at Rich

The Pritzker Center for Photography at SFMOMA (p53)

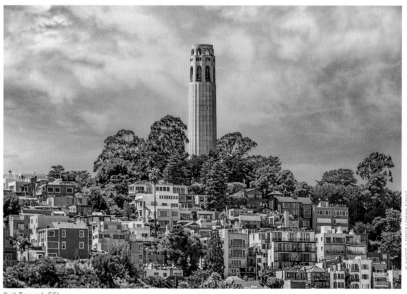

Coit Tower (p56)

Table, inventor of porcini doughnuts, miso-marrow-stuffed pasta and fried-chicken madeleines with caviar. Married co-chefs and owners Sarah and Evan Rich playfully riff on seasonal California fare, freestyling with whimsical off-menu amuse-bouches like trippy beet marshmallows or the Dirty Hippie: nutty hemp atop silky goat-buttermilk *pannacotta*, as offbeat and entrancing as Hippie Hill drum circles.

Cala Mexican, Californian $$$

(☑415-660-7701; www.calarestaurant.com; 149 Fell St; ⊙5-10pm Mon-Wed, to 11pm Thu-Sat, 11am-3pm Sun, taco bar 11am-2pm Mon-Fri; ☐6, 7, 21, 47, 49, ⓂVan Ness) Like discovering a long-lost twin, Cala's Mexico Norte cuisine is a revelation. San Francisco's Mexican-rancher roots are deeply honored here: silky bone-marrow salsa and fragrant heritage-corn tortillas grace a sweet potato slow-cooked in ashes. Brace yourself with mezcal margaritas for the ultimate California surf and turf: sea urchin with beef tongue. Original and unforgettable, even before Mayan-chocolate gelato with amaranth brittle.

🍸 DRINKING & NIGHTLIFE

For a pub crawl, start with North Beach saloons or Mission bars around Valencia and 16th Sts. The Castro has historic gay bars; SoMa adds dance clubs. Downtown and around Union Sq mix dives with speakeasies. Marina bars are preppy, while Haight bars draw mixed alterna-crowds.

🍷 Downtown, Civic Center & SoMa

Pagan Idol Lounge

(☑415-985-6375; www.paganidol.com; 375 Bush St; ⊙4pm-1am Mon-Fri, 6pm-1:30am Sat; ⒷMontgomery, ⓂF, J, K, L, M) Volcanoes erupt inside Pagan Idol every half hour, or until there's a virgin sacrifice...what, no takers? Then order your island tiki cocktail and brace for impact – these island tiki drinks are no joke. Flirt with disaster over a Hemingway Is Dead: rum, bitters and grapefruit, served in a skull. Book online to nab a hut for groups of four to six.

Bar Agricole   Bar

(📋415-355-9400; www.baragricole.com; 355 11th St; ⊙5-11pm Mon-Thu, 5pm-12am Fri & Sat, 10am-2pm & 6-9pm Sun; 🚌9, 12, 27, 47) 🍴 Drink your way to a history degree with well-researched cocktails: Whiz Bang with house bitters, whiskey, vermouth and absinthe scores high, but El Presidente with white rum, farmhouse curaçao and California-pomegranate grenadine takes top honors. This overachiever wins James Beard Award nods for spirits and eco-savvy design, plus popular acclaim for $1 oysters and $5 aperitifs, 5pm to 6pm Monday to Saturday.

Bourbon & Branch   Bar

(📋415-346-1735; www.bourbonandbranch. com; 501 Jones St; ⊙6pm-2am; 🚌27, 38) 'Don't even think of asking for a cosmo' read the House Rules at this Prohibition-era speakeasy, recognizable by its deliciously misleading Anti-Saloon League sign. For award-winning cocktails in the liquored-up library, whisper the password ('books') to be ushered through the bookcase secret passageway. Reservations required for front-room booths and Wilson & Wilson Detective Agency, the noir-themed speakeasy-within-a-speakeasy (password supplied with reservations).

🍷 North Beach & Chinatown

Comstock Saloon   Bar

(📋415-617-0071; www.comstocksaloon.com; 155 Columbus Ave; ⊙4pm-midnight Sun-Mon, to 2am Tue-Thu & Sat, noon-2am Fri; 🚌8, 10, 12, 30, 45, 🚋Powell-Mason) Relieving yourself in the marble trough below the bar is no longer advisable – Emperor Norton is watching from above – but otherwise this 1907 Victorian saloon brings back the Barbary Coast's glory days with authentic pisco punch and martini-precursor Martinez (gin, vermouth, bitters, maraschino liqueur). Reserve booths or back-parlor seating to hear on nights when ragtime-jazz bands play.

🥾 Active San Francisco

On sunny weekends, San Francisco is out kite-flying, surfing or biking. Even on foggy days, don't neglect sunscreen: UV rays penetrate San Francisco's thin cloud cover.

Hit your stride on the 10.5 mile **Coastal Trail** (www.californiacoastaltrail. info; ⊙sunrise-sunset; 🚌1, 18, 38), starting at Fort Funston, crossing 4 miles of sandy Ocean Beach and wrapping around the Presidio to the Golden Gate Bridge. Casual strollers can pick up the freshly restored trail near Sutro Baths and head around the Lands End bluffs for edge-of-the-world views and glimpses of shipwrecks at low tide.

For something a little different, discover **Emperor Norton's Fantastic Time Machine** (📋415-644-8513; www. emperornortontour.com; $20; ⊙11am & 2:30pm Thu & Sat, 11am Sun; 🚌30, 38, 🅱Powell St, Ⓜ️Powell St, 🚋Powell-Mason, Powell-Hyde). Follow the self-appointed Emperor Norton (aka historian Joseph Amster) across 2 miles of the most dastardly, scheming, uplifting and urban-legendary terrain on Earth...or at least west of Berkeley. Sunday waterfront tours depart from the Ferry Building; all others depart from Union Sq's Dewey Monument. Cash only.

Hiking towards the Golden Gate Bridge (p38)
MARGARET.W / SHUTTERSTOCK ©

Specs   Bar

(Specs Twelve Adler Museum Cafe; 📋415-421-4112; 12 William Saroyan Pl; ⊙5pm-2am; 🚌8,

🍽️ Cheap Eats in the Avenues

Work up an appetite in Golden Gate Park, then haul north for cheap and tasty ethnic eats.

Fog banks and cold wars are no match for the heartwarming powers of the **Cinderella Russian Bakery** (☑415-751-6723; www.cinderellabakery.com; 436 Balboa St; pastries $1.50-3.50, mains $7-13; � 7am-7pm; 👶☸; 🚌5, 21, 31, 33), serving treats like your baba used to make (just-baked egg-and-green-onion piroshki, hearty borscht, decadent dumplings) since 1953.

Hong Kong meets Vegas at San Francisco's most glamorous, decadent Cantonese restaurant, **Dragon Beaux** (☑415-333-8899; www.dragonbeaux.com; 5700 Geary Blvd; dumplings $4-9; � 11:30am-2:30pm & 5:30-10pm Mon-Thu, to 10:30pm Fri, 10am-3pm & 5:30-10pm Sat & Sun; 👶; 🚌2, 38). Say yes to cartloads of succulent roast meats – hello, duck and pork belly – and creative dumplings, especially XO dumplings with plump, brandy-laced shrimp in spinach wrappers

Dim sum in a San Francisco restaurant
JESSICA RUSCELLO / SHUTTERSTOCK ©

10, 12, 30, 41, 45, 🚋Powell-Mason) The walls here are plastered with merchant-marine memorabilia, and you'll be plastered too if you try to keep up with the salty characters holding court in back. Surrounded by seafaring mementos – including walrus genitalia over the bar – your order seems obvious: pitcher of Anchor Steam, coming right up. Cash only.

Li Po Bar

(☑415-982-0072; www.lipolounge.com; 916 Grant Ave; � 2pm-2am; 🚌8, 30, 45, 🚋Powell-Mason, Powell-Hyde) Beat a hasty retreat to red-vinyl booths where Allen Ginsberg and Jack Kerouac debated the meaning of life under a golden Buddha. Enter the 1937 faux-grotto doorway and dodge red lanterns to place your order: Tsingtao beer or a sweet, sneaky-strong Chinese mai tai made with *baijiu* (rice liquor). Brusque bartenders, basement bathrooms, cash only – a world-class dive bar.

Caffe Trieste Cafe

(☑415-392-6739; www.caffetrieste.com; 601 Vallejo St; � 6:30am-10pm Sun-Thu, to 11pm Fri & Sat; 📶; 🚌8, 10, 12, 30, 41, 45) Poetry on bathroom walls, opera on the jukebox, live accordion jams and sightings of Beat poet-laureate Lawrence Ferlinghetti: this is North Beach at its best, since the 1950s. Linger over legendary espresso and scribble your screenplay under the Sardinian fishing mural just as young Francis Ford Coppola did. Perhaps you've heard of the movie: *The Godfather.* Cash only.

😋 Nob Hill & Russian Hill

Tonga Room Lounge

(☑reservations 415-772-5278; www.tongaroom.com; Fairmont San Francisco, 950 Mason St; cover $5-7; � 5-11:30pm Sun, Wed & Thu, to 12:30am Fri & Sat; 🚌1, 🚋California, Powell-Mason, Powell-Hyde) Tonight's San Francisco weather: 100% chance of tropical rainstorms every 20 minutes, but only on the top-40 band playing on the island in the middle of the indoor pool – you're safe in your grass hut. For a more powerful hurricane, order one in a plastic coconut. Who said tiki bars were dead? Come before 8pm to beat the cover charge.

Top of the Mark Bar

(www.topofthemark.com; 999 California St; cover $10-15; �4:30-11.30pm Sun-Thu, to 12.30am Fri & Sat; 🚌1, 🚋California) So what if it's touristy? Nothing beats twirling in the clouds in a little cocktail dress on the city's highest dance floor. Thursday to Saturday evenings

Lombard Street (p57)

are best, when a full jazz band plays; Wednesday there's piano music. Sunday to Tuesday it's quiet, but, oh, the views! Remarkably, it's often empty at sunset – and gorgeous on fog-free evenings. Expect $15 drinks.

🟢 The Mission

%ABV — Cocktail Bar

(☎415-400-4748; www.abvsf.com; 3174 16th St; ☺2pm-2am; 🚊14, 22, Ⓑ16th St Mission, ⓂJ) As kindred spirits will deduce from the name (the abbreviation for 'percent alcohol by volume'), this bar is backed by cocktail crafters who know their Rittenhouse rye from their Japanese malt whisky. Top-notch hooch is served promptly and without pretension, including excellent Cali wine and beer on tap and original historically inspired cocktails like the Sutro Swizzle (Armagnac, grapefruit shrub, maraschino liqueur).

20 Spot — Wine Bar

(☎415-624-3140; www.20spot.com; 3565 20th St; ☺5pm-midnight Mon-Thu, to 1am Fri & Sat; 🚊14, 22, 33, Ⓑ16th St Mission) Find your California mellow at this neighborhood wine lounge in an 1895 Victorian building. After decades as Force of Habit punk-record shop – note the vintage sign – this corner joint has earned the right to unwind with a glass of Berkeley's Donkey and Goat sparkling wine and not get any guff. Caution: oysters with pickled persimmon could become a habit.

Trick Dog — Bar

(☎415-471-2999; www.trickdogbar.com; 3010 20th St; ☺3pm-2am; 🚊12, 14, 49) Drink adventurously with ingenious cocktails inspired by local obsessions: San Francisco muralists, Chinese diners or conspiracy theories. Every six months, Trick Dog adopts a new theme and the entire menu changes – proof that you can teach an old dog new tricks, and improve on classics like the Manhattan. Arrive early for bar stools or hit the mood-lit loft for high-concept bar bites.

El Rio — Club

(☎415-282-3325; www.elriosf.com; 3158 Mission St; cover free-$8; ☺1pm-2am; 🚊12, 14, 27,

Top Five for Californian Cuisine

In Situ (p61)

Benu (p62)

Rich Table (p63)

Ferry Building (p46)

Al's Place (p63)

From left: Produce at Ferry Plaza Farmers Market (p47); Piedmont Boutique, Haight & Ashbury (p57); Victorian 'Painted Ladies' (p288)

49, B 24th St Mission) Work it all out on the dance floor with San Francisco's most down and funky crowd – the full rainbow spectrum of colorful characters is here to party. Calendar highlights include Salsa Sunday, free oysters from 5:30pm Friday, drag-star DJs, backyard bands and ping-pong. Expect knockout margaritas and shameless flirting on a patio that's seen it all since 1978. Cash only.

🔵 The Haight & Hayes Valley

Smuggler's Cove   Bar

(📱415-869-1900; www.smugglerscovesf. com; 650 Gough St; ⏰5pm-1:15am; 🚌5, 21, 47, 49, M Civic Center, B Civic Center) Yo-ho-ho and a bottle of rum...wait, make that a Dead Reckoning (Nicaraguan rum, port, pineapple and bitters), unless you'll split the flaming Scorpion Bowl? Pirates are bedeviled by choice at this Barbary Coast–shipwreck tiki bar, hidden behind tinted-glass doors. With 550 types of rum and 70-plus cocktails gleaned from rum-running around the world – and $2 off 5pm to 6pm daily – you won't be dry-docked long.

Blue Bottle Coffee Kiosk   Cafe

(www.bluebottlecoffee.net; 315 Linden St; ⏰7am-6pm Mon-Sat, from 8am Sun; 👫🐾; 🚌5, 21, 47, 49, M Van Ness) Don't mock SF's coffee geekery until you've tried the elixir emerging from this back-alley garage-door kiosk. The Bay Area's Blue Bottle built its reputation with micro-roasted organic coffee – especially Blue Bottle–invented, off-the-menu Gibraltar, the barista-favorite drink with foam and espresso poured together into the eponymous short glass. Expect a (short) wait and seats outside on creatively repurposed traffic curbs.

Riddler   Wine Bar

(www.theriddlersf.com; 528 Laguna St; ⏰4-10pm Tue-Thu & Sun, to 11pm Fri & Sat; 🚌5, 6, 7, 21) Riddle me this: how can you ever thank the women in your life? As the Riddler's all-women sommelier-chef-investor team points out, champagne makes a fine start. Bubbles begin at $12 and include Veuve Cliquot, the brand named after the woman who invented riddling, the process that gives champagne its unclouded sparkle.

Aub Zam Zam   Bar

(☑415-861-2545; 1633 Haight St; ☺3pm-2am
Mon-Fri, 1pm-2am Sat & Sun; ☐6, 7, 22, 33, 43,
ⓂN) Persian arches, *One Thousand and One
Nights* murals, 1930s jazz on the jukebox
and top-shelf cocktails at low-shelf prices
have brought Bohemian bliss to Haight St
since 1941. Legendary founder Bruno used
to throw people out for ordering a vodka
martini, but he was a softie in the end, be-
queathing his beloved bar to regulars who
had become friends. Cash only.

😊 ENTERTAINMENT

San Francisco
Symphony   Classical Music

(☑box office 415-864-6000, rush-ticket hotline
415-503-5577; www.sfsymphony.org; Grove St,
btwn Franklin St & Van Ness Ave; tickets $20-150;
☐21, 45, 47, ⓂVan Ness, ⒷCivic Center) From
the moment conductor Michael Tilson
Thomas bounces up on his toes and raises
his baton, the audience is on the edge
of their seats for another thunderous
performance by the Grammy-winning San
Francisco Symphony. Don't miss signature

concerts of Beethoven and Mahler, live
symphony performances with films such as
Star Trek, and creative collaborations with
artists from Elvis Costello to Metallica.

SFJAZZ Center   Jazz

(☑866-920-5299; www.sfjazz.org; 201 Franklin
St; tickets $25-120; ⋆; ☐5, 6, 7, 21, 47, 49, ⓂVan
Ness) ✎ Jazz legends and singular talents
from Argentina to Yemen are showcased
at North America's newest, largest jazz
center. Hear fresh takes on classic jazz
albums and poets riffing with jazz combos
in the downstairs Joe Henderson Lab, and
witness extraordinary main-stage collaborations ranging from Afro-Cuban All Stars
to roots legends Emmylou Harris, Rosanne
Cash and Lucinda Williams.

Alamo Drafthouse Cinema Cinema

(☑415-549-5959; https://drafthouse.com/sf;
2550 Mission St; tickets $9-20; ⋆; ☐14, Ⓑ24th
St Mission) The landmark 1932 New Mission
cinema, now restored to its original Timothy Pfleuger–designed art-deco glory, has
a new mission: to upgrade dinner-and-a-
movie dates. Staff deliver microbrews and
tasty fare to plush banquette seats, so you

 LGBT San Francisco

It doesn't matter where you're from, who you love or who's your daddy: if you're here and queer, welcome home. San Francisco is America's pinkest city, and though New York Marys may call it the retirement home of the young – the sidewalks roll up early here – there's nowhere easier to be out and proud.

In San Francisco, you don't need to trawl the urban underworld for a gay scene. The intersection of 18th and Castro is the historic center of the gay world, but dancing queens head to SoMa for thump-thump clubs. The Mission remains the preferred 'hood of alt-chicks, dykes, trans female-to-males (FTMs) and flirty femmes.

Rainbow crosswalk in the Castro
DIEGO GRANDI / SHUTTERSTOCK ©

don't miss a moment of the premieres, cult revivals (especially Music Mondays) or San Francisco favorites from *Mrs Doubtfire* to *Dirty Harry* – often with filmmaker Q&As.

Chapel Live Music

(415-551-5157; www.thechapelsf.com; 777 Valencia St; cover $15-40; ⊙bar 7pm-2am; 🚌14, 33, Ⓜ J, Ⓑ16th St Mission) Musical prayers are answered in a 1914 California arts-and-crafts landmark with heavenly acoustics. The 40ft roof is regularly raised by shows by New Orleans brass bands, folkYEAH! Americana groups, legendary rockers like Peter Murphy and hip-hop icons such as Prince Paul. Many shows are all ages, except when comedians like W Kamau Bell test edgy material.

Oberlin Dance Collective Dance

(ODC; 🎫box office 415-863-9834, classes 415-549-8519; www.odctheater.org; 3153 17th St; drop-in classes from $15, shows $20-50; 🚌12, 14, 22, 33, 49, Ⓑ16th St Mission) For 45 years, ODC has been redefining dance with risky, raw performances and the sheer joy of movement. ODC's season runs from September to December, but its stage presents year-round shows featuring local and international artists. ODC Dance Commons is a hub and hangout for the dance community, offering 200-plus classes a week, from flamenco to vogue; all ages and skill levels welcome.

INFORMATION

SF Visitor Information Center (www.san francisco.travel/visitor-information-center) Muni Passports, activities deals, culture and event calendars.

🛈 GETTING THERE & AWAY

The Bay Area has three international airports: San Francisco (SFO), Oakland (OAK) and San Jose (SJC). Factor in additional transit time – and cost – to reach San Francisco proper from Oakland or San Jose, and note that what you save in airfare you may wind up spending on ground transportation.

If you've unlimited time, consider taking the train, instead of driving or flying, to avoid traffic hassles and excess carbon emissions.

GETTING AROUND

When San Franciscans aren't pressed for time, most walk, cycle or ride **Muni** (Municipal Transit Agency; 🎫511; www.sfmta.com) bus, streetcar and cable-car lines instead of taking a car or cab. Traffic is notoriously bad at rush hour, and parking is next to impossible in center-city neighborhoods. Avoid driving until it's time to leave town – or drive during off-peak hours.

For Bay Area transit options, departures and arrivals, call 🎫511 or check www.511.org. A detailed *Muni Street & Transit Map* is available free online.

Where to Stay

San Francisco options range from serviceable hostels and bohemian boarding houses to swanky suites in ultra-luxe hotels. Remember to plan ahead – well ahead.

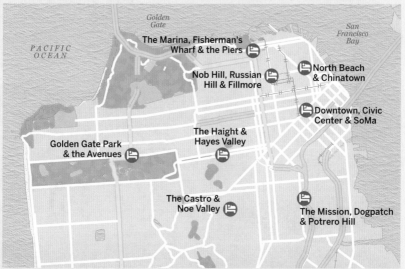

Neighborhood	Atmosphere
The Marina, Fisherman's Wharf & the Piers	Near the northern waterfront; good for kids; lots of restaurants and nightlife at the Marina; very touristy; parking at the Marina and Wharf is a nightmare.
Downtown, Civic Center & SoMa	Bustling city center with a selection of hotels; near public transportation and walkable to many sights; downtown quiet at night; Civic Center feels rough; SoMa streets are gritty at nighttime.
North Beach & Chinatown	Culturally colorful; great strolling; lots of cafes and restaurants; terrific sense of place; street noise; limited choices and transportation.
Nob Hill, Russian Hill & Fillmore	Stately, classic hotels atop Nob Hill; good restaurants and shopping in Pacific Heights and Japantown; very steep hills; parking difficult; slightly removed from major sights.
The Mission, Dogpatch & Potrero Hill	The Mission's flat terrain makes walking easier; good for biking; easy access to BART; limited choice of accommodations.
The Castro & Noe Valley	Great nightlife, especially for LGBT travelers; provides a good taste of local life; far from major tourist sights.
The Haight & Hayes Valley	Lots of bars and restaurants, near cultural sights and Golden Gate Park; limited choices.
Golden Gate Park & the Avenues	Quiet nights; good for outdoor recreation; easier parking; very far from major sights; foggy and cold in summer.

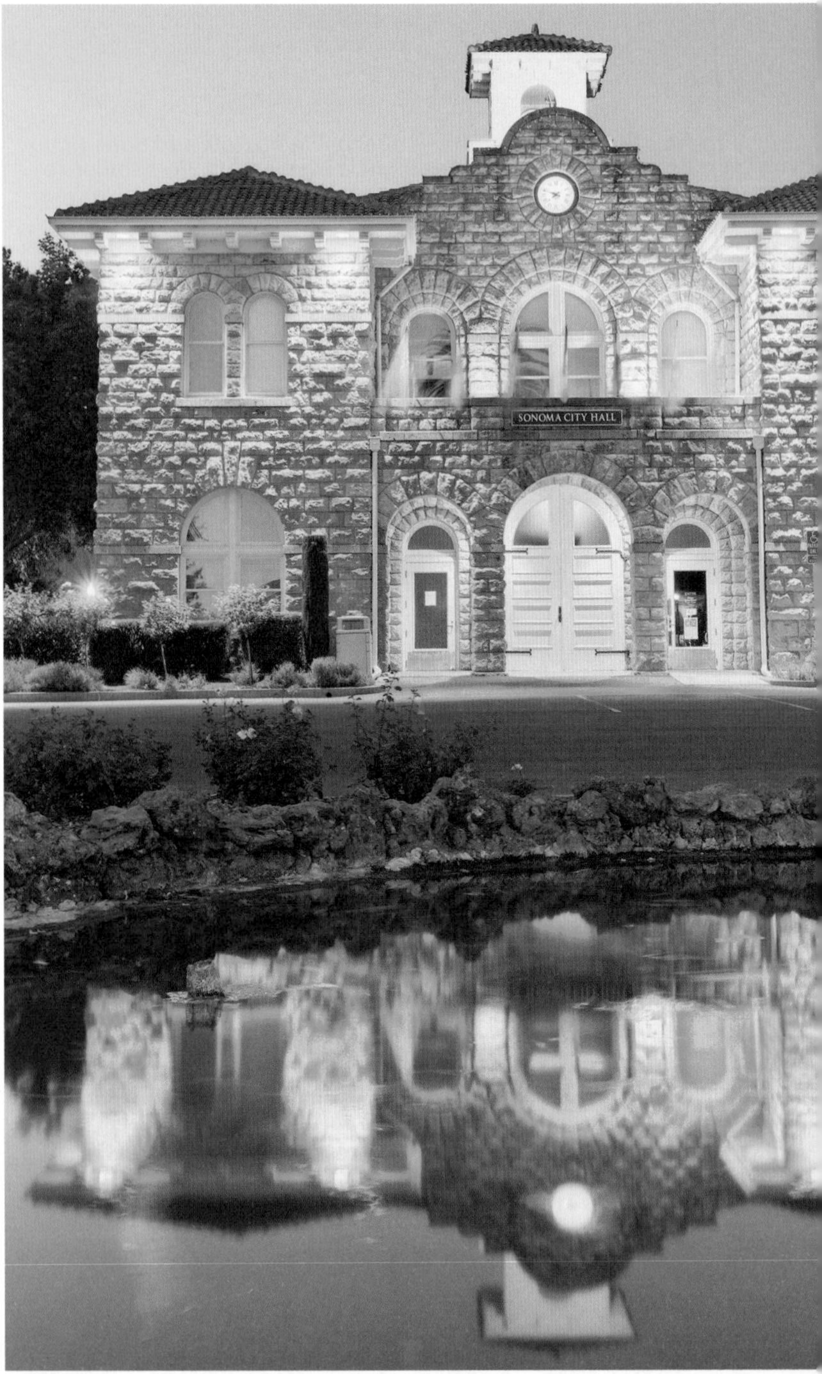

S. GREG PANOSIAN / GETTY IMAGES ©

City Hall, Sonoma Plaza (p80)

SONOMA
VALLEY

Sonoma Valley

The more laid-back, down-to-earth alternative to Napa, lovingly referred to by locals as 'Slow-noma.' Rolling hills, dotted with century-old oaks, turn the color of lion's fur under the summer sun and swaths of vineyards carpet hillsides as far as the eye can see. Anchoring the bucolic 17-mile-long valley, the town of Sonoma makes a great jumping-off point for Wine Country – it's less than 50 miles from San Francisco – and has storied 19th-century historical sights. Further up the valley, pleasantly tranquil Glen Ellen is straight from a Norman Rockwell painting.

Sonoma Valley in Two Days

Start your Wine Country adventure with coffee in **Sonoma Plaza** (p80). With two days in the area, you'll then have plenty of time to meander around the valley's quaint, vine-lined roads, stopping frequently to taste the vinous wares; be sure to hit California's oldest family-run winery, **Gundlach-Bundschu** (p79). Fans of *The Call of the Wild* should set aside time to visit **Jack London State Historic Park** (p83).

Sonoma Valley in Four Days

With two extra days, it's worth renting a bike and cruising to **Bartholomew Park** (p79), an oak-dotted preserve in a stunning natural setting with a **winery** (p79) on-site. Adventurous types can work off any alcohol-related lassitude hiking the trails of **Sugarloaf Ridge State Park** (p82). On your final evening, celebrate Sonoma Valley produce with a low-food-miles meal at **Cafe La Haye** (p82).

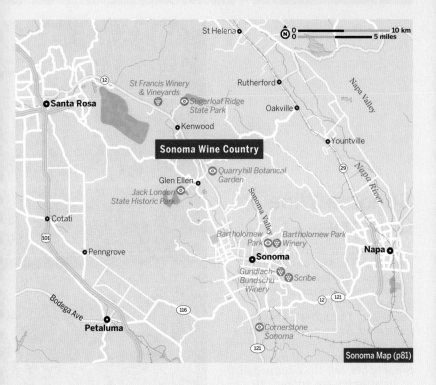

Sonoma Wine Country

Sonoma Map (p81)

Arriving in the Sonoma Valley

Car Sonoma Valley is a 90-minute drive from San Francisco. Sonoma Hwy (Hwy 12) is lined with wineries and runs from Sonoma, past Glen Ellen, through Kenwood to Santa Rosa, then on to western Sonoma County.

Bus Public transportation will get you to the valley, but is insufficient for vineyard hopping. Dial ☎511 for info or check online (www.transit.511.org).

Sleeping

For the full viticultural experience, stay at one of the many wineries dotted through the region; accommodations are often quaint and romantic. Couples will find a number of cozy cottages and inns in Glen Ellen, while Kenwood has one high-end resort and an excellent campground. There are a number of historic hotels suitable for a midrange budget around Sonoma; those counting pennies will have better luck in Santa Rosa. Off-season rates plummet.

Sonoma Wine Country

A bit less fussy and a lot less expensive than its celebrated nearby sister, Napa, this laid-back region is where wine growing began in California over 200 years ago. Though it's becoming gentrified, Sonoma lacks Napa's chic factor (and locals like it that way); the wines are more approachable, but the county's 400 or so wineries are spread out.

Great For...

❶ Need to Know

Spring and fall are the best times to visit. Summers are hot, dusty and crowded. Fall brings fine weather, harvest time and the 'crush' (grape pressing).

★ Top Tip

Don't be afraid to ask questions. Vintners love to talk. If you don't know how to taste wine, or what to look for, ask the person behind the counter to help you discover what you like.

Wine Tasting

The best way to discover the real Wine Country is to avoid factory wineries and visit family-owned boutique houses (producing fewer than 20,000 annual cases) and midsized houses (20,000 to 60,000 annual cases).

Tastings are called 'flights' and include four to six different wines. In Sonoma Valley, tastings cost about $5 to $20. You must be 21 years old to taste.

To avoid burnout, visit no more than three wineries per day. Most open daily from 10am or 11am to 4pm or 5pm, but call ahead if your heart's set on a particular place. Plan at least five hours to amble from the bottom to the top of Sonoma Valley.

Do not drink and drive. The curvy roads are dangerous and police monitor traffic.

Guided Tours

You have the most flexibility by driving your own vehicle, but to avoid drinking and driving, opt for a tour.

Billed as the anti-wine-snob tour, **Platypus Wine Tours** (www.platypustours.com) specializes in back-road vineyards, historic wineries and family-owned operations. For something a little different, **Active Wine Adventures** (www.activewineadventures. com) pairs wine and food with scenic hikes, local art, literary adventures and, most recently, microbreweries.

Another option is a guided bicycle tour. These start at around $90 per day including bikes, tastings and lunch, or contact **Sonoma Valley Cyclery** (☑707-935-3377; www.sonomacyclery.com; 20091 Broadway/Hwy 12; bikes per day from $30; ☺10am-6pm Mon-Sat, to 4pm Sun; 🚻) for do-it-yourself rentals.

Bartholomew Park Winery

Shipping

If you find you can't stop at just a bottle or two, **Bodega Shipping Co** (☏Napa 707-968-5462, Sonoma 707-343-1656; www.bodega shippingco.com) picks up wine in Sonoma Valley, packages it, and ships nationwide via UPS and FedEx, with no hidden fees. It also ships to some international destinations.

Wineries

Bartholomew Park Winery

A great bike-to winery, **Bartholomew Park** (☏707-939-3026; www.bartpark.com; 1000 Vineyard Lane, Sonoma; tasting $15; ⊙11am-4:30pm; P) ✿ occupies a 375-acre nature

Don't Miss

The vine-lined byways of the region – perfect for a lazy drive (or cycle).

INTERSECTION PHOTOS / ALAMY STOCK PHOTO ©

preserve (p80). The vineyards were originally cultivated in 1857 and now yield certified-organic, citrusy Sauvignon Blanc, Cabernet Sauvignon softer in style than Napa, and lush Zinfandel.

Gundlach-Bundschu Winery

California's oldest family-run **winery** (☏707-938-5277; www.gunbun.com; 2000 Denmark St, Sonoma; tasting $20-30, incl tour $30-60; ⊙11am-5:30pm May-Oct, to 4:30pm Nov-Apr; P) ✿ looks like a castle but has a down-to-earth vibe. Founded in 1858 by a Bavarian immigrant, its signatures are Gewürztraminer and Pinot Noir, but 'Gun-Bun' was the first American winery to produce 100% Merlot. Down a winding lane, it's a terrific bike-to winery with picnicking, hiking, a lake and frequent concerts.

St Francis Winery & Vineyards

The vineyards are scenic and all, but the real reason to visit **St Francis** (☏707-538-9463; www.stfranciswinery.com; 100 Pythian Rd at Hwy 12, Santa Rosa; tasting $15, wine & cheese pairing $25, wine & food pairing $68; ⊙10am-5pm) is the much-lauded food-pairing experience. The mouthwatering, multicourse affair is hosted by amiable and informative wine experts and includes things such as braised Kurobuta pork paired with Cab Franc and American Wagyu strip loin paired with an old-vine Zin

Scribe

With **Scribe** (☏707-939-1858; http://scribe winery.com; 2100 Denmark St, Sonoma; tasting $35, food pairing $65; ⊙11:30am-4pm Thu-Mon, by appointment only), a new generation has found its place in wine country. Bantering groups of bespectacled millennials frequent this hip winery designed to resemble a French chateau, and at outdoor picnic tables they hold forth on the terroir-driven rosé of Pinot, the skin-fermented Chardonnay and the bold Cab.

✕ Take a Break

Line your belly with superb buttermilk pancakes at Fremont Diner (p82).

Sonoma

Fancy boutiques may lately be replacing hardware stores, but Sonoma still retains an old-fashioned charm, thanks to the plaza – California's largest town square – and its surrounding frozen-in-time historic buildings. You can legally drink on the plaza – a rarity in California parks – but only between 11:30am and sunset.

⊙ SIGHTS

Sonoma Plaza   Square
(btwn Napa, Spain & 1st Sts) Smack in the center of the plaza, the Mission Revival–style city hall, built 1906–08, has identical facades on four sides, reportedly because plaza businesses all demanded City Hall face their direction. At the plaza's northeast corner, the **Bear Flag Monument** (Sonoma Plaza) commemorates the Bear Flag Revolt, which took place over 25 days in 1846. A small group of townspeople rebelled against the Mexican government and proclaimed California an independent republic. The weekly farmers market (5:30pm to 8pm Tuesday, April to October) showcases Sonoma's incredible produce.

Bartholomew Park   Park
(☑707-938-2244; www.bartholomewpark.org; 1000 Vineyard Lane; ⊙10am-4:30pm; P⊕)
FREE The top near-town outdoors destination is 375-acre Bartholomew Park, off Castle Rd, where you can picnic beneath giant oaks and hike 2 miles of trails, with hilltop vistas to San Francisco. The **Palladian Villa**, at the park's entrance, is a re-creation of Count Haraszthy's original Pompeian residence, open noon to 3pm Saturdays and Sundays. There's also a good winery (p79), independently operated. Last entry is at 4:30pm.

Cornerstone Sonoma   Gardens
(☑707-933-3010; www.cornerstonesonoma.com; 23570 Arnold Dr; ⊙10am-5pm, gardens to 4pm; P⊕) FREE This roadside, Wine Country marketplace showcases 25 walk-through

(in some cases edible) gardens, along with a bunch of innovative and adorable shops, wine-tasting parlors and on-site Sonoma Valley Visitors Bureau (p105). There's a good, if pricey, cafe, and an outdoor 'test kitchen.' Look for the enormous orange Adirondack chair at road's edge.

We especially love **Nomad Chic**, a design store that recently relocated from downtown Sonoma, and **Prohibition Spirits Distillery** (☑707-933-7507; www.prohibition-spirits.com; 23570 Arnold Dr, Sunset Gardens at Cornerstone; ⊙10am-5pm), which offers tastings of orangecello and other innovative spirits.

**Sonoma Valley
Museum of Art**   Museum
(☑707-939-7862; www.svma.org; 551 Broadway; adult/child 14-17yr/family $10/5/15; ⊙11am-5pm Wed-Sun) The 8000-sq-ft modern- and contemporary-art museum presents changing exhibitions by international and local artists, and focuses on building community around art.

✪ ACTIVITIES

Many local inns provide bicycles, and cycling is a great way to visit local wineries.

**Willow Stream Spa at
Sonoma Mission Inn**   Spa
(☑707-938-9000; www.fairmont.com/sonoma; 100 Boyes Blvd; ⊙9am-6pm) Few Wine Country spas compare with glitzy Sonoma Mission Inn. Purchasing a treatment or paying $89 (make a reservation) allows use of three outdoor and two indoor mineral pools, a gym, a sauna and a herbal steam room at the Romanesque bathhouse. No under 18s.

**Ramekins Sonoma Valley
Culinary School**   Cooking
(☑707-933-0450; www.ramekins.com; 450 W Spain St; ⊕) Offers excellent demonstrations and hands-on classes for home chefs, covering things such as hors d'oeuvres and cheese-and-wine pairings. The school also hosts culinary tours of

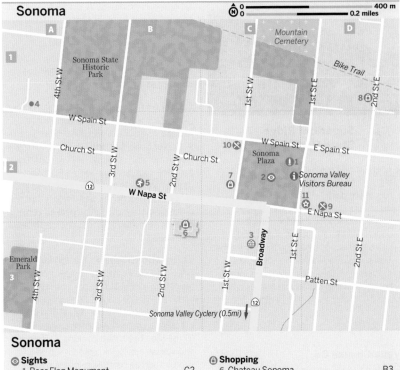

Sonoma

local farms and dinners with vintners
and chefs.

Vintage Aircraft
Company   Scenic Flights
(☏707-938-2444; www.vintageaircraft.com;
23982 Arnold Dr, Sonoma; 20min flight 1/2 people
$175/270) Scenic flights in biplanes, with an
option to add aerobatic maneuvers.

Wine Country Cyclery   Cycling
(☏707-966-6800; www.winecountrycyclery.com;
262 W Napa St; bicycle rental per day $30-75;

⊙10am-6pm) Offers hybrids, electric bikes,
road bikes and even tandem bikes. Book
ahead.

ⓐ SHOPPING

Chateau Sonoma   Homewares
(☏707-935-8553; www.chateausonoma.com;
23588 Arnold Dr; ⊙10am-5pm) France meets
Sonoma in one-of-a-kind gifts and arty
home-decor store, which recently relocated
to Cornerstone Sonoma.

 Sugarloaf Ridge State Park

There are 30 miles of fantastic hiking – when it's not blazingly hot – at this **state park** (707-833-5712; www.sugarloafpark.org; 2605 Adobe Canyon Rd, Kenwood; per car $8; P) . On clear days, Bald Mountain has drop-dead views to the sea, while the Brushy Peaks Trail peers into Napa Valley. Both are moderately strenuous; plan on a three-hour round-trip. Bikes and horses can use perimeter trails seasonally.

SUNDRY PHOTOGRAPHY / SHUTTERSTOCK ©

Vella Cheese Co Food

(707-938-3232; www.vellacheese.com; 315 2nd St E; 9:30am-6pm Mon-Fri, to 5pm Sat) Known for their jacks (made here since the 1930s), Vella specializes in dry-jack with a cocoa-powder-dusted rind. Also try Mezzo Secco, a cheese you can only find here. Staff will vacuum-pack for shipping.

Figone's Olive Oil Food

(707-282-9092; www.figoneoliveoil.com; 483 1st St W; 10am-6pm Sun-Thu, to 7pm Fri & Sat) Figone's presses its own extra-virgin olive oil and infuses some with flavors such as Meyer lemon, all free to sample.

EATING

Fremont Diner American, Southern $$

(707-938-7370; www.thefremontdiner.com; 2698 Fremont Dr; mains $9-22; 8am-3pm Mon-Wed, to 9pm Thu-Sun;) Lines snake out the door at peak times at this farm-to-table roadside diner. We prefer the indoor tables but will happily accept a picnic table to feast on buttermilk pancakes with homemade cinnamon-vanilla syrup, chicken and waffles, oyster po'boys, finger-licking barbecue and skillet-baked cornbread.

Cafe La Haye Californian $$$

(707-935-5994; www.cafelahaye.com; 140 E Napa St; mains $19-25; 5:30-9pm Tue-Sat) One of Sonoma's top tables for earthy New American cooking, La Haye only uses produce sourced from within 60 miles. Its dining room gets packed cheek-by-jowl and service can border on perfunctory, but the clean simplicity and flavor-packed cooking make it many foodies' first choice. Reserve well ahead.

El Dorado Kitchen Californian $$$

(707-996-3030; http://eldoradosonoma.com/restaurant; 405 1st St W; mains lunch $15-24, dinner $21-31; 8-11am, 11:30am-2:30pm & 5:30-9pm Mon-Thu, to 10pm Fri & Sat) The swank plaza-side choice for contemporary California-Mediterranean cooking, El Dorado showcases seasonal-regional ingredients in dishes such as seafood paella, ahi tartare and housemade pasta, served in a see-and-be-seen dining room with a big community table at its center. The happening lounge serves good small plates ($11 to $22) and craft cocktails. Make reservations.

ENTERTAINMENT

Sebastiani Theatre Cinema

(707-996-2020; www.sebastianitheatre.com; 476 1st St E) The plaza's gorgeous 1934 Mission Revival cinema screens art-house and revival films, and sometimes live theater.

INFORMATION

Sonoma Valley Visitors Bureau (866-966-1090; www.sonomavalley.com; 453 1st St E; 9am-5pm Mon-Sat, 10am-5pm Sun) Offers guides, maps, pamphlets, merchandise information on deals and events and more. There's another branch at Cornerstone Sonoma (p80).

Glen Ellen

Sleepy Glen Ellen is a snapshot of old Sonoma, with white picket fences and tiny cottages beside a poplar-lined creek. When downtown Sonoma is jammed, you can wander quiet Glen Ellen and feel far away. It's ideal for a leg-stretching stopover between wineries or a romantic overnight – the nighttime sky blazes with stars. The biggest daytime attractions are Jack London State Historic Park and Benziger winery.

◎ SIGHTS & ACTIVITIES

Jack London
State Historic Park   Park

(⌂707-938-5216; www.jacklondonpark.com; 2400 London Ranch Rd, Glen Ellen; per car $10, cottage adult/child $4/2; ◷9:30am-5pm; P⃝) Napa has Robert Louis Stevenson, but Sonoma has Jack London. This 1400-acre park frames that author's last years; don't miss the excellent on-site **museum**. Miles of **hiking trails** (some open to mountain bikes) weave through oak-dotted

woodlands, between 600ft and 2300ft elevations; an easy 2-mile loop meanders to **London Lake**, great for picnicking. On select summer evenings, the park transforms into a theater for 'Broadway Under the Stars.' Be alert for poison oak.

Changing occupations from Oakland fisherman to Alaska gold prospector to Pacific yachtsman – and novelist on the side – London (1876–1916) ultimately took up farming. He bought 'Beauty Ranch' in 1905 and moved here in 1911. With his second wife, Charmian, he lived and wrote in a small cottage while his mansion, **Wolf House**, was under construction. On the eve of its completion in 1913, it burned down. The disaster devastated London, and although he toyed with rebuilding, he died before construction got underway. His widow, Charmian, built the **House of Happy Walls**, which has been preserved as a **museum**, open 10am to 5pm. It's a half-mile walk from there to the remains of Wolf House, passing London's grave along the way. Other paths wind around the farm to the cottage (open noon to 4pm) where he lived and worked.

Jack London State Historic Park

ANDRIY BLOKHIN/SHUTTERSTOCK ©

From left: Fruit and cheese platter at a Sonoma Valley vineyard; Pinot Noir grapes in Sonoma Wine Country (p76); A vineyard in Glen Ellen (p83)

GARYTOG / GETTY IMAGES ©

GEORGE ROSE / GETTY IMAGES ©

Quarryhill Botanical Garden
Gardens

(☎707-996-3166; www.quarryhillbg.org; 12841 Hwy 12; adult/child 13-17yr $12/8; ☺9am-4pm) Just when you thought the vineyards would stretch as far as the eye could see, out of nowhere comes a world-renowned botanical garden specializing in the flora of Asia. It's a treat to stroll the trails observing specimens collected on yearly expeditions to countries throughout the far east, and to relax near the pond, contemplating the artfully created woodland landscape.

🏇 ACTIVITIES

Triple Creek Horse Outfit
Horseback Riding

(☎707-887-8700; www.triplecreekhorseoutfit. com; 2400 London Ranch Rd; 60/90min rides $80/100; ☺9am-5pm Mon-Sat) Explore Jack London State Park (p83) by horseback for stunning vistas over Sonoma Valley. Reservations required.

🛍 SHOPPING

Wine Country Chocolates Tasting Bar
Food

(☎707-996-1010; www.winecountrychoco-lates.com; 14301 Arnold Dr Suite 2, Glen Ellen; ☺10am-5pm) Sample fine chocolates of varying degrees of cacao and daily ganache selections.

🍴 EATING

Fig Cafe & Winebar
French, Californian $$

(☎707-938-2130; www.thefigcafe.com; 13690 Arnold Dr, Glen Ellen; mains $12-24, 3-course dinner $36; ☺10am-2:30pm Sat & Sun, 5-9pm Sun-Thu, 5-9:30pm Fri & Sat) The Fig's earthy California–Provençal comfort food includes flash-fried calamari with spicy lemon aioli, fig and arugula salad and *steak frites*. Good wine prices and weekend brunch give reason to return. No reservations; complimentary corkage.

GEORGE ROSE / GETTY IMAGES ©

Glen Ellen

Star Californian, Italian $$$

(📞707-343-1384; http://glenellenstar.com; 13648 Arnold Dr, Glen Ellen; pizzas $15-20, mains $24-50; ⊗5:30-9pm Sun-Thu, to 9:30pm Fri & Sat; 🅿) 🍴 Helmed by chef Ari Weiswasser, who once worked at Thomas Keller's **French Laundry** (📞707-944-2380; www.thomaskeller.com/tfl; 6640 Washington St; prix-fixe dinner $310; ⊗seatings 11am-12:30pm Fri-Sun, 5-9pm daily), this petite Glen Ellen bistro shines a light on the best of Sonoma farms and ranches. Local, organic and seasonal ingredients star in dishes such as spring-lamb ragu, whole roasted fish with broccoli di cicco or golden beets with harissa crumble. Reservations recommended.

Wednesdays are neighborhood nights, which means no corkage fee and a $35 two-course menu.

Aventine Italian $$$

(📞707-934-8911; http://glenellen.aventine hospitality.com; 14301 Arnold Dr, Glen Ellen; mains $14-28; ⊗4:30-10pm Wed-Fri, 11am-10pm Sat & Sun) The Sonoma outpost of the popular San Francisco restaurant occupies an atmospheric former gristmill with a sun-dappled outdoor patio. It serves Italian-derived dishes, including house-special Aventino: mozzarella-stuffed meatball with pesto over polenta. Make reservations.

Glen Ellen Inn American $$

(📞707-996-6409; www.glenelleninn.com; 13670 Arnold Dr, Glen Ellen; mains $16-25; ⊗11:30am-9pm Thu-Tue, 5:30-9pm Wed) Oysters, martinis and grilled steaks. Lovely garden, full bar.

REDWOOD FORESTS

Redwood Forests

This is not the legendary California of the Beach Boys' song: there are no palm-flanked beaches, and very few surfboards. The jagged edge of the continent is wild, scenic and even slightly foreboding, where spectral fog and an outsider spirit have fostered the world's tallest trees, most potent weed and a string of idiosyncratic two-stoplight towns. This is a place to traverse valleys of ancient redwood and explore hidden coves with a blanket and a bottle of local wine. But come here for the trees themselves – those majestic, otherworldly giants that make our daily problems seem very small indeed.

Redwood Forests in Two Days

With two days to see the Redwoods, it's best to road trip to **Humboldt Redwoods State Park** (p92). Stop at the quirky roadside shops along 101, before strolling agape through the primeval **Rockefeller Forest**, the world's largest grove of old-growth redwood. Spend your nights in a tent under the hushing boughs.

Redwood Forests in Four Days

Keep venturing north to the wild **Redwood National Park** (p90), where the trees are so large that the tiny towns along the road seem even smaller. Along the way, stop for a meal at Eureka's always-busy **Brick & Fire** (p97) and soak away any hiking aches and pains at the **Finnish Country Sauna and Tubs** (p95) in the region's eclectic college town, Arcata.

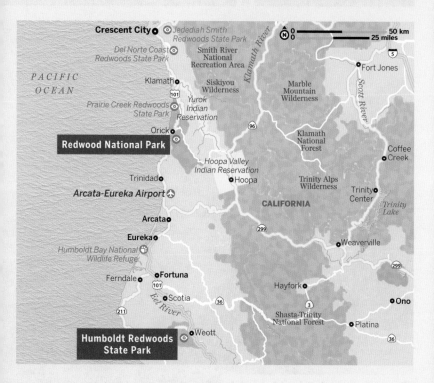

Arriving in the Redwood Forests

Arcata-Eureka Airport (www.humboldtgov.org/1396/Aviation) Located north of McKinleyville on the North Coast, signposted west of Hwy 101, and with regular services to major cities in California and Oregon, as well as further afield.

Bus Greyhound serves Eureka ($57, 6¾ hours, daily) and Arcata ($57, seven hours, daily) from San Francisco.

Sleeping

For comfortable and quaint accommodations, look to stay in Arcata, Eureka and Trinidad. Ferndale is another picture-perfect village in the region with lots of frilly B&Bs. Scores of mid-century motels line 101, but budget travelers should sleep outdoors if possible. There are plenty of options throughout the region, including backcountry options in Redwood National Park.

The coastline at Redwood National Park

ZACK FRANK / SHUTTERSTOCK ©

Redwood National & State Parks

It's hard not to get swept away by the ancient magic of this land of giant trees, some of which predate the Roman Empire by five centuries. Prepare to be impressed.

Great For...

Don't Miss

Prairie Creek Redwoods State Park's magnificent herd of elk.

Redwood National Park

This **park** (☑707-465-7335; www.nps.gov/redw; Hwy 101, Orick; [P][♿] 🅿 **FREE**) is the southernmost of the patchwork of state and federally administered lands under the umbrella of Redwood National & State Parks. A few miles north of Orick along Hwy 101, a trip inland on Bald Hills Rd will take you to **Lady Bird Johnson Grove**, with its 1-mile kid-friendly loop trail, or get you lost in the secluded serenity of **Tall Trees Grove**, which only allows a limited number of cars per day; get permits at the Orick visitor center.

Prairie Creek Redwoods State Park

Famous for some of the world's best virgin redwood groves and unspoiled coastline, this 14,000-acre **park** (www.parks.ca.gov;

Stout Grove, Jedediah Smith Redwoods State Park

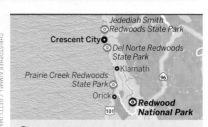

❶ Need to Know

Thomas H Kuchel Visitor Center
(📞707-465-7765; www.nps.gov/redw; Hwy 101, Orick; ⏰9am-5pm Apr-Oct, to 4pm Nov-Mar; ♿) On Hwy 101, a mile south of the town of Orick.

✕ Take a Break

Stock up on water, muesli bars and similar if you are planning on hiking in any of the parks.

★ Top Tip

Klamath, one of the tiny local settlements, is home to some seriously great roadside kitsch, for those so inclined.

Newton B Drury Scenic Pkwy; per car $8; P ♿) ✐ has spectacular scenic drives and 70 miles of mainly shady hiking trails, many of which are excellent for children. A magnificent herd of elk gathers and can often be spied grazing at the **Elk Prairie**, signposted from the highway; the best times to be sure of seeing the elk are early morning and around sunset.

Del Norte Coast Redwoods State Park

Marked by steep canyons and dense woods north of Klamath, half the 6400 acres of this **park** (📞707-465-7335; www.parks.ca.gov; Mill Creek Rd; per car $8; P) ✐ are virgin redwood, crisscrossed by miles of hiking trails. The park also fronts 8 miles of rugged coastline. Hwy 1 winds in from the coast at dramatic Wilson Beach, and traverses the

dense forest, with groves stretching as far as you can see. Picnic on the sand at False Klamath Cove. Heading north, tall trees cling precipitously to canyon walls that drop to the rocky, timber-strewn coastline.

Jedediah Smith Redwoods State Park

The northernmost park, Jedediah Smith is 9 miles northeast of Crescent City. The redwood stands are so thick that few trails penetrate this **park** (📞707-465-7335; www.parks.ca.gov; Hwy 199, Hiouchi; per car $8; ⏰sunrise-sunset; P ♿) ✐, but the outstanding 11-mile **Howland Hill Rd scenic drive** cuts through otherwise inaccessible areas (take Hwy 199 to South Fork Rd; turn right after crossing two bridges). Stop for a stroll under enormous trees in **Simpson-Reed Grove**. An easy half-mile trail, departing from the far side of the campground, crosses the Smith River via a summer-only footbridge, leading to **Stout Grove**, the park's most famous grove.

The Dyerville Giant

LUCENTIUS / GETTY IMAGES ©

Humboldt Redwoods State Park

Don't miss a magical drive through California's largest redwood park, which covers 53,000 acres –17,000 of which are old-growth – and contains some of the world's most magnificent trees.

Great For...

Don't Miss

Walking the length of the Dyerville Giant.

Avenue of the Giants

Exit Hwy 101 when you see the 'Avenue of the Giants' sign, and take this smaller alternative to the interstate; it's an incredible, 32-mile, two-lane stretch. You'll find free driving guides at roadside signboards at both the avenue's southern entrance, 6 miles north of Garberville, near Phillipsville, and at the northern entrance, south of Scotia, at Pepperwood; there are access points off Hwy 101.

Three miles north, the **California Federation of Women's Clubs Grove** is home to an interesting four-sided stone hearth designed by renowned San Franciscan architect Julia Morgan in 1931 to commemorate 'the untouched nature of the forest.'

Primeval **Rockefeller Forest**, 4.5 miles west of the avenue via Mattole Rd, appears as it did a century ago. It's the world's largest contiguous old-growth redwood

Roosevelt elk

KRIS WIKTOR / SHUTTERSTOCK ©

❶ Need to Know

📱707-946-2409; www.parks.ca.gov; Hwy 101; P ♿ ♿ **FREE**

✖ Take a Break

Stop in at **Riverbend Cellars** (📱707-943-9907; www.riverbendcellars.com; 12990 Avenue of the Giants, Myers Flat; ⏱noon-6pm) for an excellent glass of (estate-grown) El Centauro red.

★ Top Tip

Several towns have simple lodgings along the avenue, but camping is by far the best option.

forest, and contains about 20% of all such remaining trees. Walk the 2.5-mile **Big Trees Loop** (note that there is a seasonal footbridge over the river here). You quickly walk out of sight of cars and feel like you have fallen into the time of dinosaurs.

In **Founders Grove**, north of the visitor center, the **Dyerville Giant** was knocked over in 1991 by another falling tree. A walk along its gargantuan 370ft length, with its wide trunk towering above, helps you appreciate how huge these ancient trees are.

Hiking in Humboldt

The park has over 100 miles of trails for hiking, mountain-biking and horseback riding. Easy walks include short nature trails in Founders Grove and Rockefeller Forest and **Drury-Chaney Loop Trail** (with berry picking in summer). Challenging treks

include popular **Grasshopper Peak Trail**, south of the visitor center, which climbs to the 3379ft fire lookout.

Humboldt Redwoods Visitor Center

Located 2 miles south of Weott, a volunteer-staffed **visitor center** (📱707-946-2263; www.humboldtredwoods.org; Avenue of the Giants; ⏱9am-5pm Apr-Oct, 10am-4pm Nov-Mar) shows videos (three in total), sells maps and also has a small exhibition center about the local flora and fauna.

Getting There & Around

The nearest bus line stops are in Scotia to the north and Garberville to the south, both operated by the **Redwood Transit System** (📱707-443-0826; www.redwoodtransit.org). Essentially, you will need your own wheels to arrive at and to explore the park. You can also bring a bicycle and ride the entire length of the Avenue of the Giants.

Arcata

The North Coast's most progressive town, Arcata surrounds a tidy central square that fills with college students, campers, transients and tourists. Sure, it occasionally reeks of patchouli and its politics lean far left, but its earnest embrace of sustainability has fostered some of the most progressive civic action in America.

Founded in 1850 as a base for lumber camps, today Arcata is defined as a magnet for 20-somethings looking to expand their minds: either at Humboldt State University (HSU), and/or on the local highly potent marijuana. Since a 1996 state proposition legalized marijuana for medical purposes, the economy of the region has become inexorably tied to the crop.

◉ SIGHTS

Around Arcata Plaza are two National Historic Landmarks: the 1857 **Jacoby's Storehouse** (☏707-826-2426; www.facebook. com/pages/Jacoby-Storehouse; Arcata Plaza; ◷hours vary) and the 1915 **Hotel Arcata** (☏707-826-0217; www.hotelarcata.com; 708 9th St). Another great historic building is the 1914 **Minor Theatre** (☏707-822-3456; www. minortheatre.com; 1013 10th St; ◷hours vary), which some local historians claim is the oldest theater in the US built specifically for showing films.

Arcata Marsh & Wildlife Sanctuary   Wildlife Reserve

(www.cityofarcata.org; Klopp Lake) On the shores of Humboldt Bay, this sanctuary has 5 miles of walking trails and outstanding birding. The **Redwood Region Audubon Society** (☏707-826-7031; www.rras.org; donation welcome) offers guided walks on Saturdays at 8:30am, rain or shine, from the parking lot at I St's south end. Friends of Arcata Marsh offer guided tours Saturdays at 2pm from the **Arcata Marsh Interpretive Center** (☏707-826-2359; www.humboldt. edu/arcatamarsh; 569 South G St; ◷9am-5pm Tue-Sun, from 1pm Mon; ♿) **FREE**.

A storefront in Arcata

PIERRETTE GUERTIN / ALAMY STOCK PHOTO ©

ACTIVITIES

Finnish Country
Sauna and Tubs   Spa

([☎]707-822-2228; http://cafemokkaarcata.com;
495 J St; per 30min adult/child $9.75/2; [🕐]noon-
11pm Sun-Thu, to 1am Fri & Sat; [♿]) Like some
kind of Euro-crunchy bohemian dream,
these private, open-air redwood hot tubs
and sauna are situated around a small frog
pond. The staff is easygoing, and the facility
is relaxing, simple and clean. Reserve
ahead, especially on weekends.

EATING & DRINKING

Slice of Humboldt Pie Californian $

([☎]707-630-5100; 828 I St; pies $4.50-7.50;
[🕐]11am-10pm Mon-Thu, to 11pm Fri & Sat) Pies
and cider are the mainstays here, ranging
from chicken pot pie to cottage, steak and
mushroom and savory *empanadas*, including
chicken coconut curry and Thai chicken with
satay sauce. Sweet pastry treats include peanut butter fudge and traditional apple, while
the ciders cover imports and local varieties.

Wildflower Cafe & Bakery Cafe $$

([☎]707-822-0360; www.wildflowercafebakery.
com; 1604 G St; breakfast & lunch $5-8, dinner
mains $15-18; [🕐]8am-8pm Sun-Wed; [🥕]) Tops
for vegetarians, this tiny storefront serves
fab frittatas, pancakes and curries, and big
crunchy salads.

Folie Douce   Modern American $$$

([☎]707-822-1042; www.foliedoucearcata.com;
1551 G St; dinner mains $28-37, pizzas $17-24;
[🕐]11am-2pm Mon, 11am-2pm & 5:30-9pm Tue-Thu,
11am-2pm & 5:30-10pm Fri & Sat) [🌿] Just a slip
of a place, but with an enormous reputation. The short but inventive menu features
seasonally inspired bistro cooking, from
Asian to Mediterranean, with an emphasis
on local organics. Wood-fired pizzas are renowned and desserts are pretty special, as
well. A slice of artichoke heart cheesecake
perhaps? Dinner reservations essential.

Six Rivers Brewery   Microbrewery

([☎]707-839-7580; www.sixriversbrewery.com;
1300 Central Ave, McKinleyville; [🕐]11:30am-

 The Economics of the Humbolt Herb

With an estimated one-fifth of Humboldt County's population farming its
world-famous weed, a good chunk of the
economy here has run, for decades, as
bank-less, tax-evading and cash only –
but it's also been prosperous enough to
strongly support many local businesses.
Back in the 1990s farmers could expect
to get around $6000 a pound for their
crops but since medical marijuana has
become legal the price has dropped radically, to just above $1000 per pound.
In November 2016 a further law was
passed legalizing recreational cannabis
use in the state, which some feel may
lead to prices plummeting still further
and, more ominously, the possibility of
large farms and corporations putting
the small farmers out of business.

Marijuana, the 'Humboldt herb'
ERIS AND EDRINGTON CO / SHUTTERSTOCK ©

11:30pm Sun & Tue-Thu, to 12:30am Fri & Sat,
from 4pm Mon) One of the first female-owned
breweries in California, the 'brew with a
view' kills it in every category: great beer,
amazing community vibe, occasional live
music and delicious hot wings. The spicy
chili-pepper ale is amazing. At first glance
the menu might seem like ho-hum pub
grub, but portions are fresh and huge. They
also make a helluva pizza.

INFORMATION

California Welcome Center ([☎]707-822-3619;
www.arcatachamber.com; [🕐]9am-5pm) At the
junction of Hwys 299 and 101; has area info.

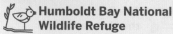
Humboldt Bay National Wildlife Refuge

This pristine **wildlife refuge** (☏707-733-5406; www.fws.gov/refuge/humboldt_bay; 1020 Ranch Rd, Loleta; ⊙8am-5pm; [P][♿]) ✔[FREE] protects wetland habitats for more than 200 species of birds migrating annually along the Pacific Flyway. Between the fall and early spring, when Aleutian geese descend en masse to the area, more than 25,000 geese might be seen in a cackling gaggle outside the visitor center.

A marsh wren
PHOTOGRAPHY BY ADRI / SHUTTERSTOCK ©

Eureka

One hour north of Garberville, on the edge of the giant Humboldt Bay, lies Eureka, the largest bay north of San Francisco. With a strip-mall sprawl surrounding a lovely historic downtown, it wears its role as the county seat a bit clumsily. Despite a diverse and interesting community of artists, writers, pagans and other free-thinkers, Eureka's wild side slips out only occasionally – the Redwood Coast Jazz Festival at the end of March or the summer concerts on the F Street Pier – but mostly, Eureka goes to bed early. Make for Old Town, a small historic district with good shopping and a revitalized waterfront.

SIGHTS

Morris Graves Museum of Art   Museum
(☏707-442-0278; www.humboldtarts.org; 636 F St; $5; ⊙noon-5pm Wed-Sun; [♿]) Across Hwy

101, this excellent museum shows rotating Californian artists and hosts performances inside the 1904 **Carnegie library**, the state's first public library. If you are around for a while, it also hosts art workshops and classes for adults and kids.

Romano Gabriel Wooden Sculpture Garden   Gardens
(315 2nd St) The coolest thing to gawk at downtown is this collection of whimsical outsider art that's enclosed by ageing glass. For 30 years, wooden characters in Gabriel's front yard delighted locals. After he died in 1977, the city moved the collection here.

Kinetic Museum Eureka   Museum
(☏707-786-3443; http://kineticgrandchampionship.com/kinetic-museum-eureka; 518 A St; admission by donation; ⊙2:15-6:30pm Fri-Sun, also 6-9pm 1st Sat of month; [♿]) Come see the fanciful, astounding, human-powered contraptions used in the annual Kinetic Grand Championship race from Arcata to Ferndale. Shaped like giant fish and UFOs, these colorful piles of junk propel racers over roads, water and marsh during the May event.

⊕ ACTIVITIES

Blue Ox Millworks & Historic Park   Historic Building
(☏707-444-3437; www.blueoxmill.com; 1 X St; adult/child 6-12yr $10/5; ⊙9am-5pm Mon-Fri year-round, plus 9am-4pm Sat Apr-Nov; [♿]) One of only a few of its kind in America, here antique tools and mills are used to produce authentic gingerbread trim for Victorian buildings. One-hour self-guided tours take you through the mill and historical buildings, including a blacksmith shop and 19th-century skid camp. Kids love the oxen. Be sure to leave time to peruse the gift shop.

Harbor Cruise   Cruise
(Madaket Cruises; ☏707-445-1910; www.humboldtbaymaritimemuseum.com; 1st St; narrated cruises adult/child $22/18; ⊙1pm, 2:30pm & 4pm Wed-Sat, 1pm & 2:30pm Sun-Tue mid-May–mid-Oct; [♿]) Board the 1910 *Madaket*,

Cruising Humboldt Bay aboard the *Madaket*

America's oldest continuously operating passenger vessel, and learn the history of Humboldt Bay. Docked at the foot of C St, it originally ferried mill workers and passengers until the Samoa Bridge opened in 1971. The $10 sunset cocktail cruise serves from the smallest licensed bar in the state, and there's also a 75-minute wildlife cruise.

😋 EATING

Cafe Nooner   Mediterranean $

(📞707-443-4663; www.cafenooner.com; 409 Opera Alley; mains $10-14; ⏱11am-4pm Sun-Wed, to 8pm Thu-Sat; 🍴) Exuding a cozy bistro-style ambience with red-and-white checkered tablecloths and jaunty murals, this perennially popular restaurant serves natural, organic and Med-inspired cuisine with choices that include a Greek-style *meze* platter, plus kebabs, salads and soups. There's a healthy kids menu, as well.

Brick & Fire   Californian $$

(📞707-268-8959; www.brickandfirebistro. com; 1630 F St, Eureka; dinner mains $14-23; ⏱11:30am-9pm Mon & Wed-Fri, 5-9pm Sat &

Sun; 🍸) Eureka's best restaurant is in an intimate, warm-hued, bohemian-tinged setting that is almost always busy. Choose from thin-crust pizzas, delicious salads (try the pear and blue cheese) and an ever-changing selection of appetizers and mains that highlight local produce and wild mushrooms.

Restaurant 301   Californian $$$

(📞707-444-8062; www.carterhouse.com; 301 L St; mains $24-40; ⏱5-8:30pm) 🌿 Part of the excellent Carter House Inn, Eureka's top table, romantic, sophisticated 301 serves a contemporary Californian menu, using produce from its organic gardens (tours available). The five-course tasting menu ($62, with wine pairings $107) is a good way to taste local seasonal food in its finest presentation.

ℹ️ INFORMATION

Eureka Chamber of Commerce (📞707-442-3738; www.eurekachamber.com; 2112 Broadway; ⏱8:30am-5pm Mon-Fri; 🍸) The main visitor information center is on Hwy 101.

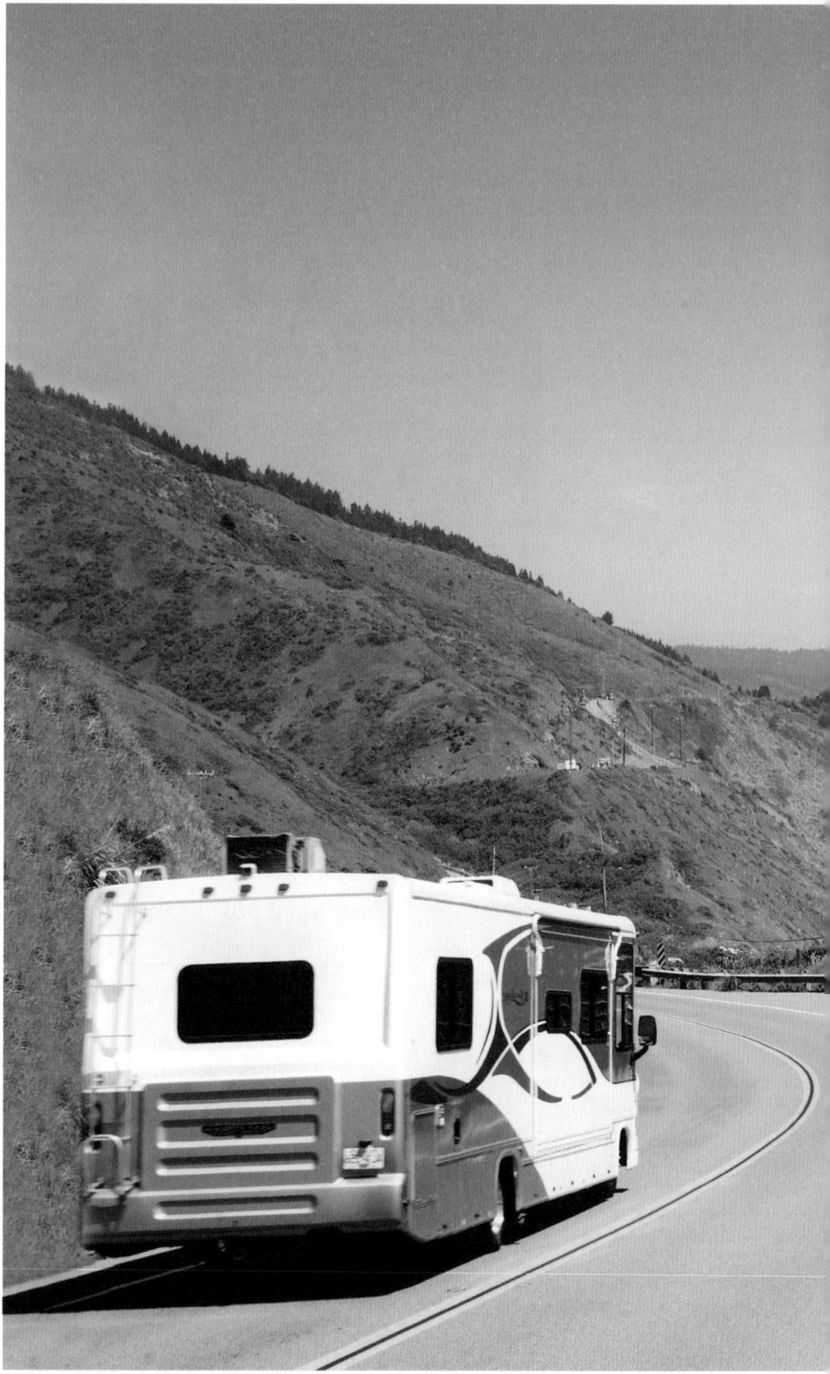

COASTAL
HIGHWAY 1

Coastal Highway 1

Down south it's called the 'PCH,' or Pacific Coast Hwy, but North Coast locals simply call it Hwy 1. However you label it, get ready for a fabulous coastal drive, which cuts a winding course on isolated cliffs high above the crashing surf. Compared to the famous Big Sur coast, the serpentine stretch of Hwy 1 up the North Coast is more challenging, more remote and seemingly more authentic, passing farms, fishing towns and hidden beaches. Drivers use roadside pullouts to scan the hazy Pacific horizon for migrating whales and explore a coastline dotted with rock formations that are relentlessly pounded by the surf.

Coastal Highway 1 in Two Days

With two days, set your sites on **Mendocino** (p102), the most picturesque town on this stretch of coast, and home to the iconic **Café Beaujolais** (p103). Take your time to get here, twisting up Hwy 1 and exploring all the **beaches** (p104) along the way (when it's time to go home, cut over to Hwy 101 for a straight shot home).

Coastal Highway 1 in Four Days

From Mendocino you can really explore some of California's most rugged coastline in depth. Spend half a day at the **Mendocino Coast Botanical Gardens** (p108) and looking for sea glass at **Glass Beach** (p108) in Fort Bragg. If you plan to take Hwy 1 back south, make time for a bowl of clam chowder at the **fish market** (p107) in Bodega Bay.

Map showing the Mendocino and Sonoma Coast region, including MacKerricher State Park, Fort Bragg, Caspar, Mendocino, Willits, Mendocino National Forest, Snow Mountain Wilderness, Elk, Ukiah, Point Arena Lighthouse, Point Arena, Boonville, Clear Lake, Clearlake, Gualala, Healdsburg, Russian River Valley, Dry Creek Valley, Goat Rock, Shell Beach, Jenner, Duncan's Landing, Portuguese Beach, Bodega Bay, Salmon Creek Beach, Sonoma Coast State Beach, Santa Rosa, Sonoma Valley, Napa Valley, Lake Berryessa, Sonoma, Napa.

Arriving on Coastal Highway 1

Although Hwy 1 is popular with cyclists and there are bus connections operated by the Mendocino Transit Authority (www.mendocinotransit.org), you will almost certainly need a car to explore this region. Windy Hwy 1 hugs the coast, then cuts inland and ends at Leggett, where it joins Hwy 101. Neither Amtrak nor Greyhound serve cities on coastal Hwy 1.

Sleeping

Bodega Bay, Mendocino and Fort Bragg are all full of quality B&Bs, but they're pricey. As a transit hub for the north coast, Fort Bragg has the most inexpensive chain hotels and motels. The region also has a number of great camping options, though you'll want to reserve ahead in the summer.

Mendocino Headlands State Park

WESTEND61 / GETTY IMAGES ©

Mendocino

Leading out to a gorgeous headland, Mendocino is the North Coast's salt-washed perfect village, with B&Bs surrounded by rose gardens, white-picket fences and New England–style redwood water towers.

Built by transplanted New Englanders in the 1850s, Mendocino thrived late into the 19th century, with ships transporting redwood timber from here to San Francisco. The mills shut down in the 1930s, and the town was rediscovered in the 1950s by artists and bohemians. Today the culturally savvy, politically aware, well-traveled citizens welcome visitors, but eschew corporate interlopers.

Mendocino Headlands State Park

This **state park** (☎707-937-5804; www.parks.ca.gov; Ford St) **FREE** surrounds the village, with trails that crisscross bluffs and rocky coves. Ask at the visitor center about guided weekend walks, including spring wildflower explorations and whale-watching jaunts.

Great For...

Don't Miss

A walk along the headland among berry bramble and wildflowers.

❶ Need to Know

Ford House Museum & Visitor Center
(☎707-537-5397; www.mendoparks.org;
45035 Main St; ☉11am-4pm)

✕ Take a Break

Stop by **Mendocino Cafe** (☎707-937-
6141; www.mendocinocafe.com; 10451
Lansing St; lunch mains $12-16, dinner mains
$21-33; ☉11:30am-8pm; 🛜🅿) for an
alfresco lunch on the ocean-view deck.

★ Top Tip

To avoid crowds, come midweek or in
the low season, when the vibe is mel-
lower – and prices more reasonable.

Big River Tidal Estuary

Northern California's longest undeveloped
estuary has no highways or buildings,
only beaches, forests, marshes, streams,
abundant wildlife and historic logging
sites. Friendly outfitter **Catch a Canoe**
(☎707-937-0273; www.catchacanoe.com; 44850
Comptche-Ukiah Rd, Stanford Inn by the Sea; 3hr
kayak, canoe or bicycle rental adult/child $28/14;
☉9am-5pm; 🛝) rents bikes, kayaks and
canoes (including redwood outriggers) for
trips up the 8-mile estuary. Bring a picnic,
and pack a camera to capture majestic blue
herons and the ramshackle remnants of
century-old train trestles.

Mendocino Celebrations

Enjoy wine and chowder tastings,
whale-watching and plenty of live music

at the **Mendocino Whale Festival** (www.
mendowhale.com; ☉early Mar). During the
summer orchestral and chamber music
concerts take place on the headlands, as
a part of the **Mendocino Music Festival**
(www.mendocinomusic.com; ☉mid-Jul; 🛝).

Mendocino Dining

The influx of Bay Area weekenders has
fostered an excellent dining scene that
enthusiastically espouses organic, sustainable principles.

For a special-occasion dinner, Mendocino's iconic, beloved country-Cal–French
Café Beaujolais (☎707-937-5614; www.
cafebeaujolais.com; 961 Ukiah St; lunch mains
$10-18, dinner mains $23-38; ☉11:30am-2:30pm
Wed-Sun, dinner from 5:30pm daily; 🅿) ✿
occupies an 1893 farmhouse restyled into
a monochromatic urban-chic dining room.
The locally sourced menu changes with the
seasons, but the Petaluma duck confit is a
gourmand's delight.

Shell Beach

Sonoma Coast State Beach

Bring binoculars, a picnic and a flexible agenda. The hidden coves and rocky headlands of Sonoma Coast make it a stunningly gorgeous place to while away some time.

Stretching 17 miles north from Bodega Head to Vista Trail, four miles north of Jenner, the glorious Sonoma Coast State Beach is a series of beaches separated by several beautiful rocky headlands. Some beaches are tiny, hidden in little coves, while others stretch far and wide. Most are connected by vista-studded coastal hiking trails along the bluffs.

Exploring the Coast

From Bodega Bay, head to **Salmon Creek Beach** (3095 Hwy 1, Bodega Bay; P), situated around a lagoon and with good waves for surfing. **Portuguese Beach** (btwn Bodega Bay & Jenner; P) is another lovely option and boasts sheltered coves between rocky outcroppings.

Duncan's Landing (6947 Cliff Ave, Bodega Bay; P), on a rocky headland where small

Great For...

Don't Miss

Goat Rock's lethargic colony of harbor seals hauled out on the sand.

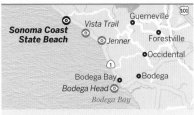

❶ Need to Know

Sonoma Coast beaches are beautiful, but the surf is often too treacherous to even wade; keep an eye on children.

✕ Take a Break

Stop in for a coffee, a pastry and expansive Russian River views at Café Aquatica.

★ Top Tip

Exploring this area makes an excellent day-long adventure, but facilities are nonexistent, so bring water, food and a fully charged cell phone.

boats will unload in the morning, is an excellent place to go wandering for wildflowers in the spring. A hop and a skip north, a boardwalk and trail leads out to **Shell Beach** (Shell Beach Rd, Jenner; Ⓟ), perfect for tide-pooling and beachcombing.

If you only have time for one beach, pull over at **Goat Rock** (5400-5900 N Hwy 1, Jenner; Ⓟ), famous for its colony of harbor seals, lazing in the sun at the mouth of the Russian River. The immense arched sea stack in the distance is said to have earned its name from goat herds that grazed here over a century ago.

Just north of the river in Jenner is the lovely **Café Aquatica** (Ⓙ707-865-2251; 10439 Hwy 1; pastries & sandwiches $4-10; ⊙8am-5pm; 🛜✍), the kind of North Coast coffee shop you've been dreaming of, with fresh pastries and fog-lifting organic coffee.

Sonoma Coast Accommodations

Unless you are willing to hammer down tent pegs, you will need to base yourself in Bodega Bay or Jenner.

If you are up for camping, **Wright's Beach** (Ⓙ800-444-7275; www.reserveamerica.com; 7095 Hwy 1; tent & RV sites $35, day use $8; Ⓟ) is the best campground, even though sites lack privacy and there are no hot showers. There are just 27 sites, but they can be booked six months in advance, and numbers one to 12 are right on the beach. Closer to Bodega Bay, **Bodega Dunes** (Ⓙ800-444-7275; www.reserveamerica.com; 3095 Hwy 1, Ranch Rd, Bodega Bay; tent & RV sites $35, day use $8; Ⓟ) is the largest campground in the Sonoma Coast State Beach system of parks with close to 100 sites. Sites are in high dunes and have hot showers, but be warned – the foghorn sounds all night.

Bodega Bay

Bodega Bay is the first pearl in a string of sleepy fishing towns that line the North Coast and was the setting of Hitchcock's terrifying 1963 avian psycho-horror flick *The Birds*. The skies are free from blood-thirsty gulls today (though you'd best keep an eye on the picnic); it's Bay Area week-enders who descend en masse for extraor-dinary beaches, tide pools, whale-watching, fishing, surfing and seafood.

◉ SIGHTS

Bodega Head   Viewpoint
(Bay Flat Rd) At the peninsula's tip, Bodega Head rises 265ft above sea level. It's great for whale-watching. Landlubbers enjoy hiking above the surf, where several good trails include a 3.75-mile trek to Bodega Dunes Campground and a 2.2-mile walk to Salmon Creek Ranch. Head west from Hwy 1 onto Eastshore Rd, then turn right at the stop sign onto Bay Flat Rd.

Ren Brown Collection Gallery   Gallery
(☎707-875-2922; www.renbrown.com; 1781 Hwy 1; ☺10am-5pm Wed-Sun) The renowned collection of modern Japanese prints and California works at this small gallery is a tranquil escape from the elements. Check out the Japanese garden at the back.

✪ ACTIVITIES

Chanslor Ranch   Horseback Riding
(☎707-875-3333, 707-875-2721; www.horsen aroundtrailrides.com; 2660 N Hwy 1; rides from $125; ☺10am-5pm; ◉) Just north of town, this friendly outfit leads expeditions along the coastline and the rolling inland hills. Ron, the trip leader, is an amiable, sun-weathered cowboy straight from central casting; he recommends tak-ing the Salmon Creek ride or calling ahead for moonlight rides, weather permitting. The 90-minute beach rides are justifiably popular.

Bodega Bay

BILDAGENTUR ZOONAR GMBH / SHUTTERSTOCK ©

Bodega Bay Sportfishing
Center Fishing, Whale-Watching

(📞707-875-3495; www.bodegacharters.com; 1410b Bay Flat Rd; fishing trips $135, whale-watching adult/child $50/35; 🚗) Beside the Sandpiper Cafe, this outfit organizes full-day fishing trips and three-hour whale-watching excursions. It also sells bait, tackle and fishing licenses. Call ahead to ask about recent sightings.

EATING

Fishetarian
Fish Market Californian $

(📞707-480-9037; www.fishetarianfishmarket.com; 599 Hwy 1; mains from $12; ⏱11am-6pm Mon-Thu & Sun, to 7pm Fri & Sat; 🅿🚗🐾) A fish market, deli and great place to eat, with reggae on the soundtrack, an outdoor deck near the water, and an expansive menu that includes colorful and imaginative organic salads, fried tofu (or calamari) with home-made fries, oysters, fish tacos, crab cakes and a fine clam chowder. Also serves craft beers on tap and decadent desserts.

Spud Point Crab
Company Seafood $

(📞707-875-9472; www.spudpointcrab.com; 1860 Westshore Rd; mains $6.75-12; ⏱9am-5pm; 🅿🚗) In the classic tradition of dockside crab shacks, Spud Point serves salty-sweet crab sandwiches and *real* clam chowder (that consistently wins local culinary prizes). You can also buy a crab to take home if you fancy. Eat at picnic tables overlooking the marina. Take Bay Flat Rd to get here.

Drakes Californian $$$

(📞888-875-2250; www.drakesbodegabay.com; 103 Hwy 1, Bodega Bay Lodge & Spa; mains $25-28, appetizers $8-17; ⏱7am-10pm; 🅿📶) This sophisticated spot offers a choice of dining experiences. The Drakes Sonoma Coast Kitchen offers breakfast and dinner, the latter concentrating on such classics as pan-seared duck breast and Black Angus rib-eye steak with accompaniments like orange and almond relish and Parmesan mash. The Fireside Lounge offers a relaxed setting for lighter bites including Pacific oysters and garlic fries.

 Bloodthirsty Birds of Bodega Bay

Bodega Bay has the enduring claim to fame as the setting for Alfred Hitchcock's *The Birds*. Although special effects radically altered the actual layout of the town, you still get a good feel for the supposed site of the farm owned by Mitch Brenner (played by Rod Taylor). The once-cozy **Tides Wharf & Restaurant** (📞707-875-3652; www.innatthetides.com; 835 Hwy 1; breakfast $9-24, lunch $17-30, dinner $25-38; ⏱7:30am-9:30pm Mon-Thu, 7:30am-10pm Fri, 7am-10pm Sat, 7am-9:30pm Sun; 🅿🚗), where much avian-caused havoc occurs in the movie, is still there, but since 1962 it has been transformed into a vast restaurant complex. Venture 5 miles inland to the tiny town of Bodega and you'll find two icons from the film: the schoolhouse and the church. Both stand just as they did in the movie – a crow overhead may make the hair rise on your neck.

TOMSMITH585 / GETTY IMAGES ©

INFORMATION

Sonoma Coast Visitor Center (📞707-875-3866; www.bodegabay.com; 850 Hwy 1; ⏱9am-5pm Mon-Thu & Sat, to 6pm Fri, 10am-5pm Sun) Opposite the Tides Wharf. Stop by for the best help on the coast and a copy of the *North Coaster*, a small-press indie newspaper of essays and brilliant insights on local culture.

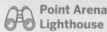

Point Arena Lighthouse

This 1908 **lighthouse** (☑707-882-2809; www.pointarenalighthouse.com; 45500 Lighthouse Rd; adult/child $7.50/1; ☺10am-3:30pm mid-Sep–mid-May, to 4:30pm mid-May–mid-Sep; P) is the tallest on the US West Coast, standing 10 stories high. It's also the only lighthouse in California you can ascend. Check in at the museum, then climb 145 steps to the top and see the Fresnel lens and the jaw-dropping view.

The lighthouse is around 70 miles north of Bodega Bay and 45 miles south of Fort Bragg.

WESTEND61 / GETTY IMAGES ©

Fort Bragg

In the past, Fort Bragg was Mendocino's ugly stepsister, home to a lumber mill, a scrappy downtown and blue-collar locals who gave a cold welcome to outsiders. Since the mill closure in 2002, the town has started to reinvent itself, slowly warming to a tourism-based economy, with the downtown continuing to develop as a wonderfully unpretentious alternative to Mendocino. Drive past the chain stores and seek out downtown, where you'll find better hamburgers and coffee, old-school architecture and residents eager to show off their little town.

◎ SIGHTS

Mendocino Coast Botanical Gardens   Gardens

(☑707-964-4352; www.gardenbythesea.org; 18220 N Hwy 1; adult/child/senior $14/5/10; ☺9am-5pm Mar-Oct, to 4pm Nov-Feb; P) ✤ This gem of Northern California displays native flora, rhododendrons and heritage roses. The succulent display alone is amazing and the organic garden is harvested by volunteers to feed area residents in need. The serpentine paths wander along 47 seafront acres south of town. Primary trails are wheelchair accessible.

Northcoast Artists Gallery   Gallery

(www.northcoastartists.org; 362 N Main St; ☺10am-6pm) An excellent local arts cooperative where 20 full-time members work in photography, glass, woodworking, jewelry, painting, sculpture, textiles and printmaking. Openings are held on the first Friday of the month. Visit the www.mendocino.com website for a comprehensive list of galleries throughout Mendocino County.

Glass Beach   Beach

(Elm St) Named for (what's left of) the sea-polished glass in the sand, remnants of its days as a city dump, this beach is now part of **MacKerricher State Park** (☑707-964-9112; www.parks.ca.gov; Fort Bragg). Take the headlands trail from Elm St, off Main St, but leave the glass, visitors are not supposed to pocket souvenirs (although, strictly speaking, it is not against the law).

◉ ACTIVITIES

Skunk Train   Historic Train

(☑707-964-6371; www.skunktrain.com; 100 W Laurel St; adult/child $84/42; ☺9am-3pm; ⚑) Fort Bragg's pride and joy, the vintage train got its nickname in 1925 for its stinky gas-powered steam engines, but today the historic steam and diesel locomotives are odorless. Passing through redwood-forested mountains, along rivers, over bridges and through deep mountain tunnels, the trains run from both Fort Bragg and Willits to the midway point of Northspur, where they turn around.

If you want to go to Willits, plan to spend the night. The depot is downtown at the foot of Laurel St, one block west of Main St.

WOLLERTZ / SHUTTERSTOCK ©

Glass Beach

⊗ EATING

Taka's Japanese Grill   Japanese $
(☎707-964-5204; 250 N Main St; mains $10.50-17; ☺11:30am-3pm & 4:30-9pm; ℗) Although it may look fairly run-of-the-mill, this is an exceptional Japanese restaurant. The owner is a former grader at the Tokyo fish market so the quality is tops and he makes a weekly run to San Francisco to source freshly imported seafood. Sushi, teriyaki dishes, noodle soups and pan-fried noodles with salmon, beef or chicken are just a few of the options.

Piaci Pub & Pizzeria   Italian $$
(☎707-961-1133; www.piacipizza.com; 120 W Redwood Ave; mains $8-20; ☺11am-9:30pm Mon-Thu, to 10pm Fri & Sat, 4-9:30pm Sun) Fort Bragg's must-visit pizzeria is as well-known for its sophisticated wood-fired, brick-oven pizzas as it is for its long list of microbrews. Try the 'Gustoso' – with chevre, pesto and seasonal pears – all carefully orchestrated on a thin crust. Piaci is tiny, loud and fun,

with much more of a bar atmosphere than a restaurant. Expect to wait at peak times.

Cucina Verona   Italian $$$
(☎707-964-6844; www.cucinaverona.com; 124 E Laurel St; mains $26-30; ☺9am-9pm) A re-al-deal Italian restaurant with never-fail traditional dishes, plus a few with a Californian tweak, like butternut squash lasagne and artichoke bruschetta. The atmosphere is as comforting as the cuisine, with dim lighting, a warm color scheme and unobtrusive live music most evenings. There is an extensive microbrewery selection on offer, as well as local and imported wines.

ⓘ INFORMATION

Fort Bragg-Mendocino Coast Chamber of Commerce (☎707-961-6300; www.mendocino coast.com; 332 S Main St; ☺10am-5pm Mon-Fri, to 3pm Sat;) The chamber of commerce has lots of helpful information about this stretch of coast and what's on. Its online guide is also worth checking out.

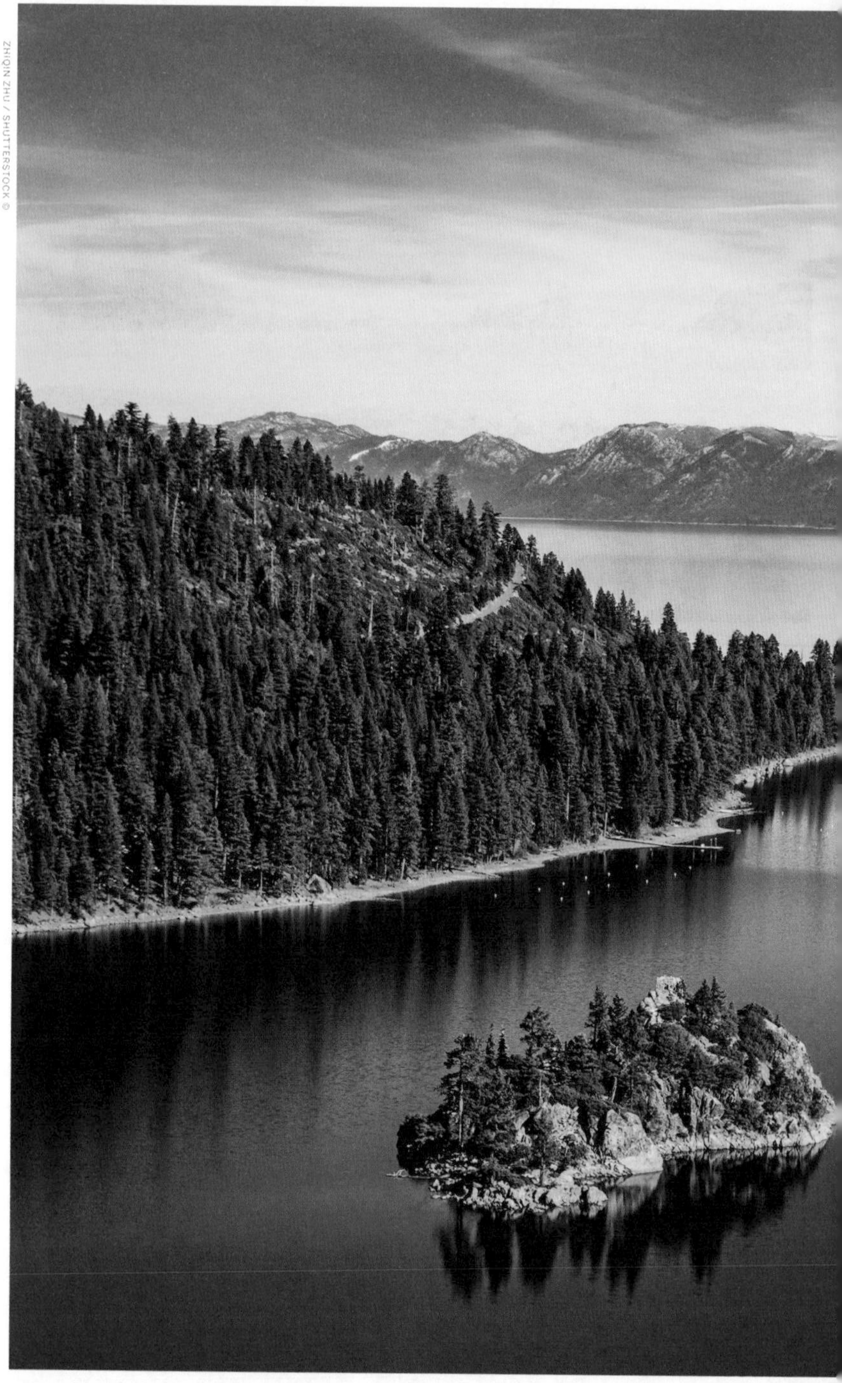

ZHIQIN ZHU / SHUTTERSTOCK ©

Emerald Bay State Park (p122)

LAKE TAHOE

Lake Tahoe

Shimmering in myriad shades of blue and green, Lake Tahoe is the USA's second-deepest lake and, at 6255ft above sea level, it is also one of the highest-elevation lakes in the country. The horned peaks surrounding the lake, which straddles the California–Nevada state line, are year-round destinations. The sun shines on Tahoe three out of every four days. Swimming, boating, kayaking, windsurfing, stand up paddle surfing and other water sports take over in summer, as do hiking, camping and wilderness backpacking adventures. Winter brings bundles of snow, perfect for hitting Tahoe's top-tier ski and snowboard resorts.

Lake Tahoe in Two Days

A two-day itinerary is entirely dependent on the season: in winter you'll want to spend at least one day on the **slopes** (p114), whereas **getting out onto the lake** (p125) is essential in summer. Regardless of the season a nice long drive along the shore will take in breathtaking scenery, but be warned: driving the entirety of the spellbinding 72-mile scenic shoreline will give you quite a workout behind the wheel.

Lake Tahoe in Four Days

With two more days, you'll have more time for exploring the outdoors, either on the winter slopes or on a summer hike to the Alpine lakes and high-mountain meadows of the **Desolation Wilderness** (p120). For a little less exertion, head south and explore **Vikingsholm Castle** (p122) in Emerald Bay State Park. Ensure you set aside an evening for superb Italian food at **Cafe Fiore** (p125).

Snow Sports

Emerald Bay State Park

Arriving in Lake Tahoe

Car From late fall through early spring, drivers should always pack snow chains. Chains can be purchased and installed in towns along the I-80 and Hwy 50.

Bus and train Greyhound buses from Reno, Sacramento and San Francisco run to Truckee, and you can also get the daily Zephyr train here from the same destinations. From Truckee, TART (www.laketahoetransit.com) buses run to the north, west and east shore of the lake.

Sleeping

If you're not staying at one of the ski resorts, the best bet is one of the many vacation rentals that are scattered around the lake. These vary wildly, from plush retreats with spas to rustic log cabins. If you're here in summer, ski resort prices plummet, but the most memorable stay will be under the stars in the Desolation Wilderness backcountry.

Snow Sports

Lake Tahoe has phenomenal skiing, with thousands of acres of the white stuff beckoning at more than a dozen resorts. Winter-sports complexes range from the giant, jet-set slopes of Squaw Valley, Heavenly and Northstar, to no-less-enticing insider playgrounds like Sugar Bowl and Homewood. Tahoe's simply got a hill for everybody, from kids to kamikazes.

Great For...

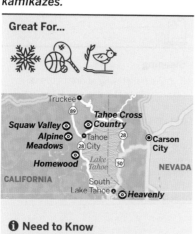

ℹ Need to Know

For a party and crowds, head for the south shore; for a quieter getaway, check out the north shore options.

★ Top Tip

The Bay Area Ski Bus (www.bayarea
skibus.com) from San Francisco and
Sacramento allows you to leave the
headache of driving the I-80 to others.

Ski season generally runs November to April, although it can start as early as October and continue until the last storm whips through in May or even June. All resorts have ski schools, equipment rental and other facilities; check the websites for snow conditions, weather reports and free ski-season shuttle buses from area lodgings.

Deals & Discounts

Midweek and half-day afternoon discounts on lift tickets are usually available, but expect higher prices on weekends and holidays. In San Francisco, Sports Basement (https://shop.sportsbasement.com) sells deeply discounted lift tickets.

Parents should ask about the interchangeable 'Parent Predicament' lift tickets offered by some resorts, which let one parent ski while the other one hangs with the kids, then switch off later.

Top Winter Resorts

Heavenly

The 'mother' of all Tahoe mountains, **Heavenly** (☎775-586-7000; www.skiheavenly.com; 4080 Lake Tahoe Blvd; adult/child 5-12yr/youth 13-18yr $135/79/113; ☺9am-4pm Mon-Fri, from 8:30am Sat, Sun & holidays; ⛷) boasts the most acreage, the longest run (5.5 miles), great tree skiing and the biggest vertical drop around. Follow the sun by skiing on the Nevada side in the morning, moving to the California side in the afternoon. Two terrain parks won't strand snowboarders of any skill level, with the High Roller for experts only. Stats: 28 lifts, 3500 vertical feet, 97 runs.

View of Lake Tahoe from the mountains

Squaw Valley

Few ski hounds can resist the siren call of this mega-sized, world-class, see-and-be-seen **resort** (⌀530-452-4331; www.squaw.com; 1960 Squaw Valley Rd, off Hwy 89, Olympic Valley; adult/child 5-12yr/youth 13-22yr $124/75/109; ⏵9am-4pm Mon-Fri, from 8:30am Sat, Sun & holidays; ⛷), which hosted the 1960 Winter Olympic Games. Hard-core skiers thrill to white-knuckle cornices, chutes and bowls, while beginners practice their turns in a separate area on the upper mountain. There's also a great après-ski scene, and relatively short chairlift waits. Stats: 29 lifts, 2850 vertical feet, over 170 runs.

> **Don't Miss**
>
> The outdoor exhibition skate rink at Squaw Valley's High Camp (p126).

GEARTOOTH PRODUCTIONS / SHUTTERSTOCK ©

Alpine Meadows

Though now owned by neighboring Squaw (tickets are good at both resorts and a free shuttle connects them), **Alpine** (⌀530-452-4356; www.skialpine.com; 2600 Alpine Meadows Rd, off Hwy 89; adult/child under 13yr/youth 13-22yr $124/75/109; ⏵9am-4pm) remains a no-nonsense resort with challenging terrain but without the fancy village, attitude or crowds. It gets more snow than Squaw and it's the most backcountry-friendly around. Boarders jib down the mountain in a terrain park designed by Eric Rosenwald. Stats: 13 lifts, 1800 vertical feet, over 100 runs.

Homewood

Larger than it looks from the road, this **resort** (⌀530-525-2992; www.skihomewood.com; 5145 Westlake Blvd, off Hwy 89; adult/child 5-12yr/youth 13-19yr $83/35/65; ⏵9am-4pm; ⛷), 6 miles south of Tahoe City, proves that bigger isn't always better. Locals and in-the-know visitors cherish the awesome lake views, laid-back ambience, smaller crowds, tree-lined slopes, open bowls (including the excellent but expert 'Quail Face') and a high-speed quad that gets things moving. Families love the wide, gentle slopes. Stats: eight lifts, 1650 vertical feet, 64 runs.

Tahoe Cross Country

Run by the nonprofit Tahoe Cross Country Ski Education Association, this **center** (⌀530-583-5475; www.tahoexc.org; 925 Country Club Dr, off N Lake Blvd/Hwy 28; adult/child under 12yr/youth 13-17yr $24/free/20; ⏵8:30am-5pm; ⛷), about 3 miles north of Tahoe City, has 40 miles of groomed tracks (23 trails) that wind through lovely forest, suitable for all skill levels. Group lessons come with good-value equipment-rental packages; half-day and twilight trail-pass discounts are also available.

> **✗ Take a Break**
>
> Warm up slopeside in **Le Chamois & Loft Bar** (www.squawchamois.com; 1970 Squaw Valley Rd; mains $7-17; ⏵11am-6pm Mon-Fri, to 8pm Sat & Sun, bar open to 9pm or 10pm; ⛷) after skiing Squaw Valley.

Tahoe Rim Trail (p121)

Hiking & Backpacking

With stunning granite-topped hills and incredible views, there's no better way to connect with this incredible natural wonderland than to explore it on a hike or overnight backpacking trip.

Great For...

Don't Miss

Looking up from the path – the vistas really are as breathtaking as the hills.

ⓘ Need to Know

Self-serve wilderness permits for day hikers only are freely available at trailheads. Overnight permits can be reserved online (www.recreation.gov) and may be subject to quotas.

Hiking South Lake Tahoe

Many miles of summer hiking trails start from the top of the gondola at Heavenly (p116). On the Nevada side of the state line, **Lam Watah Nature Trail** meanders for just over a mile each way, winding underneath pine trees and beside meadows and ponds, starting from the community park off Kahle Dr.

Several easy kid- and dog-friendly hikes begin near the United States Forest Service (USFS) Taylor Creek Visitor Center off Hwy 89, including the **Rainbow Trail** and rolling 1-mile **Moraine Trail** near Fallen Leaf Lake. Up at cooler elevations, the mile-long round-trip to **Angora Lakes** is another popular trek with kids, especially because it ends by a sandy swimming beach and a summer snack bar selling ice-cream treats.

Hiking the Desolation Wilderness

Sculpted by powerful glaciers aeons ago, this relatively compact **wilderness area** (www.fs.usda.gov/detail/eldorado/special places/) spreads south and west of Lake Tahoe and is the most popular in the Sierra Nevada. It's a 100-sq-mile wonderland of polished granite peaks, deep-blue alpine lakes, glacier-carved valleys and pine forests that thin quickly at the higher elevations. In summer, wildflowers nudge out from between the rocks.

All this splendor makes for some exquisite backcountry exploration. Six major trailheads provide access from the Lake Tahoe side: Glen Alpine (near Lily Lake, south of Fallen Leaf Lake), Tallac (opposite the entrance to Baldwin Beach), Echo Lakes (near Echo Summit on Hwy 50), Bayview,

Tahoe Rim Trail

Eagle Falls and Meeks Bay. Tallac and Eagle Falls get the most traffic, but solitude comes quickly.

Hiking the Granite Chief Wilderness

Explore the fabulous trails of the **Granite Chief Wilderness** north and west of Tahoe City. For maps and trailhead directions, stop by the visitor center. Recommended day hikes include the moderately strenuous **Five Lakes Trail** (over 4 miles round-trip), which starts from Alpine Meadows Rd off Hwy 89 heading toward Squaw Valley, and the easy trek to **Paige Meadows**, leading onto the **Tahoe Rim Trail** (www.tahoerimtrail.

> ✕ **Take a Break**
>
> Grab healthy food for the trail from New Moon Natural Foods (p126).

HAIRBALLUSA / GETTY IMAGES ©

org) **FREE**. Paige Meadows is also good terrain for novice mountain bikers and snowshoeing. Wilderness permits are not required, even for overnight trips, but free campfire permits are needed, even for gas stoves. Leashed dogs are allowed on these trails.

Hiking Around Truckee

Truckee is a great base for treks in the **Tahoe National Forest**, especially around **Donner Summit**. One popular 5-mile hike reaches the summit of 8243ft **Mt Judah** for awesome views of **Donner Lake** (www.donnerlakemarina.com; P ♿) and the surrounding peaks. A longer, more strenuous ridge-crest hike (part of the **Pacific Crest Trail**) links **Donner Pass** to Squaw Valley (15 miles each way), skirting the base of prominent peaks, but you'll need two cars for this shuttle hike.

Donner Summit is also a major rock-climbing mecca, with over 300 traditional and sport-climbing routes. To learn the ropes, so to speak, take a class with **Alpine Skills International** (☎530-582-9170; www.alpineskills.com; 11400 Donner Pass Rd).

Hiking Squaw Valley

Several hiking trails radiate out from High Camp (p126), or try the lovely, moderate **Shirley Lake Trail** (round-trip 5 miles), which follows a sprightly creek to waterfalls, granite boulders and abundant wildflowers. It starts at the mountain base, near the end of Squaw Peak Rd, behind the cable-car building. Leashed dogs are allowed.

> ★ **Top Tip**
>
> Using bear-proof food-storage canisters is strongly advised in all wilderness areas. Borrow canisters for free from the USFS offices.

Vikingsholm Castle

SUDARSHAN26 / SHUTTERSTOCK ©

Emerald Bay State Park

This gorgeous natural landmark is one of the lake's most beautiful little corners, drawing families to its beach in summer and hosting snowshoeing adventures in winter.

Great For...

Don't Miss

The gorgeous green-water views from the east window of the tea house on Fannette Island.

Sheer granite cliffs and a jagged shoreline hem in glacier-carved Emerald Bay, a teardrop cove that will have you digging for your camera. Its most captivating aspect is the water, which changes from cloverleaf green to light jade depending on the angle of the sun. Fannette Island, a picture-perfect little speck of granite, is set perfectly in its center. You'll spy panoramic pullouts all along Hwy 89, including at **Inspiration Point**. Just south, the road shoulder evaporates on both sides, revealing a postcard-perfect view of Emerald Bay and Cascade Lake to the south.

Vikingsholm Castle

Aside from the natural splendor, the focal point of the park is **Vikingsholm Castle** (http://vikingsholm.com; tour adult/child 7-17yr

❶ Need to Know

📞530-541-6498; www.parks.ca.gov

✕ Take a Break

Stash some local fruit snacks from Grass Roots Natural Foods (p124) before heading to the park.

★ Top Tip

To get here on public transport, catch the **Emerald Bay Trolley** (📞531-541-7149; www.tahoetransportation.org; fare $2; ♿) from the South Y Transit Center.

$10/8; ⏱10:30am-3:30pm or 4pm late May–Sep; 🅿♿), Heiress Lora Knight's majestic mansion on the bay, a rare example of ancient Scandinavian-style architecture. Completed in 1929, it has trippy design elements aplenty, including sod-covered roofs that sprout wildflowers in late spring and a three-story tower. The mansion is reached by a steep 1-mile trail, which also leads by a visitor center. You can take a 30-minute tour of the interior of the house, which still has much of the original furnishings. While Knight is best known today for this incredible building, the eccentric figure was also one of the primary financial backers of Charles Lindbergh's non-stop solo flight across the Atlantic in 1927.

Fannette Island

Knight's tract of land here also included Tahoe's only island, the brush-covered, uninhabited Fannette. The island holds the vandalized remains of a tiny 1920s teahouse. Knight would occasionally motorboat guests here from the castle. Fannette Island is accessible by boat or kayak, except during Canada goose nesting season (typically February to mid-June). You can rent boats at Meeks Bay or South Lake Tahoe; from the latter, you can also catch narrated bay cruises or speedboat tours.

Eagle Falls Trail

If you want an adventure on land, hit this hiking trail, which gives you a chance to see the summer wildflowers on a steep 2-mile alpine hike. It's a there-and-back trail from Emerald Bay Rd to Eagle Lake, via spectacular falls. In winter, when Emerald Bay is serene and empty, you can also rent snow shoes to explore the route.

South Lake Tahoe & Stateline

Highly congested and arguably overdeveloped, South Lake Tahoe is a chockablock commercial strip bordering the lake and framed by picture-perfect alpine mountains. At the foot of the world-class Heavenly mountain resort (p116), and buzzing from the gambling tables in the casinos just across the border in Stateline, NV, Lake Tahoe's south shore draws visitors with a cornucopia of activities, lodging and restaurant options, especially for summer beach access and tons of powdery winter snow.

◎ SIGHTS

Tallac Historic Site   Historic Site

(www.tahoeheritage.org; Tallac Rd; optional tour adult/child $10/5; ☉10am-4pm daily mid-Jun–Sep, Fri & Sat late May–mid-Jun; 🎨) **FREE** Sheltered by a pine grove and bordering a wide, sandy beach, this national historic site sits on the archaeologically excavated grounds of the former Tallac Resort, a swish vacation retreat for San Francisco's high society around the turn of the 20th century. Feel free to just amble or cycle around the breezy forested grounds, today transformed into a community arts hub, where leashed dogs are allowed.

✪ ACTIVITIES

Nevada Beach   Swimming

(per car $7) A sweeping sandy beach with a timber picnic area and a shack selling ice creams and drinks.

Camp Richardson Corral & Pack Station   Horseback Riding

(☏530-541-3113; www.camprichardsoncorral. com; Emerald Bay Rd/Hwy 89; trail rides $50-168; 🚸) In continuous operation since 1934, this camp offers trail and wagon rides and magical winter sleigh trips.

🛍 SHOPPING

Grass Roots Natural Foods   Food & Drinks

(http://grassrootstahoe.com; 2030 Dunlap Dr; ☉9am-8pm) 🌿 This store sells a wealth of organic produce, lifestyle products and grocery goods, plus sandwiches and fresh pizzas.

Tallac Historic Site

RICHARD CUMMINS / GETTY IMAGES ©

EATING & DRINKING

Cafe Fiore   Italian $$
(☑530-541-2908; www.cafefiore.com; 1169 Ski
Run Blvd; mains $18-34; ☺5:30-9pm) Serving
upscale Italian without pretension, this
tiny romantic eatery pairs succulent pasta,
seafood and meats with an award-winning
300-vintage wine list. Swoon over the veal
scaloppine, homemade white-chocolate
ice cream and near-perfect garlic bread.
With only seven tables (a baker's dozen in
summer when the candle-lit outdoor patio
opens), reservations are essential.

Freshie's   Fusion $$
(☑530-542-3630; www.freshiestahoe.com; 3330
Lake Tahoe Blvd; mains $14-28; ☺11:30am-9pm;
☑) From vegans to seafood lovers, everybody should be able to find a favorite on the
extensive menu at this Hawaiian fusion joint
with sunset upper-deck views. Most of the
produce is local and organic, and the blackened fish tacos are South Lake Tahoe's best.
Check the webcam to see if there's a wait.

Brewery at Lake Tahoe   Brewery
(www.brewerylaketahoe.com; 3542 Lake Tahoe
Blvd; ☺11am-10:30pm) Crazy-popular brewpub
pumps its signature Bad Ass Ale into grateful
local patrons, who may sniff at bright-eyed
out-of-towners. The barbecue is dynamite
and a roadside patio opens in summer. Don't
leave without a bumper sticker!

ⓘ INFORMATION

Lake Tahoe Visitors Authority (☑800-288-
2463; www.tahoesouth.com; 169 Hwy 50,
Stateline, NV; ☺9am-5pm Mon-Fri) A full range of
tourist information.

Tahoe City

The western shore's commercial hub, Tahoe
City straddles the junction of Hwys 89 and
28, making it almost inevitable that you'll find
yourself breezing through here at least once
during your round-the-lake sojourn. The
town is handy for grabbing food and supplies
and renting sports gear. It's also the closest

Take a Cruise on Lake Tahoe

Two paddle steamers, operated by **Lake
Tahoe Cruises** (☑800-238-2463; www.
zephyrcove.com; 900 Ski Run Blvd; adult/
child from $55/20; ☑), ply Lake Tahoe's
'big blue' year-round with a variety
of sightseeing, drinking, dining and
dancing cruises, including a narrated
two-hour daytime trip to Emerald Bay.

Sunset champagne and happy-hour
floats aboard a sailing catamaran with
Woodwind Cruises (☑775-588-3000;
www.tahoecruises.com; 760 Hwy 50, NV,
Zephyr Cove Marina; 1hr cruise adult/child
2-12yr from $49/18) are the perfect way to
chill after a sunny afternoon lazing on
the beach. Five daily departures during
summer; reservations recommended.

A Lake Tahoe cruise
ASIF ISLAM/SHUTTERSTOCK ©

lake town to Squaw Valley (p117). The
main drag, N Lake Blvd, is chockablock with
outdoor outfitters, touristy shops and cafes.

◎ SIGHTS

Gatekeeper's Museum & Marion Steinbach Indian Basket Museum   Museum
(☑530-583-1762; www.northtahoemuseums.
org; 130 W Lake Blvd/Hwy 89; adult/child under
13yr $5/free; ☺10am-5pm daily late May-Sep,
11am-4pm Fri & Sat Oct-Apr) In a reconstructed
log cabin close to town, this museum has
a small but fascinating collection of Tahoe
memorabilia, including Olympics history
and relics from the early steamboat era and
tourism explosion around the lake. In the

High Camp & the Olympic Museum

At the top of a steep cable car in Squaw Valley, **High Camp** (☏800-403-0206; http://squawalpine.com; cable car adult/child 5-12yr/youth 13-22yr $39/15/25, all-access pass $46/19/38; ☺11am-4:30pm; ⚽) boasts a heated seasonal outdoor swimming lagoon (adult/child $14/8), an 18-hole disc-golf course (free), two high-altitude tennis courts (racquet rentals and ball purchase available), and a roller-skating rink ($14/8) that doubles as an ice-skating rink in winter. Several hiking trails begin here.

Cable-car tickets include admission to the **Olympic Museum** (11am to 4pm Saturday and Sunday), a fun retro exploration of the 1960 Olympics, featuring a film and much memorabilia.

The lagoon at High Camp
SACRAMENTO BEE / GETTY IMAGES ©

museum's newer wing, uncover an exquisite array of Native American baskets collected from over 85 indigenous California tribes.

Commons Beach   Park
(400 N Lake Blvd) Commons Beach is a small, attractive park with sandy and grassy areas, picnic tables, barbecue grills, a climbing rock and playground, as well as free summer concerts (www.concertsatcommons beach.com) and outdoor movie nights. Leashed dogs welcome.

⊕ ACTIVITIES

Truckee River Raft Rentals Rafting
(☏530-583-0123; www.truckeeriverraft.com; 185 River Rd; adult/child 6-12yr $30/25; ☺8:30am-

3:30pm Jun-Sep; ⚽) The Truckee River here is gentle and wide as it flows northwest from the lake – perfect for novice paddlers. This outfit rents rafts for the 5-mile float from Tahoe City to the **River Ranch Lodge** (☏530-583-4264; http://riverranchlodge.com; Hwy 89 at Alpine Meadows Rd; mains patio & cafe $8-13, restaurant $22-30; ☺lunch Jun-Sep, dinner year-round, call for seasonal hours), including transportation back to town. Reservations strongly advised.

✖ EATING & DRINKING

Fat Cat   Californian $
(www.tahoefatcat.com; 599 N Lake Blvd; mains $9-17; ☺11am-9pm, bar to 2am; ⚽) This casual, family-run restaurant with local art splashed on the walls does it all: from-scratch soups, heaped salads, sandwiches, incredible burgers, pasta bowls and plenty of fried munchies for friends to share. Look for live indie music on Friday and Saturday nights.

New Moon Natural Foods   Deli, Health Food $
(505 W Lake Blvd; mains $6-12; ☺9am-8pm Mon-Sat, 10am-7pm Sun; ☑) ✔ A tiny but well-stocked natural-foods store, its gem of a deli concocts scrumptious ethnic food to go, all packaged in biodegradable and compostable containers. Try the fish tacos or Thai salad with organic greens and spicy peanut sauce.

Dockside 700 Wine Bar & Grill   American $$
(☏530-581-0303; www.dockside700.com; 700 N Lake Blvd; lunch $10-17, dinner $14-32; ☺11:30am-8pm Mon-Thu, to 9pm Fri-Sun; ⚽⚽) On a lazy summer afternoon, grab a table on the back deck that overlooks the boats bobbing at Tahoe City Marina. Barbecue chicken, ribs and steak light a fire under dinner (reservations advised), alongside seafood pastas and pizzas.

Tahoe Mountain Brewing Co   Brewery
(www.tahoebrewing.com; 475 N Lake Blvd; ☺11:30am-10pm) Brewed in nearby Truckee, the Sugar Pine Porter, barrel-aged sours and award-winning Paddleboard Pale Ale here pair

Rafting on Truckee River

splendidly with sweet potato fries, burgers and other pub grub on the lake-facing patio.

INFORMATION

Tahoe City Downtown Association (www.visitta hoecity.org; 425 N Lake Blvd; ⏰9am-5pm Mon-Thu) Tourist information and online events calendar.

Tahoe City Visitors Information Center (☎530-581-6900; www.gotahoenorth.com; 100 N Lake Blvd; ⏰9am-5pm) At the Hwy 89/28 split.

GETTING THERE & AWAY

Just south of the Hwy 28/89 split, the modern new **Tahoe City Transit Center** (www.nextbus.com/ tahoe; 870 Cabin Creek Rd, off Hwy 89) is the main bus terminal, with a comfy waiting room. Behind it you'll find trailhead parking for the **Tahoe Rim Trail** (p121) and various bike path routes. Regular buses connect the town with other spots on the lake.

Homewood

This quiet and very alpine-looking resort hamlet, associated with the ski resort

(p117) of the same name, is popular with summertime boaters and, in winter, skiers and snowboarders. **West Shore Sports** (☎530-525-9920; www.westshoresports.com; 5395 W Lake Blvd; ⏰8am-5pm) rents out all the winter and summer gear you'll need.

EATING

West Shore Café Californian **$$** (☎530-525-5200; www.westshorecafe.com; 5160 W Lake Blvd; mains $12-33; ⏰11am-9:30pm mid-Jun–Sep, 5-9:30pm Oct–mid-Jun) At the **West Shore Inn's** (r/ste from $199/349; ❄🤶) cozy restaurant, chef Mike Davis whips up worthy meals using fresh produce and ranched meats, from burgers to Arctic char with spaghetti squash and hedgehog mushrooms.

GETTING THERE & AWAY

Tahoe Area Rapid Transit (TART; ☎530-550-1212; www.laketahoetransit.com; 10183 Truckee Airport Rd; single/day pass $2/4) operates buses along the north shore as far as Incline Village.

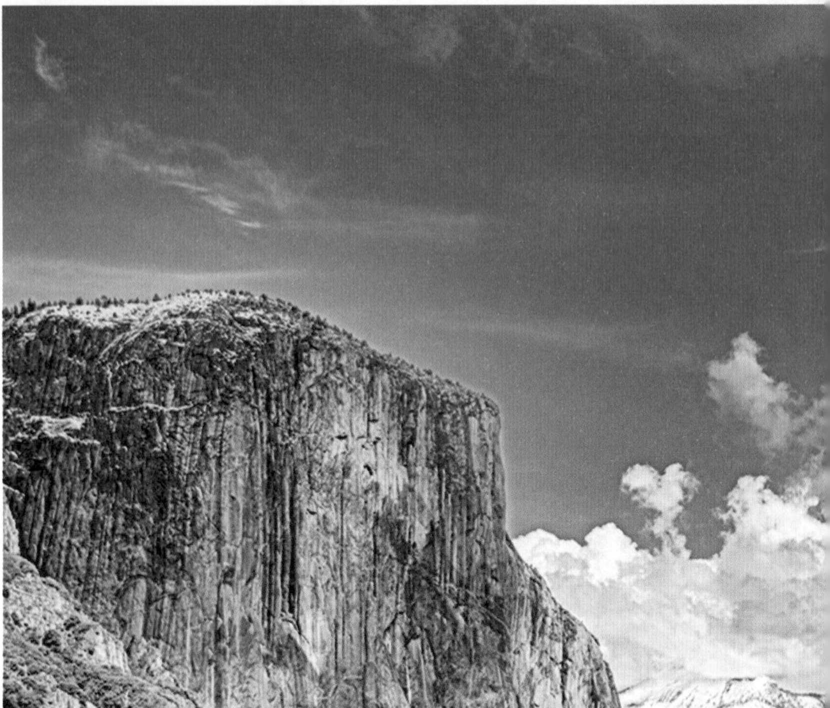

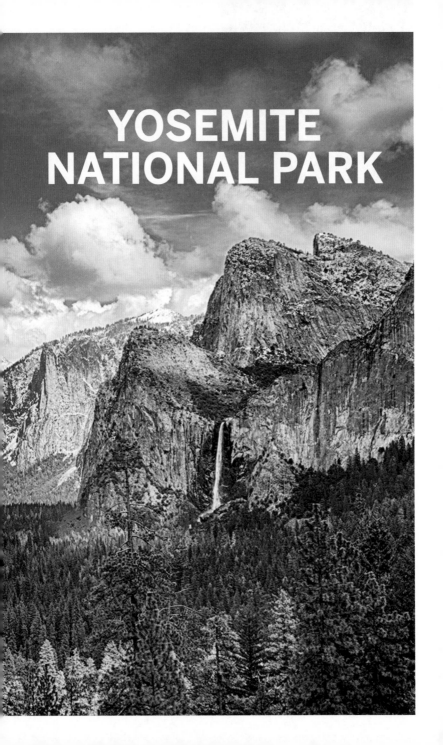

Yosemite National Park

The jaw-dropping head-turner of America's national parks, and a Unesco World Heritage Site, Yosemite (yo-sem-it-ee) garners the devotion of all who enter. From the waterfall-striped granite walls buttressing Yosemite Valley to the skyscraping sequoias of Mariposa Grove, the place inspires a sense of awe. But lift your eyes above the crowds and you'll feel your heart instantly moved by unrivalled splendors: the haughty profile of Half Dome, the hulking presence of El Capitan, the drenching mists of Yosemite Falls and the gemstone lakes of the high country's subalpine wilderness.

Yosemite National Park in Two Days

With two days in Yosemite, you'll want to head straight to the valley, where you can stand agape at the twin marvels of **Half Dome** (p134) and El Capitan, and enjoy a drink or two at the comfortable **Majestic Bar** (p135). Make the most of day two with a short hike to see some of the valley's **waterfalls** (p136).

Yosemite National Park in Four Days

Get deeper into this incredible park by cruising the twisting two-lane blacktop of CA 120 to Yosemite's high country and **Tuolumne Meadows** (p140). On the way, make time for the incredible views at **Olmsted Point** (p134). If you're particularly ambitious, hike up to **Glacier Point** (p132) for a bird's-eye view of the valley's monuments or try a night or two in the backcountry.

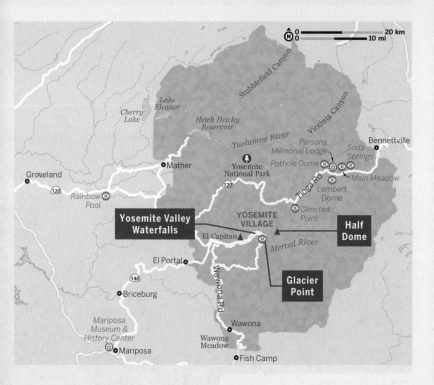

Arriving in Yosemite National Park

Car Yosemite is accessible year-round from the west (via Hwys 120 W and 140) and south (Hwy 41), and also in summer from the east (via Hwy 120 E). Yosemite's entrance fee is $30 per vehicle (or $15 for those on a bicycle or on foot) and is valid for seven consecutive days.

Bus and train Yosemite can easily be reached by public transportation. Greyhound buses and Amtrak trains serve Merced, west of the park, where they are met by buses operated by Yosemite Area Regional Transportation System (YARTS; www.yarts.com).

Sleeping

Camping, even in a busy campground near Yosemite Village, enhances the being-out-in-nature feeling. Backcountry wilderness camping is for the prepared and adventurous. All noncamping reservations within the park are handled by Aramark/Yosemite Hospitality (www.travelyosemite.com); reservations are critical from May to early September. There are a few quality hotels in Groveland proper, a variety of accommodations to the east along Hwy 120 in the Stanislaus National Forest, and a number of chain options in Mariposa.

Sunrise over Half Dome (p134), viewed from Glacier Point

KRIS WIKTOR / SHUTTERSTOCK ©

Glacier Point

With granite peaks stretching out into the distance, Glacier Point offers one of the most commanding views in the state, including a bird's-eye view of El Capitan and Half Dome.

History

Almost from the park's inception, Glacier Point has been a popular destination. It used to be that getting up here was a major undertaking. That changed once the Four Mile Trail opened in 1872. A wagon road to the point was completed in 1882, and the current Glacier Point Rd was built in 1936. The cozy Glacier Point Trailside Museum was one of the park's first projects, a humble little stone hut that offers a great shelter from a passing storm.

The View

If you drove up here, the views from 7214ft Glacier Point might make you feel like you cheated – superstar sights present themselves with your having made hardly any physical effort. A quick mosey up the paved

Great For...

Don't Miss

The granite faces of the Sierra bathed in warm, golden light at sunset.

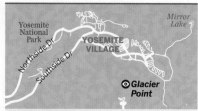

❶ Need to Know

The road to the point is closed in winter; the best time to visit is late spring, as soon as the road is cleared, for the best waterfall flows.

✕ Take a Break

Pack a picnic and amble over to the Glacier Point amphitheater, an ideal setting with incredible panoramas.

★ Top Tip

In the summer, a free shuttle leaves Badger Pass for Glacier Point every 20 minutes.

At the tip of the point is **Overhanging Rock**, a huge granite slab protruding from the cliff edge like an outstretched tongue, defying gravity and once providing a scenic stage for daredevil extroverts. Through the years, many famous photos have been taken of folks performing handstands, high kicks and other wacky stunts on the rock. The precipice is now off-limits.

Getting There

Nearby, if you're still craving views, you can hike to the summit of Sentinel Dome (8122ft), the shortest and easiest trail up one of Yosemite's granite domes. For those unable to visit Half Dome's summit, Sentinel offers an equally outstanding 360-degree perspective of Yosemite's wonders, and the 2.2-mile round-trip hike only takes about an hour. A visit at sunrise or sunset or during a full moon is spectacular.

path from the parking lot and you'll find the entire eastern Yosemite Valley spread out before you, from **Yosemite Falls** to **Half Dome**, as well as the distant peaks that ring Tuolumne Meadows. Half Dome looms practically at eye level, and if you look closely, you can spot hikers on its summit.

To the left of Half Dome lies the glacially carved **Tenaya Canyon**, and to its right are the wavy white ribbons of **Nevada Falls** and **Vernal Falls**. On the valley floor, the Merced River snakes through green meadows and groves of trees. If you're not afraid of heights, sidle up to the railing, hold on tight and peer 3200ft straight down at Half Dome Village. **Basket Dome** and **North Dome** rise to the north of the valley, and **Liberty Cap** and the **Clark Range** can be seen to the right of Half Dome.

Half Dome at sunrise

DAVID KIENE / GETTY IMAGES ©

Half Dome

Yosemite's most distinctive natural monument, this beautifully broken slab of granite is 87 million years old and has a 93% vertical grade – the sheerest cliff in North America.

Great For...

Don't Miss

The view of the back side of Half Dome from **Olmsted Point**, midway between the May Lake turnoff and Tenaya Lake.

The Story of Half Dome

According to Native American legend, one of Yosemite Valley's early inhabitants went down from the mountains to Mono Lake, where he wed a Paiute named Tesaiyac. The journey back to the valley was difficult, and by the time they reached what was to become Mirror Lake, Tesaiyac had decided that she wanted to go back to her people at Mono Lake. However, her husband refused to live on such barren land with no oak trees from which to get acorns.

With a heart full of despair, Tesaiyac began to run toward Mono Lake, and her husband followed her. When the powerful spirits heard quarreling in Yosemite, they became angry and turned the two into stone: he became North Dome and she became Half Dome. The tears she cried

❶ Need to Know

Rangers check for valid permits at the base of the Half Dome cables.

✕ Take a Break

Settle in for a drink at the cozy **Majestic Bar** (www.travelyosemite.com; Majestic Yosemite Hotel, 1 Ahwahnee Dr, Yosemite Valley; ⊙11am-10pm) inside the Majestic Yosemite Hotel.

★ Top Tip

If you want to climb the dome, check www.nps.gov/yose/planyourvisit/hd permits.htm for the latest information.

made marks as they ran down her face, thus forming Mirror Lake.

Climbing & Hiking

Climbers come from around the world to grapple with its legendary north face, but good hikers can reach its summit via a 17-mile round-trip trail from Yosemite Valley. The trail gains 4900ft in elevation and has cable handrails for the last 200yd.

The hike can be done in a day but is more enjoyable if you break it up by camping along the way (Little Yosemite Valley is the most popular spot).

Half Dome Permits

To stem lengthy lines (and increasingly dangerous conditions) on the vertiginous cables of Half Dome, the park now requires that all day hikers obtain a permit in advance.

Preseason permit lottery (www.recreation.gov) Lottery applications ($10) for the 300 daily spots must be completed in March, with confirmation notification sent in mid-April; an additional fee of $10 per person confirms the permit. Applications can include up to six people and seven alternate dates.

Daily lottery Approximately 50 additional permits are distributed by lottery two days before each hiking date. Apply online or by phone (☎877-444-6777) between midnight and 1pm Pacific Time; notification is available late that same evening. It's easier to score weekday permits.

Backpackers Those with Yosemite-issued wilderness permits that reasonably include Half Dome can request Half Dome permits (from $12.50 per person) without going through the lottery process.

Bridalveil Fall

WAYNE HSIEH78 / SHUTTERSTOCK ©

Yosemite Valley Waterfalls

Yosemite's waterfalls mesmerize even the most jaded traveler, especially when the spring runoff turns them into spectacularly thunderous cataracts.

Great For...

Don't Miss

Cooling off in the refreshing mist of Vernal Falls in the peak of summer.

Yosemite Falls

West of Yosemite Village, Yosemite Falls is considered among the tallest waterfalls in North America, dropping 740m (2425ft) in three tiers. Because it faces the open meadows, you'll be able to see this gorgeous cascade from vantage points throughout the valley. A slick trail leads to the bottom or, if you prefer solitude, you can clamber up the Yosemite Falls Trail, which puts you atop the falls after a grueling 3.4 miles. The falls are usually mesmerizing, especially when the spring runoff turns them into thunderous cataracts, but most are reduced to a trickle by late summer.

Bridalveil Fall

At the southwestern end of the valley, Bridalveil Fall tumbles 620ft. The Ahwah-

❶ Need to Know

People have been swept away in Yosemite's falls; be extremely cautious around wet footpaths and railings.

✕ Take a Break

The **Village Store** (Yosemite Village; ⏱8am-8pm, to 10pm summer) has health-food items and organic produce to fuel a waterfall-bound walk.

★ Top Tip

Bring rain gear or expect to get soaked when the falls are heavy.

---

neechee people call it Pohono (Spirit of the Puffing Wind), as gusts often blow the fall from side to side, even lifting water back up into the air. The waterfall usually runs year-round, though it's often reduced to a whisper by midsummer.

Park at the large lot where Wawona Rd (Hwy 41) meets Southside Dr. From the lot, it's a quarter-mile walk to the base of the fall. The path is paved but probably too rough for wheelchairs, and there's a somewhat steep climb at the very end. Avoid climbing on the slippery rocks at the fall's base – no one likes a broken bone.

Vernal & Nevada Falls

At Vernal Falls, one of Yosemite's most iconic, the thundering waters of the Merced River tumble 317ft down on the way to meet

Yosemite Valley below. Mist Trail, the paved path to the falls, is one of the park's most popular. At the top of the falls, the view is jaw-dropping (and a little scary). Continue a short distance further on the trail and you'll come to Emerald Pool and Silver Apron. Both of these may look temping on a sweltering summer day, but stay out; it is extremely dangerous to swim here. You can continue over a small bridge and take in a short stretch of the famed John Muir Trail, which will lead back to Yosemite Valley in about four miles. This alternate return has big rewards with incredible views of Liberty Cap (look for climbers in summer) and Nevada Falls.

Spectacular views await from Nevada Falls, ricocheting 594ft as part of the 'Giant Staircase' leading the Merced River down into Yosemite Valley. Most people take the Mist Trail (you pass Vernal Fall on the way), but the John Muir Trail also gets you to the top.

ℹ️ INFORMATION

DANGERS & ANNOYANCES

Yosemite is prime black-bear habitat. Follow park rules on proper food storage and utilize bear-proof food lockers when parked overnight. Mosquitoes can be pesky in summer, so bug spray's not a bad idea. And please don't feed those squirrels. They may look cute but they've got a nasty bite.

MEDICAL SERVICES

Yosemite Medical Clinic (☏209-372-4637; 9000 Ahwahnee Dr, Yosemite Village; ⏱9am-7pm daily late-May–late Sep, to 5pm Mon-Fri late Sep-late May) A 24-hour emergency service is available.

TOURIST INFORMATION

Yosemite Valley Visitor Center (☏209-372-0200; 9035 Village Dr, Yosemite Village; ⏱9am-5pm; ♿) The main tourist-information center, with exhibits and free film screenings in the theater. Give yourself plenty of time, as lines are long in summer. Issues wilderness permits from November to April when the **Wilderness Center** (☏209-372-0745; Yosemite Village; ⏱8am-5pm May-Oct) is closed.

ℹ️ GETTING THERE & AWAY

CAR

Yosemite is accessible year-round from the west (via Hwys 120 W and 140) and south (Hwy 41), and in summer also from the east (via Hwy 120 E). Roads are plowed in winter, but snow chains may be required at any time. In 2006 a mammoth rockslide buried part of Hwy 140, 6 miles west of the park; traffic there is restricted to vehicles under 45ft. Big Oak Flat Rd was closed for several months after a 'slide', really of an entire hillside, in February 2017.

Gas up year-round at Wawona inside the park (you'll pay dearly), at El Portal on Hwy 140 just outside its western boundary or Lee Vining at the junction of Hwys 120 and 395 outside the park in the east. In summer, gas is also sold at Crane Flat – the gas station in Tuolumne Meadows is now closed.

PUBLIC TRANSPORTATION

Yosemite is one of the few national parks that can easily be reached by public transportation. Greyhound (p310) buses and Amtrak (p314) trains serve Merced, west of the park, where

Yosemite Valley

they are met by buses operated by the **Yosemite Area Regional Transportation System** (YARTS; ☎877-989-2787; www.yarts.com), and you can buy Amtrak tickets that include the YARTS segment all the way into the park. Buses travel to Yosemite Valley along Hwy 140 several times daily year-round, stopping along the way.

In summer (roughly June through September), another YARTS route runs from Mammoth Lakes along Hwy 395 to Yosemite Valley via Hwy 120. One-way tickets to Yosemite Valley are $13 ($9 child and senior, three hours) from Merced and $18 ($15 child and senior, 3½ hours) from Mammoth Lakes – less if boarding in between.

YARTS fares include the park-entrance fee, making them a super bargain, and drivers accept credit cards.

❶ GETTING AROUND

BICYCLE

Bicycling is an ideal way to take in Yosemite Valley. You can rent a wide-handled cruiser (per hour/day $12.50/30.50) or a bike with an attached child trailer ($19/56.50) at the **Yosemite Valley Lodge** or **Half Dome Village** (⊘9am-6pm Mar-Oct). Strollers and wheelchairs are also rented here.

CAR

Roadside signs with red bears mark the many spots where bears have been hit by motorists, so think before you hit the accelerator, and follow the pokey posted speed limits. Valley visitors are advised to park and take advantage of the Yosemite Valley Shuttle Bus. Even so, traffic in the valley can feel like rush hour in LA.

Glacier Point and Tioga Rds are closed in winter.

Village Garage (☎209-372-8320; Tecoya Rd; ⊘8am-5pm) provides emergency repairs and even gasoline when you're in an absolute fix.

Groveland

From the Big Oak Flat entrance to Yosemite, it's 22 miles to Groveland, an adorable town with restored gold rush–era buildings and lots of visitor services.

 Guided Tours of Yosemite

The nonprofit **Yosemite Conservancy** (☎209-379-2317; www.yosemiteconservancy. org) has scheduled tours of all kinds, plus custom trips.

First-timers often appreciate the two-hour **Valley Floor Tour** (☎209-372-1240; www.travelyosemite.com; adult/child $35/25; ⊘year-round; 👪), which runs year-round and covers the valley's highlights.

For other options, stop at the tour and activity desks at **Yosemite Valley Lodge** (☎209-372-1240; ⊘7:30am-7pm), Half Dome Village or Yosemite Village, call ☎209-372-4386 or check www. travelyosemite.com.

Valley Floor Tour
BARBARA DAVIDSON / GETTY IMAGES ©

◎ SIGHTS & ACTIVITIES

Rainbow Pool Natural Pool
(www.fs.usda.gov/stanislaus) About 15 miles east of Groveland, in the Stanislaus National Forest, Rainbow Pool is a popular swimming hole with a small cascade; it's signed on the south side of Hwy 120.

ARTA River Trips Rafting
(☎800-323-2782, 209-962-7873; www.arta.org; 24000 Casa Loma Rd) Nonprofit rafting outfitter runs one-day and multiday Tuolumne River trips, as well as day trips on the Merced River.

Sierra Mac Rafting
(☎209-591-8027; www.sierramac.com; 27890 Hwy 120) One of two outfitters running the experts-only Cherry Creek; offers other Tuolumne and Merced River trips. Marty McDonnell, Sierra Mac's owner, has been

 Dazzling Tuolumne Meadows

About 55 miles from Yosemite Valley via Tioga Rd (or Hwy 120 E), 8600ft **Tuolumne Meadows** is the largest sub-alpine meadow in the Sierra. It provides a dazzling contrast to the valley, with its lush open fields, clear blue lakes, ragged granite peaks and domes, and cooler temperatures. If you come during July or August, you'll find a painter's palette of wildflowers decorating the shaggy meadows.

The main meadow is about 2.5 miles long and lies on the northern side of Tioga Rd between **Lembert Dome** and **Pothole Dome**. The 200ft scramble to the top of the latter – preferably at sunset – gives you great views of the meadow. An interpretive trail leads from the stables to muddy **Soda Springs**, where carbonated water bubbles up in red-tinted pools. The nearby **Parsons Memorial Lodge** has a few displays.

Hikers and climbers will find a paradise of options around Tuolumne Meadows, which is also the gateway to the High Sierra camps.

PUNG / SHUTTERSTOCK ©

river guiding since the 1960s. Sierra Mac's staging office is perched on a hill 13 miles east of town.

 EATING & DRINKING

Burgers, sandwiches and pizza aren't in short supply. Groveland also has a chef-driven contemporary American restaurant and a Mexican place – both are recommended.

If heading to campgrounds or accommodations further east, you can stock up on groceries at the town supermarket.

Mar-Val Supermarket $
(209-962-7452; 1900 Main St; 7am-10pm, to 9pm winter) This large grocery store at the eastern end of town is a good place to stock up on food and supplies before heading into Yosemite.

Fork & Love Restaurant Modern American $$
(www.forkandlove.com; 18736 Main St; mains $17-28; 6-9pm Thu-Sat, 9am-1pm Sun Mar-Nov) Scarce in these parts, 'local, organic and sustainable' is done right at this rustically refined restaurant in a historic saloon space in the **Hotel Charlotte** (209-962-6455; www.hotelcharlotte.com; r $149-249;). The small plates, as well as the mains, like pork spatzle, carne masala (black Angus beef with homemade masala sauce) and artichoke fried rice, are innovative and best enjoyed by sharing.

Iron Door Grill & Saloon Bar
(209-962-6244; www.iron-door-saloon.com; 18761 Main St; restaurant 7am-10pm, bar 11am-2am, shorter hours winter) Claiming to be the oldest bar in the state, the Iron Door is a dusty, atmospheric place, with swinging doors, a giant bar, high ceilings, mounted animal heads and hundreds of dollar bills tacked to the ceiling. There's live music summer-weekend nights, and the adjacent, more contemporary dining room serves good steaks, ribs and pasta dishes (mains $9.50 to $25).

 INFORMATION

USFS Groveland Ranger Station (209-962-7825; www.fs.usda.gov/stanislaus; 24545 Hwy 120; 8am-4:30pm Mon-Sat Jun-Aug, reduced hours Sep-May) About 8 miles east of Groveland; offers recreation information for the surrounding Stanislaus National Forest and nearby Tuolumne Wild and Scenic River Area.

There are two banks with ATMs and a gas station 1.5 miles west of town.

 JON CHICA / SHUTTERSTOCK ©

Mariposa

GETTING THERE & AWAY

YARTS (209-388-9589, 877-989-2787; www.yarts.com) buses run year-round along Hwy 140 into Yosemite Valley ($3 one way, 1¾ hours), stopping at the Mariposa visitor center. Tickets include admission to Yosemite.

Mariposa

About halfway between Merced and Yosemite Valley, Mariposa (Spanish for 'butterfly') is the largest and most interesting town near Yosemite National Park. Established as a mining and railroad town during the gold rush, it has the oldest courthouse in continuous use (since 1854) west of the Mississippi, loads of Old West pioneer character and a couple of museums dedicated to the area's history.

SIGHTS

Mariposa Museum & History Center
Museum

(209-966-2924; www.mariposamuseum.com; 5119 Jessie St; adult/child $5/free; 10am-4pm;) Mariposa's past comes alive, well, as much as possible, considering the fairly fusty objects displayed in this museum. Menus, logbooks, train tickets, photos etc are organized in small diorama-style rooms to tell the stories of specific historical epochs or people. Some gems, like actual gold-miners' letters, can be found if you have the time.

Several period buildings and a Yosemite Miwok bark house can be visited on the museum grounds.

EATING & DRINKING

Happy Burger
Diner $

(209-966-2719; www.happyburgerdiner.com; Hwy 140, cnr 12th St; mains $8-14; 5:30am-9pm;) Burgers, fries and shakes served with a heavy dose of nostalgic Americana. Happy Burger, decorated with old LP album covers, and boasting the largest menu in the Sierra, offers one of the cheaper meals in town. Besides burgers, there are sandwiches, Mexican food, salads and a ton of sinful ice-cream desserts. Free computer terminal inside and a 'doggy dining area' outdoors.

BURACHET / SHUTTERSTOCK ©

JIM LUNDGREN / ALAMY STOCK PHOTO ©

From left: Half Dome (p134) at night; Cascades below
Vernal Falls (p137); Hiking with views of Half Dome

Savoury's American $$

(☑209-966-7677; 5034 Hwy 140; mains $17-35;
⊙5-9:30pm, closed Wed winter; ⚹) Upscale yet
casual Savoury's is the best restaurant in
town. Black lacquered tables and contemporary art create tranquil window dressing
for dishes like wild-mushroom ravioli,
Cajun-spiced New York steak with pan-seared
onions, and crab cakes with cilantro-lime aioli.

Charles Street
Dinner House Steak $$$

(☑209-966-2366; www.charlesstreetdinner
house.net; cnr Hwy 140 & 7th St; mains $19-32;
⊙11am-2pm & 5-10pm Tue-Sat, 9am-1pm Sun)
As old school as it gets: expect wooden
booths, wagon wheels for decor and
hearty steaks on the menu. But it's classic
fare done well and the portions are large
enough to satisfy the heartiest appetite.

The Alley Bar

(☑209-742-4848; www.thealleylounge.com; 5027
Hwy 140; ⊙4-10pm Mon-Thu, to midnight Fri &
Sat) Californian wines and craft beers are
served up in a sophisticated, contemporary
space inside this bar. But it's the lovely backyard beer garden, open in warm months,

that puts the Alley over the top. Nibble on
Bavarian soft pretzels ($9) and smoked
salmon ($14) while enjoying the laid-back
atmosphere. Live music some nights.

Bett's Gold Coin
Sports Tavern Bar

(☑209-966-2388; http://bettsgoldcoin.com;
5021 Hwy 140; ⊙10am-10pm Sun-Thu, to 1am
Fri & Sat) Housed in a 19th-century historic
building, Bett's is a warm and lively place
with a handsome horseshoe bar and large
nautical-themed wall murals. With a full
menu offering burgers ($12), sandwiches
($9) and more elaborate fare, Bett's is
as good for a meal as it is for a drink. Live
music weekend nights.

ⓘ INFORMATION

John C Fremont Hospital (☑209-966-3631;
www.jcf-hospital.com; 5189 Hospital Rd; ⊙24hr)
Emergency room.

Mariposa County Visitor Center (☑209-966-
7081; cnr Hwys 140 & 49; ⊙8:30am-5:30pm;
⚹) Helpful staff and racks of brochures; public
restrooms.

ONNES / SHUTTERSTOCK ©

ⓘ GETTING THERE & AWAY

YARTS (☏209-388-9589, 877-989-2787; www.
yarts.com) buses run year-round along Hwy 140
into Yosemite Valley ($3 one way, 1¾ hours),
stopping at the Mariposa visitor center. Tickets
include admission to Yosemite.

Merced River Canyon

The approach to Yosemite via Hwy 140
is one of the most scenic routes to the
park, especially the section that meanders
through Merced River Canyon. The springtime runoff makes this a spectacular spot
for **river rafting**. Right outside the Arch
Rock entrance, and primarily inhabited by
park employees, **El Portal** makes a convenient Yosemite base.

✖ EATING

June Bug Cafe   Californian $$
(☏206-966-6666; www.yosemitebug.com/cafe.
html; Yosemite Bug Rustic Mountain Resort, 6979

Hwy 140, Midpines; mains $8-22; ⊙7-10am, 11am-
2pm & 6-9pm;) Guests of all ages and
backgrounds at the **Yosemite Bug resort**
(☏209-966-6666; www.yosemitebug.com; 6979
Hwy 140, Midpines; dm $30, tent cabins from $65,
r with/without bath from $165/95; P♿@🌐) ♪
convene at this friendly cafe to share sto-
ries and delicious, freshly prepared meals,
beer and wine in the evenings, and live
music some nights. More than a half-dozen
healthy and hearty dishes are on the white-
board menu and served cafeteria-style.

ⓘ GETTING THERE & AWAY

While Hwy 140, the road through the canyon,
is quite beautiful, unless you're up at the crack
of dawn it can get crowded at the height of
summer.

YARTS buses from Mariposa stop at Midpines
($1 one way) and El Portal ($3 one way) on their
way to Yosemite Valley.

Pfeiffer Beach (p149)

BIG SUR

Big Sur

Big Sur is more a state of mind than a place to pinpoint on a map, and when the sun goes down, the moon and the stars are the area's natural streetlights. (If summer's fog hasn't extinguished them.) Raw beauty and an intense maritime energy characterize this land shoehorned between the Santa Lucia Range and the Pacific.

In the 1950s and '60s, Big Sur became a retreat for artists and writers, including Henry Miller and Beat Generation visionaries such as Lawrence Ferlinghetti. Today Big Sur attracts artists, new-age mystics, and city slickers seeking to unplug on this emerald-green edge of the continent.

Big Sur in Two Days

It's easy to spend two days driving Hwy 1 between San Francisco and Los Angeles. The opportunities for jaw-dropping vistas are around every bend, so plan lots of time for pulling the car over to take some pictures. Among the many along-the-route beaches, it's **Pfeiffer Beach** (p149) that is the most spectacular. Stop in for a drink at **Alvarado Street Brewery** (p151) on the way south.

Big Sur in Four Days

Two extra days on the road will allow more time for beach-combing and photo-snapping. Check out the lighthouse at **Point Sur State Historic Park** (p148), walk along **Sand Dollar Beach** (p149) and take a hike in the **Los Padres National Forest** (p149). Two other essential stops are the **Henry Miller Memorial Library** (p154) and the vainglorious **Hearst Castle** (p152).

 Arriving in Big Sur

Car Big Sur is best explored by car; note that even if your driving skills are up to these narrow switchbacks, others' aren't: expect to average 35mph or less along the route.

Bus MST (www.mst.org) bus 22 ($3.50, 1¼ hours) travels from Monterey via Carmel and Point Lobos as far south as Nepenthe restaurant, stopping en route at Andrew Molera State Park and the Big Sur River Inn.

 Where to Stay

Big Sur lodgings are dotted along Hwy 1, but there aren't a lot of rooms overall, so demand often exceeds supply and prices can be steep. In summer and on weekends, reservations are essential. Camping is currently available at four of Big Sur's state parks and two United States Forest Service (USFS) campgrounds along Hwy 1.

Bixby Bridge

OLEKSANDR TELESNIUK / 500PX ©

Driving Highway 1

One of the most spectacular drives in North America, Hwy 1 twists along the edge of the continent with rugged coastline, mist-shrouded cliffs, dense forests, crashing waterfalls and remote beaches all waiting to be discovered.

Great For...

Don't Miss

Watching waves crash through the rock formation at Pfeiffer State Beach.

Point Sur State Historic Park

A little over 6 miles south of **Bixby Bridge** (one of the world's highest single-span bridges), Point Sur rises like a velvety green fortress out of the sea. It looks like an island, but is actually connected to land by a sandbar. Atop the volcanic rock sits an 1889 stone light station, which was staffed until 1974. During three-hour **guided tours** (☎831-625-4419; www.pointsur.org; off Hwy 1; adult/child 6-17yr from $12/5; ☺tours usually at 1pm Wed, 10am Sat & Sun Oct-Mar, 10am & 2pm Wed & Sat, 10am Sun Apr-Sep, also 10am Thu Jul & Aug) FREE, ocean views and tales of the lighthouse keepers' family lives are engrossing. Call ahead to confirm all tour schedules and show up early because space is limited (no reservations, so credit cards accepted).

ⓘ Need to Know

Driving this narrow highway is very slow going. Allow about three hours to cover the distance between the Monterey Peninsula and San Luis Obispo (excluding stops).

✕ Take a Break

Try to decide which beer to indulge in at Maiden Publick House (p155).

★ Top Tip

Check current highway conditions with CalTrans (www.dot.ca.gov) and fill up your gas tank beforehand.

Pfeiffer Beach

This phenomenal, crescent-shaped and dog-friendly **beach** (☎831-667-2315; www. fs.usda.gov/lpnf; end of Sycamore Canyon Rd; per car $10; ◷9am-8pm; P♿☎) is known for its huge double-rock formation, through which waves crash with life-affirming power. It's often windy, and the surf is too dangerous for swimming, but dig down into the wet sand – it's purple! That's because manganese garnet washes down from the craggy hillsides above. To get here from Hwy 1, make a sharp right onto Sycamore Canyon Rd.

Julia Pfeiffer Burns State Park

If you're chasing waterfalls, swing into this state park named for a Big Sur pioneer. From the parking lot, the 1.3-mile round-trip **Overlook Trail** rushes downhill toward the ocean, passing through a tunnel underneath Hwy 1. Everyone comes to photograph 80ft-high **McWay Falls**, which tumbles year-round over granite cliffs and freefalls into the sea – or the beach, depending on the tide. The park entrance is on the east side of Hwy 1, about 8 miles south of Nepenthe restaurant (p155).

Los Padres National Forest

The tortuously winding 40-mile stretch of Hwy 1 south of Lucia to Hearst Castle (p152) is sparsely populated, rugged and remote, mostly running through national forest lands. Around 5 miles south of Kirk Creek Campground is **Sand Dollar Beach**, a crescent-shaped strip of sand protected from winds by high bluffs and Big Sur's longest sandy beach. Nearby is beachcomber-worthy **Jade Cove**, and it's a short drive south to **Salmon Creek Falls**, tucked uphill in a forested canyon.

Monterey

Working-class Monterey is all about the sea, with the town's world-class aquarium overlooking Monterey Bay National Marine Sanctuary, which protects dense kelp forests and a sublime variety of marine life.

◎ SIGHTS

Monterey Bay Aquarium   Aquarium

(ⓘinfo 831-648-4800, tickets 866-963-9645; www.montereybayaquarium.org; 886 Cannery Row; adult/child 3-12yr/youth 13-17yr $50/30/40; ⊙10am-6pm; 🐾) 🐟 Monterey's most mesmerizing experience is its enormous aquarium, built on the former site of the city's largest sardine cannery. All kinds of aquatic creatures are featured, from kid-tolerant sea stars and slimy sea slugs to animated sea otters and surprisingly nimble 800lb tuna. The aquarium is much more than an impressive collection of glass tanks – thoughtful placards underscore the bay's cultural and historical contexts.

Monterey State Historic Park   Historic Site

(ⓘinfo 831-649-7118; www.parks.ca.gov) **FREE** Old Monterey is home to an extraordinary assemblage of 19th-century brick and adobe buildings, administered as Monterey State Historic Park, and all found along a 2-mile self-guided walking tour portentously called the 'Path of History.' You can inspect dozens of buildings, many with charming gardens; expect some to be open while others aren't, according to a capricious schedule dictated by unfortunate state-park budget cutbacks.

🍴 EATING & DRINKING

Tricycle Pizza   Pizza $

(www.tricyclepizza.com; 899 Lighthouse Ave; pizza $11-13; ⊙3-9pm Wed-Fri, noon-9pm Sat) One of Monterey's favorite food trucks has graduated to a bricks and mortar location along Lighthouse Ave. Tricycle's crusty wood-fired pizza is still cooked in the original truck on-site, but there's now the option of takeout or dining in a hip, industrial

Monterey State Historic Park

space nearby. Try the sausage and mushroom with organic oregano, wood-fired mushrooms and fennel sausage.

Monterey's Fish House Seafood $$

(☑831-373-4647; www.montereyfishhouse.com; 2114 Del Monte Ave; mains $11-25; ⊘11:30am-2:30pm Mon-Fri & 5-9:30pm daily) Watched over by photos of Sicilian fishermen, dig into oak-grilled or blackened swordfish, barbecued oysters or, for those stout of heart, the Mexican squid steak. Reservations are essential (it's *so* crowded), but the vibe is island-casual: Hawaiian shirts seem to be de rigueur for men.

Alvarado Street
Brewery Craft Beer

(☑831-655-2337; www.alvaradostreetbrewery.com; 426 Alvarado St; ⊘11:30am-10pm Sun-Wed, to 11pm Thu-Sat) Vintage beer advertising punctuates Alvarado Street's brick walls, but that's the only concession to earlier days at this excellent craft-beer pub. Innovative brews harness new hop strains, sour and barrel-aged beers regularly fill the taps, and superior bar food includes Thai-curry mussels and truffle-crawfish mac 'n' cheese. In summer, adjourn to the alfresco beer garden out back.

A Taste of Monterey Wine Bar

(www.atasteofmonterey.com; 700 Cannery Row; tasting flights $14-22; ⊘11am-6pm Sun-Thu, to 8pm Fri-Sat) Sample medal-winning Monterey County wines from as far away as the Santa Lucia Highlands while soaking up dreamy sea views, then peruse thoughtful exhibits on barrel-making and cork production. Shared plates, including crab cakes and smoked salmon, provide a tasty reason to linger.

ⓘ INFORMATION

Monterey Visitor Center (☑831-657-6400; www.seemonterey.com; 401 Camino el Estero; ⊘9am-6pm Mon-Sat, to 5pm Sun, closes 1hr earlier Nov-Mar) Free tourist brochures; ask for a *Monterey County Literary & Film Map*.

🔭 Whale-Watching at Monterey Bay

You can spot whales off the coast of Monterey Bay year-round. The season for blue and humpback whales runs from April to early December, while gray whales pass by from mid-December through to March. Tour boats depart from **Fisherman's Wharf** (☑831-375-4658; www.montereybaywhalewatch.com; 84 Fisherman's Wharf; 3hr tour adult/child 4-12yr from $44/29; ⚓) and **Moss Landing** (☑info 831-917-1042, tickets 888-394-7810; www.sanctuarycruises.com; 7881 Sandholdt Rd; tours $45-55; ⚓) ✈. Reserve trips at least a day in advance; be prepared for a bumpy, cold ride.

A humpback whale, Monterey Bay
CHASE DEKKER / SHUTTERSTOCK ©

ⓘ GETTING THERE & AWAY

Monterey is 43 miles south of Santa Cruz and 177 miles north of San Luis Obispo.

Carmel-by-the-Sea

With borderline fanatical devotion to its canine citizens, quaint Carmel has the well-manicured feel of a country club. Founded as a seaside resort in the 1880s – fairly odd, given that its beach is often blanketed in fog – Carmel quickly attracted famous artists and writers, such as Sinclair Lewis and Jack London, and their hangers-on. Artistic flavor survives in more than 100 galleries that line downtown's immaculate streets.

Explore
Hearst Castle

Hearst Castle (info 805-927-2020, reservations 800-444-4445; www.hearstcastle. org; 750 Hearst Castle Rd; tours adult/child 5-12yr from $25/12; ⊙from 9am; P 🚹), the former home of 19th- and 20th-century newspaper magnate William Randolph Hearst, is a fantasy estate furnished with statues from ancient Greece and Moorish Spain, accented by shimmering pools and fountains, and surrounded by flowering gardens and the ruins of what was, in Hearst's day, the world's largest private zoo.

From the 1920s into the '40s, Hearst and Marion Davies, his longtime mistress (Hearst's wife refused to grant him a divorce), entertained a steady stream of the era's biggest movers and shakers. Invitations were highly coveted, but Hearst had quirks – he despised drunkenness, and guests were forbidden to speak of death.

California's first licensed female architect, Julia Morgan, based the main building, Casa Grande, on the design of a Spanish cathedral, and over the decades she catered to Hearst's every design whim, deftly integrating the spoils of his fabled European shopping sprees.

To see anything of this historic monument, you have to take a tour; reservations are recommended in advance year-round. There are three main tours: the guided portion of each lasts about an hour, after which you're free to wander the gardens and terraces and soak up views.

◉ SIGHTS

Mission San Carlos
Borromeo de Carmelo   Church

(📞831-624-1271; www.carmelmission.org; 3080 Rio Rd; adult/child 7-17yr $6.50/2; ⊙9:30am-7pm; 🚹) Monterey's original mission was established by Franciscan friar Junípero Serra in 1770, but poor soil and the corrupting influence of Spanish soldiers forced the move to Carmel two years later. Today this is one of California's most strikingly beautiful missions, an oasis of solemnity bathed in flowering gardens. The mission's adobe chapel was later replaced with an arched basilica made of stone quarried in the Santa Lucia Mountains. Museum exhibits are scattered throughout the meditative complex.

Point Lobos State
Natural Reserve   State Park

(📞831-624-4909; www.pointlobos.org; Hwy 1; per car $10; ⊙8am-7pm, to 5pm early Nov–mid-Mar; P 🚹) 🐾 They bark, they bathe and they're fun to watch – sea lions are the stars here at Punta de los Lobos Marinos (Point of the Sea Wolves), almost 4 miles south of Carmel, where a dramatically rocky coastline offers excellent tide-pooling. The full perimeter hike is 6 miles, but shorter walks take in wild scenery too, including **Bird Island**, shady cypress groves, the historical **Whaler's Cabin** and the **Devil's Cauldron**, a whirlpool that gets splashy at high tide.

⊕ ACTIVITIES

17-Mile Drive   Scenic Drive

(www.pebblebeach.com; per car/bicycle $10/ free) Once promoted as 'Mother Nature's Drive-Thru,' the 17-Mile Drive is a spectacularly scenic private toll road (motorcyclists prohibited) that loops around the Monterey Peninsula, connecting Pacific Grove with Pebble Beach and Carmel-by-the-Sea.

Mission San Carlos Borromeo de Carmelo

 EATING & DRINKING

Corkscrew Cafe — Cafe $$

(☏831- 659-8888; www.corkscrewcafe.com; 55 W Carmel Valley Rd; mains $15-26; ☺noon-9pm Wed-Mon) Just possibly Carmel Valley's coziest eatery, the Corkscrew Cafe combines a rustic wine-country vibe and a Mediterranean-influenced menu – think wood-fired salmon, pizza, and mushroom and lamb pasta – with a stellar local wine list. Relax into a Carmel Valley evening under the market umbrellas in the pleasant garden, and don't leave without checking out the quirky corkscrew museum.

Cultura Comida y Bebida — Mexican $$

(☏831-250-7005; www.culturacarmel.com; Dolores St btwn 5th & 6th Aves; mains $19-32; ☺11:30am-midnight Thu-Sun, 5pm-midnight Mon-Tue) Located near art galleries in a brick-lined courtyard, Cultura Comida y Bebida is a relaxed bar and eatery inspired by the food of Oaxaca in Mexico. Pull up a seat at the elegant bar and sample a vertical tasting of mezcal, or partner Monterey squid tostadas and oak-roasted trout with cilantro, lime and garlic with Californian and French wines.

Valley Greens Gallery — Craft Beer

(☏831-620-2985; www.valleygreensgallery.com; 16e E Carmel Valley Rd; 4-beer tasting flights $12; ☺3-9pm Mon-Tue, 3-10pm Wed-Thu, 1-11pm Fri-Sat, 1-9pm Sun) One part funky art gallery and two parts craft-beer bar, Valley Greens is a standout destination amid Carmel Valley's laid-back main drag. Four rotating beer taps deliver some real surprises from smaller Californian breweries, old-school reggae and foosball tables create a fun ambience, and open-mike night from 6pm on Tuesdays is always worth catching.

Barmel — Wine Bar

(☏831-626-2095; www.facebook.com/Barmel ByTheSea; San Carlos St, btwn Ocean & 7th Aves; ☺2pm-2am Mon-Fri, 1pm-2am Sat-Sun) Shaking up Carmel's conservative image and adding a dash of after-dark fun is this cool little Spanish-themed courtyard bar.

From left: Jellyfish at Monterey Bay Aquarium (p150); Nepenthe; Cormorants gathered at Point Lobos State Natural Reserve (p152)

There's live music from 7pm to 9pm from Thursday to Saturday, robust cocktails and an energetic, younger vibe.

ℹ️ INFORMATION

Carmel Chamber of Commerce (📞831-624-2522; www.carmelcalifornia.org; San Carlos St, btwn 5th & 6th Aves; ⊙10am-5pm) **Free** maps and brochures, including local art gallery guides.

ℹ️ GETTING THERE & AWAY

Carmel is about 5 miles south of Monterey via Hwy 1.

Along Highway 1

◉ SIGHTS

Henry Miller Memorial Library Arts Center
(📞831-667-2574; www.henrymiller.org; 48603 Hwy 1; donations accepted; ⊙10am-5pm) **FREE**

Novelist Henry Miller was a Big Sur denizen from 1944 to 1962. More of a beatnik memorial, alt-cultural venue and bookshop, this community gathering spot was never Miller's home. The house belonged to Miller's friend, painter Emil White, until his death and is now run by a nonprofit group. Stop by to browse and hang out on the front deck. It's 0.4 miles south of Nepenthe restaurant.

⚙️ ACTIVITIES

Esalen Hot Springs Hot Springs
(📞831-667-3047; www.esalen.org; 55000 Hwy 1; per person $30; ⊙by reservation) At the private Esalen Institute, clothing-optional baths fed by a natural hot spring sit on a ledge above the ocean. We're confident you'll never take another dip that compares scenery-wise, especially on stormy winter nights. Only two small outdoor pools perch directly over the waves, so once you've stripped and taken a quick shower, head outside immediately. Credit cards only.

EATING & DRINKING

Big Sur Deli & General Store
Deli $

(☑831-667-2225; www.bigsurdeli.com; 47520 Hwy 1; snacks $2-12; ☺7am-8pm) With the most reasonable prices in Big Sur, this family-owned deli slices custom-made sandwiches and piles up tortillas with carne asada, pork *carnitas*, veggies or beans and cheese. The small market carries camping food, snacks and beer and wine.

Nepenthe
Californian $$$

(☑831-667-2345; www.nepenthebigsur.com; 48510 Hwy 1; mains $18-50; ☺11:30am-4:30pm & 5-10pm; ☑♿) Nepenthe comes from a Greek word meaning 'isle of no sorrow,' and indeed, it's hard to feel blue while sitting by the fire pit on this aerial terrace. Just-okay California cuisine (try the renowned Ambrosia burger) takes a backseat to the views and Nepenthe's history – Orson Welles and Rita Hayworth briefly owned a cabin here in the 1940s. Reservations essential.

Maiden Publick House
Pub

(☑831-667-2355; Village Center Shops, Hwy 1; ☺3pm-2am Mon-Thu, from 1pm Fri & from 11am Sat-Sun) Just south of the Big Sur River Inn, this dive has an encyclopedic beer bible and motley local musicians jamming, mostly on weekends. Sixteen rotating taps and three pages of bottled brews create havoc for the indecisive drinker.

ℹ INFORMATION

Big Sur Chamber of Commerce (☑831-667-2100; www.bigsurcalifornia.org; Hwy 1; ☺9am-1pm Mon, Wed & Fri)

Big Sur Station (☑831-667-2315; www.bigsurcalifornia.org/contact.html; 47555 Hwy 1; ☺9am-4pm) Multi-agency ranger station with information and maps for state parks and the Los Padres National Forest.

SANTA BARBARA

Santa Barbara

Locals call it the 'American Riviera,' and honestly that's not too much of a stretch: Santa Barbara is so picturesque, you just have to sigh. Waving palm trees, sugar-sand beaches, boats bobbing by the harbor – it'd be a travel cliché if it wasn't the plain truth.

California's 'Queen of the Missions' is a beauty, as are downtown's red-roofed, whitewashed adobe buildings, all rebuilt in harmonious Spanish Colonial Revival style after a devastating earthquake in 1925. Come aspire to the breezy, rich-and-famous lifestyle over a long weekend of sipping wine and lazing on the beach.

Santa Barbara in Two Days

Spend your first morning exploring Santa Barbara's historic **mission** (p160). After lunch – tacos from **Corazon Cocina** (p172), perhaps – visit the **county courthouse** (p168) for murals on the 2nd floor and 360-degree views from the clock tower. Set day two aside to visit a **beach or three** (p162) and head to **Stearns Wharf** (p168) for sunset. After dark, follow the siren call of cocktails to **Good Lion** (p175).

Santa Barbara in Four Days

With two extra days, head up to **Santa Barbara's Wine Country** (p166). On the way, detour off Hwy 54 to visit centuries-old cave art at the **Chumash Painted Cave** (p164). Spend the night in Chumash or Solvang, hit a couple more wineries, then head back to town for a celebratory dinner at **Bouchon** (p174).

Santa Barbara Map (p170)

Arriving in Santa Barbara

Santa Barbara Airport Nine miles west of downtown via Hwy 101; a taxi downtown costs about $30 to $35 plus tip.

Bus and Train Santa Barbara Airbus (www.sbairbus.com) shuttles between Los Angeles International Airport (LAX) and Santa Barbara ($49, 2½ hours). Greyhound operates a few direct buses daily to LA ($15, three hours) and San Francisco ($40, nine hours). Amtrak trains run south to LA ($31, 2½ hours) and north to Oakland ($43, 8¾ hours).

Sleeping

Prepare for sticker shock: even basic motel rooms by the beach command over $200 in summer. Don't arrive without reservations and expect to find anything reasonably priced, especially on weekends. A good selection of renovated motels are tucked between the harbor and Hwy 101, just about walking distance to everything.

SHIPPEE / SHUTTERSTOCK ©

Mission Santa Barbara

When the setting sun warms the brick facade and the Pacific breeze carries the scent of eucalyptus from the surrounding hills, California's 'Queen of the Missions' is magical.

Great For...

Don't Miss

Peering into the padre's bedroom, with its thin blanket, chess set and quiet air of contemplation.

Mission Santa Barbara reigns above the city on a hilltop perch over a mile north of downtown. Its proud Ionic facade, an architectural homage to an ancient Roman chapel, is topped by an unusual twin bell tower. Inside the mission's 1820 stone church, there are striking examples of Chumash artwork, including a unique abalone-encrusted altar dated to the 1790s. There are also a pair of magnificent paintings, two of the largest of any of the California missions. The *Assumption and Coronation of the Virgin* is thought to have originated in the Mexico City studio of Miguel Mateo Maldonado y Cabrera. The origins of the other, *The Crucifixion,* are unknown. In the cemetery the elaborate mausoleums of early California settlers stand out, while the graves of thousands of Chumash lie largely forgotten.

NAGEL PHOTOGRAPHY / SHUTTERSTOCK ©

❶ Need to Know

☎805-682-4713; www.santabarbaramission.
org; 2201 Laguna St; adult $9, child 5-17yr $4;
⊙9am-5pm, last entry 4:15pm; Ⓟ👬

✕ Take a Break

Head back downtown to the Good Lion
(p175) for a post-Mission cocktail.

★ Top Tip

Make the most of your visit by joining
one of the entertaining and educational
docent-led tours.

The mission was established on December 4 (the feast day of St Barbara),
1786, as the 10th California mission. Of
California's original 21 Spanish colonial
missions, it's the only one that escaped
secularization under Mexican rule. Continuously occupied by Catholic priests since
its founding, the mission is still an active
parish church.

Touring the Mission

The self-guided tour of the mission starts
in the pretty garden before heading to the
cemetery. Among the graves, you'll find a
commemorative plaque inscribed with the
Christian baptismal name Juana María,
the Native American girl made famous in
Scott O'Dell's Newbery Medal–winning
Island of the Blue Dolphins. She was left
behind on San Nicolas Island during the
early 19th century, when her people were
forced off the Channel Islands, just off
the coast. She survived mostly alone on
the island for 18 years, living in a whale-
bone hut, until she was discovered by a
seal hunter in 1853. By the time she was
brought to the Santa Barbara Mission she
was the last of her people, no one could
understand her language and she died just
seven weeks later.

Next up is the church itself, followed by
a series of rooms turned into a museum
and exhibiting Chumash baskets, a
missionary's bedroom and time-capsule
black-and-white photos showing the last
Chumash residents of the Mission and the
damage done to the buildings after the
1925 earthquake.

Excellent docent-guided tours are usually given every Tuesday to Friday at 11am,
and Saturday at 10:30am; no reservations
are taken.

To get here from downtown, take MTD
bus 6 or 11, then walk five blocks uphill.

East Beach

Santa Barbara Beaches

With mile after mile of perfect sand, lots of variety and a Mediterranean vibe, Santa Barbara's beaches are reason enough to visit.

Great For...

Don't Miss

A spot of tide-pooling (low tide only) at Thousand Steps Beach, accessible from Shoreline Park.

East Beach

Santa Barbara's largest and most popular beach is **East Beach** (www.santabarbaraca. gov/gov/depts/parksrec; E Cabrillo Blvd; 👪), a long, sandy stretch sprawling east of Stearns Wharf, with volleyball nets for pick-up games, a children's play area and a snack bar. On Sunday afternoons, artists set up booths along the sidewalk, near the bike path.

West Beach

West Beach (W Cabrillo Blvd; 👪) is a central, palm-tree-backed stretch of sand, right next to Stearns Wharf and the harbor (swimming isn't advisable). It's also the setting for large outdoor city events such as Fourth of July celebrations. West Beach is also a great place to check out public

❶ Need to Know

Don't expect a sunset over the Pacific; most Santa Barbara beaches face south rather than west.

✕ Take a Break

Stop at Boathouse (p173), right on Arroyo Burro Beach, for cocktails with water views.

★ Top Tip

To cruise from beach to beach by bike, Wheel Fun Rentals (www.wheelfun rentalssb.com) has two locations close to Stearns Wharf (p168).

art, and there's historical and interpretive signage. No dogs are allowed.

Leadbetter Beach

One of Santa Barbara's most popular beaches, **Leadbetter Beach** (☏805-564-5418; Shoreline Dr, at Loma Alta Dr; per vehicle $2; P🚻) is always busy with surfers, wind- and kite-surfers, joggers and sunbathers. Facilities include reservable picnic areas and showers. It's also a great place to rent a board from **Paddle Sports Center** (☏805-617-3425; http://paddlesportsca.com; 117b Harbor Way; SUP/kayak rental from $20/12; ⏰usually 8am-6pm) and try your hand at stand up paddle surfing.

Shoreline Park

For great views across the city, mountains and ocean (with the chance to spot whales in season and dolphins year-round), come to **Shoreline Park** (Shoreline Dr; ⏰8am-sunset; P🚻🐕) FREE, southwest of Santa Barbara. There are restrooms, picnic tables and a children's playground, and dogs are welcome.

Arroyo Burro Beach

Swim (lifeguards on duty), stroll or just picnic on this gem of a **stretch of sand** (Hendry's; ☏805-568-2460; www.county-ofsb.org/parks; Cliff Dr, at Las Positas Rd; ⏰8am-sunset; P🚻🐕), 5 miles southwest of Santa Barbara. It's flat, wide, away from tourists and great for kids, who can go tide-pooling. It's also a popular local surf spot and the eastern section is dog-friendly. The flat, long beach and selection of driftwood make it perfect for a game of fetch, and there's even a dog wash in the parking lot.

Sand Dollar Beach, Los Padres National Forest (p165)

DANITA DELIMONT / GETTY IMAGES ©

Driving Highway 154

A gorgeous drive through the Santa Ynez Mountains and Santa Barbara's celebrated wine country, Highway 154 is proof that the journey can be more rewarding than the destination.

Great For...

Don't Miss

Checking out statues of the Little Mermaid and Hans Christian Andersen in Solvang.

As Hwy 154 climbs from the coast, you'll leave oh-so civilized Santa Barbara behind and enter the rugged Santa Ynez Mountains and Wine Country.

First stop on the route, just 12 miles from the busy city, is a chance to look back at pre-European California in the shape of the **Chumash Painted Cave** (www.parks. ca.gov; Painted Cave Rd, off Hwy 154; ⊘dawn-dusk) **FREE**. This tiny, off-the-beaten-path historic site shelters pictographs painted by Chumash tribespeople over 400 years ago. The sandstone cave is protected from graffiti and vandalism by a metal screen, so bring a flashlight to get a good look. The turnoff is off Hwy 154 below San Marcos Summit, about 6 miles from Hwy 101. The 2-mile twisting side road to the site is extremely narrow, rough and steep (no

ⓘ Need to Know

Take it slow. This route is beautiful but the drive has some treacherous sections.

✕ Take a Break

Solvang's **First & Oak** (☏805-688-1703; www.firstandoak.com; 409 First St, Mirabelle Inn; mains $12-23; ☺5:30-8:45pm) offers innovative meals in an elegant but cozy setting.

★ Top Tip

From basic camping to lake-view yurts, Cachuma Lake is a great place to spend the night.

RVs). Look for a small signposted pull-off on your left.

Continue along Painted Cave Rd to get back on the 154, but only for some 6 miles before a left-side turnoff leads to historic **Cold Spring Tavern** (☏805-967-0066; www.coldspringtavern.com; 5995 Stagecoach Rd; mains breakfast & lunch from $11, dinner from $22; ☺11am-close Mon-Fri, from 8am Sat & Sun), a good stop for lunch, especially if the barbecue is on. Check out the odd but charming assortment of Western memorabilia while you wait for your order.

Sidetrack off the 154 just a few miles north of the tavern for a trip to Paradise (road), taking you into **Los Padres National Forest** (☏805-967-3481; www.fs.usda.gov/lpnf; 3505 Paradise Rd; daily pass per car $5; ☺8am-4:30pm Mon-Fri, also 8am-4:30pm

Sat late May–early Sep; 🚻) 🏊. The forest stretches for hundreds of miles, with this stretch offering swimming spots and hikes for burning off those barbecue calories. **Camping** (☏877-444-6777; www.recreation.gov; Paradise Rd, off Hwy 154; campsites $30) is an option if you want to stay longer, or for even more water-based activities, continue along the 154 for a few more miles to **Cachuma Lake** (☏805-568-2460; www.countyofsb.org/parks; per vehicle $10, 2hr cruise adult/child $17/7; ☺6am-sunset; 🚻🏊). The lake might be artificial (it was created by the construction of a dam in the 1950s), but it's still a pretty spot.

Once past the lake you're well and truly in Santa Barbara Wine Country, with vineyards scattered throughout the surrounding area. Enjoy a few tastings before winding up in the incongruous but charming Danish village of Solvang, with plenty of places to indulge a taste for Scandinavian sweets and lay your head for the night.

Santa Ynez Valley

Santa Barbara Wine Country

Oak-dotted hillsides, winding country lanes, rows of grapevines stretching toward the horizon – it's hard not to gush about the Santa Ynez and Santa Maria Valleys and the Santa Rita Hills wine regions.

Great For...

Don't Miss

La Purisíma Mission, one of Southern California's most evocative.

This is an area made for do-it-yourself exploring. With around 100 local wineries, visiting can seem daunting, but simply choose a region and hit the road.

Santa Ynez Valley

One of California's top viticulture regions, the Santa Ynez Valley is a compact area comprising a handful of small towns and dozens of vineyards. Put on the map back in 2004 by the movie *Sideways,* the area still draws the crowds and it's a hugely pleasant place to stay in upmarket lodgings, eat at high-quality restaurants and, of course, enjoy the many fine wines produced here. Los Olivos is the cutest town, Buellton the most down-to-earth, with incongruous Danish Solvang and tiny Santa Ynez and Ballard in between. Popular wineries cluster between Los Olivos and Solvang

Windmill house in Solvang

SARAH CAMILLE / SHUTTERSTOCK ©

Rancho Sisquoc Winery

Santa Maria Valley

101

Los Alamos

Los Padres National Forest

Los Olivos

Santa Rita Hills 246

Lompoc

Buellton

Solvang

Santa Ynez Valley

Santa Ynez

154

1

❶ Need to Know

Santa Barbara Wine Country (www. sbcountywines.com) This comprehensive website has excellent info on the region and how to make the most of a trip.

✕ Take a Break

Rancho Sisquoc Winery (☏805-934-4332; www.ranchosisquoc.com; 6600 Foxen Canyon Rd; tastings $10; ⊙10am-4pm Mon-Thu, to 5pm Fri-Sun) is a tranquil gem and well worth the extra mileage.

along Alamo Pintado Rd and Refugio Rd, south of Roblar Ave and west of Hwy 154.

Santa Maria Valley

The scenic Foxen Canyon Wine Trail runs north from Hwy 154, just west of Los Olivos, deep into the heart of the rural Santa Maria Valley. It's a must-see for oenophiles or anyone wanting to get off the beaten path. For the most part, it follows Foxen Canyon Rd, though a couple of top spots lie close to Santa Maria town.

Santa Rita Hills

When it comes to country-road scenery, eco-conscious farming practices and top-notch Pinot Noir, the less-traveled Santa Rita Hills region holds its own. Almost a dozen tasting rooms line an easy driving loop west of Hwy 101 via Santa Rosa Rd and Hwy

246. Be prepared to share the roads with cyclists and an occasional John Deere tractor. More artisan winemakers hide out in the industrial warehouses of Buellton near Hwy 101 and further afield in Lompoc, where you can also visit **La Purísima Mission** (☏805-733-3713; www.lapurisimamission.org; 2295 Purísima Rd, Lompoc; per car $6; ⊙9am-5pm, tours at 1pm Wed-Sun & public holidays Sep-Jun, daily Jul & Aug; 🅿️👫) 🐾, founded in 1787.

Wine Tours

Full-day wine-tasting tours average $120 to $160 per person; most leave from Santa Barbara, and some require a minimum number of participants. Wine Edventures (www.welovewines.com), Sustainable Vine Wine Tours (www.sustainablevinewinetours. com) and Santa Barbara Wine Country Cycling Tours (www.winecountrycycling. com) are great options. The website www. sbcountywines.com has lots more.

⊙ SIGHTS

Santa Barbara County Courthouse Historic Building

(📞805-962-6464; http://sbcourthouse.org; 1100 Anacapa St; ⊗8am-5pm Mon-Fri, 10am-5pm Sat & Sun) **FREE** Built in Spanish–Moorish Revival style in 1929, the courthouse features hand-painted ceilings, wrought-iron chandeliers and tiles from Tunisia and Spain. On the 2nd floor, step inside the hushed mural room depicting Spanish-colonial history, then head up to El Mirador, the 85ft clock tower, for arch-framed panoramas of the city, ocean and mountains.

MOXI Museum

(Wolf Museum of Exploration + Innovation; 📞805-770-5000; www.moxi.org; 125 State St; adult/child $14/10; ⊗10am-5pm; 🚼) Part of the regeneration of this neglected strip of State St, Moxi's three floors are filled with hands-on displays covering science, arts and technology themes will lure families in, even when it's not raining outside. If all that interactivity gets too much, head to the roof terrace for views across Santa Barbara and a nerve-challenging walk across a glass ceiling.

Santa Barbara Historical Museum Museum

(📞805-966-1601; www.santabarbaramuseum.com; 136 E De La Guerra St; ⊗10am-5pm Tue-Sat, from noon Sun) **FREE** Embracing a romantic cloistered adobe courtyard, this peaceful little museum tells the story of Santa Barbara. Its endlessly fascinating collection of local memorabilia ranges from the simply beautiful, such as Chumash woven baskets and Spanish Colonial–era textiles, to the intriguing, such as an intricately carved coffer that once belonged to Junípero Serra. Learn about the city's involvement in toppling the last Chinese monarchy, among other interesting lessons in local history.

Stearns Wharf Waterfront

(www.stearnswharf.org; ⊗open daily, hours vary; 🅿🚼) **FREE** The southern end of State St gives way to Stearns Wharf, a rough wooden pier lined with souvenir shops, snack stands and seafood shacks. Built in

Santa Barbara County Courthouse

1872, it's the oldest continuously operating wharf on the West Coast, although the actual structure has been rebuilt more than once. During the 1940s it was co-owned by tough-guy actor Jimmy Cagney and his brothers. If you have kids, take them inside the Sea Center.

Santa Barbara Botanic Garden
Gardens

(☑805-682-4726; www.sbbg.org; 1212 Mission Canyon Rd; adult $12, child 2-12yr $6, youth 13-17yr $8; ☉9am-6pm Mar-Oct, to 5pm Nov-Feb; P🚻🐾) Take a soul-satisfying jaunt around this 40-acre botanic garden, devoted to California's native flora. Miles of partly wheelchair-accessible trails meander past cacti, redwoods and wildflowers and by the old mission dam, originally built by Chumash tribespeople to irrigate the mission's fields. Guided tours (included with admission) depart at 11am and 2pm on Saturday and Sunday, and 2pm on Monday. Leashed, well-behaved dogs are welcome.

🟢 ACTIVITIES

Santa Barbara Adventure Company
Kayaking

(☑805-884-9283; www.sbadventureco.com; 32 E Haley St; ☉office 8am-5pm Mon-Sat; 🚻) The name says it all: if you want a company that provides a whole host of well-organized adventures, then you've come to the right place. It offers everything from Channel Island kayaking ($179) to surf lessons ($89), and bike tours (from $119) to horseback riding ($150).

Surf Happens
Surfing

(☑805-966-3613; http://surfhappens.com; 13 E Haley St; 2hr private lesson from $160; 🚻) Welcoming families, beginners and 'Surf Happens Sisters,' these highly reviewed classes and camps led by expert staff incorporate the Zen of surfing. In summer, you'll begin your spiritual wave-riding journey. Make reservations in advance. The office is based in downtown Santa Barbara.

👪 Santa Barbara for Children

Santa Barbara abounds with family-friendly fun for kids of all ages. **MOXI** (p168) is Santa Barbara's newest hands-on, kid-friendly attraction.

Santa Barbara Museum of Natural History (☑805-682-4711; www.sbnature. org; 2559 Puesta del Sol; adult $12, child 2-12yr $7, youth 13-17yr $8, incl planetarium show $16/12/12; ☉10am-5pm; P🚻) Giant skeletons, an insect wall and a pitch-dark planetarium.

Santa Barbara Maritime Museum (☑805-962-8404; www.sbmm.org; 113 Harbor Way; adult $8, child 6-17yr $5; ☉10am-5pm Thu-Tue; P🚻) Peer through a periscope, reel in a virtual fish or check out the model ships.

Santa Barbara Zoo (☑805-962-6310; www.sbzoo.org; 500 Ninos Dr; adult $17, child under 13yr $10; ☉10am-5pm; P🚻) This small zoo has 146 species covering all creatures great and small.

Sea Center (☑805-962-2526; www. sbnature.org; 211 Stearns Wharf; adult $8.50, child 2-12yr $6, youth 13-17yr $7.50; ☉10am-5pm; P🚻) From touch tanks and crawl-through aquariums to whale sing-alongs.

Chase Palm Park (www.santabarbaraca. gov/gov/depts/parksrec; 323 E Cabrillo Blvd; ☉sunrise-10pm; 🚻) **FREE** Antique carousel rides ($2) plus a shipwreck-themed playground.

Penguins, Santa Barbara Zoo

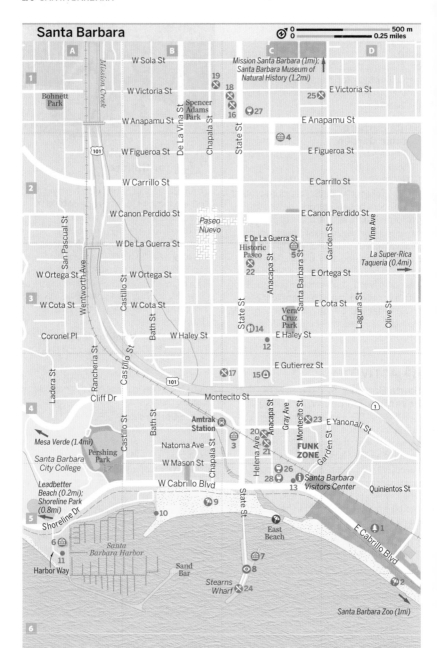

Santa Barbara

0 — 500 m
0 — 0.25 miles

Santa Barbara

TOURS

Architectural Foundation of Santa Barbara   Walking

(☑805-965-6307; www.afsb.org; adult $10, child under 12yr free; ⊙10am Sat & Sun weather permitting) Take time out of your weekend for a fascinating 90-minute guided walking tour of downtown's art, history and architecture. No reservations required; call or check the website for meet-up times and places.

Santa Barbara Trolley   Bus

(☑805-965-0353; www.sbtrolley.com; adult $22, child 3-12yr $8; ⊙10am-3pm; 🚺) 🖉 Biodiesel-fueled trolleys make a narrated 90-minute one-way loop stopping at 14 major tourist attractions around the city, including the mission and the zoo. They start from the visitor center (hourly departures 10am to 3pm) and the hop-on, hop-off tickets are valid all day (and one consecutive day) – pay the driver directly, or buy discounted tickets online in advance.

One child aged 12 years or under rides free with each paid adult rider. Your ticket also gives you savings on admission to several Santa Barbara attractions and shops.

Condor Express   Cruise

(☑805-882-0088; www.condorcruises.com; 301 W Cabrillo Blvd; 2½/4½hr cruises adult from $50/99, child 5-12yr from $30/50; 🚺) Take a whale-watching excursion aboard the high-speed catamaran *Condor Express*. Whale sightings are guaranteed, so if you miss out the first time, you'll get a free voucher for another cruise.

🄰 SHOPPING

Downtown's **State St** is packed with shops of all kinds, and even chain stores conform to the red-roofed architectural style. For more local art galleries and indie shops, dive into the **Funk Zone**, east of State St, tucked in south of Hwy 101.

REI   Sports & Outdoors

(☑805-560-1938; www.rei.com; 321 Anacapa St; ⊙10am-9pm Mon-Fri, to 7pm Sat, to 6pm Sun) If you forgot your tent or rock-climbing carabiners at home, the West Coast's most popular independent co-op outdoor retailer is the place to pick up outdoor recreation gear, active clothing, sport shoes and topographic maps.

Santa Barbara Art Walks

Prime time for downtown gallery hopping is **First Thursday** (www. santabarbaradowntown.com), from 5pm to 8pm on the first Thursday of every month, when art galleries on and off State St throw open their doors for new exhibitions, artists' receptions, wine tastings and live music, all free. Closer to the beach but similar in aim is the **Funk Zone Art Walk** (http://funkzone. net), happening on a bimonthly basis from 5pm to 8pm and featuring free events and entertainment at offbeat art galleries, bars and restaurants.

Santa Barbara Museum of Art
CSFOTOIMAGES / GETTY IMAGES ©

 EATING

Corazon Cocina   Mexican $

(☏805-845-0282; www.facebook.com/ sbcorazoncocina; 38 W Victoria St; ⊙11am-9pm Tue-Sat, to 8pm Sun & Mon) The usual Mexican crowd-pleasers are all here (tacos *al pastor,* quesadillas, agua fresca) but made to such perfection that previous versions pale in comparison. Head into the Santa Barbara Public Market and prepare to get food drunk (and to wait a while – it's popular).

Arigato Sushi   Japanese $

(☏805-965-6074; www.arigatosb.com; 1225 State St; rolls from $7; ⊙5:30-10pm Sun-Thu, to 10:30pm Fri & Sat; ❄☏) Phenomenally popular Arigato Sushi always has people milling around waiting for a table (no reservations taken), but it's worth the

wait. Traditional and more unusual sushi, including lots of vegetarian options, plus salads and a dizzying array of hot and cold starters will make you order a sake pronto just to help you get through the menu.

Lucky Penny   Pizza $

(☏805-284-0358; www.luckypennysb.com; 127 Anacapa St; pizzas $10-16; ⊙11am-9pm Sun-Thu, to 10pm Fri & Sat; ☏) Shiny exterior walls covered in copper pennies herald a brilliant pizza experience inside this Funk Zone favorite, right beside the Lark (p174). Always jam-packed, it's worth the wait for a crispy pizza topped with a variety of fresh ingredients, many vegetarian-friendly, or a wood-oven-fired lamb-and-pork-meatball sandwich. The coffee is taken seriously too.

Backyard Bowls   Health Food $

(☏805-845-5379; www.backyardbowls.com; 331 Motor Way; items $5-11; ⊙7am-5pm Mon-Fri, from 8am Sat & Sun; ☏) ✎ This eco-minded little shop serves up real-fruit smoothies and heaping acai bowls with all kinds of health-conscious add-ons such as fresh berries, granola, coconut milk, honey, bee pollen, almonds and loads of other locally sourced, sustainably harvested ingredients.

Metropulos   Deli $

(☏805-899-2300; www.metrofinefoods.com; 216 E Yanonali St; dishes $2-10; ⊙8:30am-5pm Mon-Fri, 10am-5pm Sat) Before a day at the beach, pick up custom-made sandwiches and fresh salads at this gourmet deli in the Funk Zone. Artisan breads, imported cheeses, cured meats, and California olives and wines will be bursting out of your picnic basket.

La Super-Rica Taqueria   Mexican $

(☏805-963-4940; 622 N Milpas St; ⊙11am-9pm Thu-Mon) It's small, there's usually a line and the decor is basic, but all that's forgotten once you've tried the most authentic Mexican food in Santa Barbara. The fish tacos, tamales and other Mexican staples

Stearns Wharf (p168)

have been drawing locals and visitors here for decades, and were loved by TV chef and author Julia Child.

McConnell's Fine Ice Creams
Desserts $

(☎805-324-4402; www.mcconnells.com; 728 State St; pints from $10; ☻11am-10pm Sun-Thu, to 11pm Fri & Sat; ♠) Just try walking past this place on State St if you have a sweet tooth. A Santa Barbara institution since 1949, McConnell's uses local milk and other ingredients to produce an array of flavors, from the classics, such as chocolate and vanilla, to the adventurous, like Turkish coffee, and cardamom and gingersnaps.

Santa Barbara Shellfish Company
Seafood $$

(☎805-966-6676; http://shellfishco.com; 230 Stearns Wharf; dishes $4-19; ☻11am-9pm; ♠♠) 'From sea to skillet to plate' sums up this end-of-the-wharf seafood shack that's more of a buzzing counter joint than a sit-down restaurant. Chase away the seagulls as you chow down on garlic-baked clams, crab cakes and coconut-fried shrimp at wooden picnic tables outside. Awesome lobster bisque, ocean views and the same location for almost 40 years.

Mesa Verde
Vegan $$

(☎805-963-4474; http://mesaverderestaurant. com; 1919 Cliff Dr; mains $15-21; ☻11am-9pm; ♠) ✿ Perusing the menu is usually a quick job for vegetarians – but not at Mesa Verde. There are so many delicious, innovative all-vegan dishes on offer here (the tacos with jackfruit are a highlight) that meat-avoiding procrastinators will be in torment. If in doubt, pick a selection and brace yourself for flavor-packed delights. Meat-eaters welcome (and possibly converted).

Boathouse
Californian $$

(☎805-898-2628; http://boathousesb.com; 2981 Cliff Dr; mains from $14; ☻7:30am-close; ♠♠) Water views and ocean air accompany your healthy dining at the Boathouse, right on Arroyo Burro Beach (p163). The outdoor patio is great for enjoying a cocktail and fancy salad with other beachgoers, while

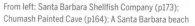
From left: Santa Barbara Shellfish Company (p173); Chumash Painted Cave (p164); A Santa Barbara beach

the walls inside display photos paying homage to the area's surfing and rowing heritage.

Lark Californian $$$

(☑805-284-0370; www.thelarksb.com; 131 Anacapa St; shared plates $7-17, mains $19-48; ⏱5-10pm Tue-Sun, bar to midnight) ✦ There's no better place in Santa Barbara County to taste the bountiful farm and fishing goodness of this stretch of SoCal coast. Named after an antique Pullman railway car, this chef-run restaurant in the Funk Zone morphs its menu with the seasons, presenting unique flavor combinations such as crispy Brussels sprouts with dates or harissa-and-honey chicken. Make reservations.

Yoichi's Japanese $$$

(☑805-962-6627; www.yoichis.com; 230 E Victoria St; set 7-course menu $100; ⏱5-10pm Tue-Sun) Headline: *kaiseki* (traditional Japanese multicourse dining) comes to Santa Barbara and wows locals. It might have limited hours, take a chunk out of your wallet and need to be booked way in advance, but none of that has stopped

Yoichi's being hailed as one of Santa Barbara's best (and slightly hidden away) eating experiences.

Bouchon Californian $$$

(☑805-730-1160; www.bouchonsantabarbara. com; 9 W Victoria St; mains $26-36; ⏱5-9pm Sun-Thu, to 10pm Fri & Sat) ✦ The perfect, unhurried follow-up to a day in the Wine Country is to feast on the bright, flavorful California cooking at pretty Bouchon (meaning 'wine cork'). A seasonally changing menu spotlights locally grown farm produce and ranched meats that marry beautifully with almost three-dozen regional wines available by the glass. Lovebirds, book a table on the candlelit patio.

🍷 DRINKING & NIGHTLIFE

Figueroa Mountain Brewing Co Bar

(☑805-694-2252; www.figmtnbrew.com; 137 Anacapa St; ⏱11am-11pm Sun-Thu, to midnight Fri & Sat) Father and son brewers have brought their gold-medal-winning hoppy IPA, Danish red lager and double IPA from Santa

Barbara's Wine Country to the Funk Zone. Knowledgeable staff will help you choose before you clink glasses on the taproom's open-air patio while acoustic acts play. Enter on Yanonali St.

Good Lion   Cocktail Bar

(☎805-845-8754; www.goodlioncocktails.com; 1212 State St; ⊙4pm-1am) Grab a cocktail at the beautiful, blue-tiled bar, then grab a book from the shelves and settle into a leather banquette in this petite place that has a cool Montmartre–turn-of-the-20th-century feel (candles on the tables and absinthe in many of the cocktails helps with the Parisian atmosphere).

Brass Bear   Craft Beer

(☎805-770-7651; www.brassbearbrewing.com; 28 Anacapa St; ⊙noon-9pm Wed, Sun & Mon, to 10pm Thu, to 11pm Fri & Sat; 🍴🍽) Large glasses of wine and beer and a great grilled cheese make this cozy place, located up an alley off Anacapa (follow the murals), a worthy detour. Friendly staff add to the convivial atmosphere. Just be careful not to drink too much and end up taking some of the for-sale art on the walls home with you.

Municipal Winemakers   Bar

(☎805-931-6864; www.municipalwinemakers. com; 22 Anacapa St; tastings $12; ⊙11am-8pm Sun-Wed, to 11pm Thu-Sat; 🍽) Dave, the owner of Municipal Winemakers, studied the vine arts in Australia and France before applying his knowledge in this industrially decorated tasting room and bar. Pale Pink rosé is a staple and hugely popular – enjoy a bottle on the large patio. For food, you can't beat the cheese plate, or at weekends a burger van parks outside.

❶ INFORMATION

Santa Barbara Visitors Center (☎805-568-1811, 805-965-3021; www.santabarbaraca.com; 1 Garden St; ⊙9am-5pm Mon-Sat, 10am-5pm Sun, closes 1hr earlier Nov-Jan) Pick up maps and brochures while consulting with the helpful but busy staff. The website offers free downloadable DIY touring maps and itineraries, from famous movie locations to wine trails, art galleries and outdoors fun. Self-pay metered parking lot nearby.

Zabriskie Point

SYLVIA BENTLE FOTOGRAFIE / SHUTTERSTOCK ©

Death Valley National Park

The very name evokes all that is harsh, hot and hellish – a punishing, barren and lifeless place. Yet Death Valley puts on a truly spectacular show of flourishing, other-worldly natural splendor.

Great For...

Don't Miss

Sunrise at Zabriskie Point, the location of the cover of U2's *Joshua Tree* album.

Singing sand dunes, water-sculpted canyons, extinct volcanic craters, palm-shaded oases, stark mountains rising to 11,000ft and plenty of endemic wildlife. This is a land of superlatives, holding the US records for hottest temperature (134°F/57°C), lowest point (Badwater, 282ft below sea level) and largest national park outside Alaska (more than 5000 sq miles).

Stunning Views

Dante's View

At 5475ft, the view from Dante's of the entire southern Death Valley basin from the top of the Black Mountains is absolutely brilliant, especially at sunrise or sunset. On very clear days, you can simultaneously see the highest (Mt Whitney) and lowest (Badwater) points in the contiguous USA. Allow about 1½ hours for the 26-mile

Death Valley National Park

Independence •   Beatty •

Lone Pine •   Furnace Creek •

Stovepipe Wells Village   Death Valley Junction •

NEVADA

Shoshone •   Tecopa •   Las Vegas

CALIFORNIA

ℹ Need to Know

760-786-3200; www.nps.gov/deva; 7-day-pass per car $25; ⊘24hr; P🚻 ♿

✕ Take a Break

Sip a cocktail on the patio of Inn Dining Room (p179).

★ Top Tip

Stop by the **Furnace Creek Visitor Center** (760-786-3200; www.nps.gov/deva; 8am-5pm; 📶🚻) for tourist info and to watch the 20-minute *Seeing Death Valley* movie.

round-trip from the turnoff at Hwy 190, east of Furnace Creek.

Zabriskie Point

Early morning is the best time to visit Zabriskie Point for spectacular views across golden badlands eroded into waves, pleats and gullies. It was named for a manager of the Pacific Coast Borax Company and also inspired the title of Michelangelo Antonioni's 1970s movie.

Badwater Basin

The lowest point in North America (282ft below sea level), Badwater Basin is an eerily beautiful landscape of crinkly salt flats. Here you can walk out onto a constantly evaporating bed of salty, mineralized water that's otherworldly in its beauty, then look up at the big blue sky arcing overhead. It's

about 17 miles south of Furnace Creek on Hwy 190.

Mesquite Flat Sand Dunes

The most accessible dunes in Death Valley, Mesquite Flat is an undulating sea of sand rising up to 100ft high next to Hwy 190 near Stovepipe Wells Village. The dunes are at their most photogenic at sunrise or sunset when bathed in soft light and accented by long, deep shadows.

Scenic Drives

About 9 miles south of Furnace Creek, the 9-mile, one-way **Artists Drive** scenic loop offers 'wow' moments around every turn; it's best done in the late afternoon when exposed minerals and volcanic ash make the hills erupt in fireworks of color.

Another option, about 2 miles outside the park boundary, is the spectacular one-way backcountry **Titus Canyon Rd**, leading to Hwy 190 in 27 miles of rough track. The road climbs, dips and winds to a crest in the Grapevine Mountains, then slowly descends back to the desert floor past a ghost town, petroglyphs and canyon narrows.

Hiking

The best time for hiking is November to March. Stay off the trail in summer, except on higher-elevation mountain trails, which are usually snowed in during winter. Constructed paths are rare in Death Valley and all but the easiest hikes may require some scrambling or bouldering. An adequate water supply is essential; one gallon per day per person in summer and half a gallon in winter are recommended.

Wildrose Peak

This moderate-to-strenuous trail begins near the charcoal kilns, off Wildrose Canyon Rd and ascends to Wildrose Peak (9064ft).

The 8.4-mile round-trip hike is best in spring or fall. The elevation gain is 2200ft, but great views start about halfway up.

Mosaic Canyon Trail

West of Stovepipe Wells Village, a 2.3-mile gravel road leads to Mosaic Canyon, where you can hike and scramble past smooth multihued rock walls. Colors are sharpest at midday.

Telescope Peak

The park's most demanding summit is Telescope Peak (11,049ft), with views that plummet to the desert floor. The 14-mile round-trip trail climbs 3000ft above Mahogany Flat, off upper Wildrose Canyon Rd. Summiting in winter requires ice-axe, crampons and winter-hiking experience.

Driving through Death Valley National Park

Cuisine

There are restaurants and stores for stocking up on basic groceries and camping supplies in Furnace Creek, Stovepipe Wells Village and Panamint Springs.

Inn Dining Room

This formal **restaurant** (☑760-786-2345; www.furnacecreekresort.com/dining; Inn at Furnace Creek, off Hwy 190; breakfast $10-17, mains lunch $10-14, dinner $27-58; ☺7-10:30am & noon-2pm Mon-Sat, 7-10am & 5:30-9pm Sun mid-Oct–mid-May; 🅿🛜) delivers continental cuisine with stellar views of the Panamint Mountains. For a more chilled ambience, enjoy breakfast, lunch or cocktails on the patio. Reservations are key for dinner when a 'no shorts or tank tops' policy kicks in.

Toll Road Restaurant

Above-par cowboy cooking happens at this **ranch house** (☑760-786-2387; www.deathvalleyhotels.com; 51880 Hwy 190, Stovepipe Wells Village; mains $12.50-34; ☺7-10am & 5:30-9pm; 🅿🛜). Many of the mostly meaty mains are made with local ingredients, such as mesquite honey, prickly pear and piñons.

Accommodations

Camping is plentiful (the national park service operates nine campgrounds, including four tucked into the Panamint Mountains), but if you're looking for a place with a roof, in-park options are limited, pricey and often booked solid in springtime. Alternative bases are the gateway towns of Beatty (40 miles from Furnace Creek), Lone Pine (40 miles), Death Valley Junction (30 miles) and Tecopa (70 miles).

Getting There & Away

There is no public transport to Death Valley. Coming from Las Vegas, it's about 120 miles via Hwy 160 or 140 miles via I-95 and Hwy 373. Coming from Hwy 395, you can reach Furnace Creek in about 100 miles from Lone Pine via Hwy 190 or in 120 miles from Ridgecrest via Hwys 178 and 190. From I-15, get off at Baker and head 115 miles north via Hwy 127.

> ★ **Top Tip**
> Stock up on luscious dates in the middle of the desert at **China Ranch Date Farm** (☑760-852-4415; www.chinaranch.com; China Ranch Rd; ☺9am-5pm; 🅿👣).

MARK READ / LONELY PLANET ©

> ✕ **Take a Break**
> Is it a mirage? No, it's the pint-sized **Death Valley Brewing** (☑760-852-4273; www.deathvalleybrewing.com; 102 Old Spanish Trail; ☺noon-6pm Fri-Sun Nov-Apr), all set to quench your thirst.

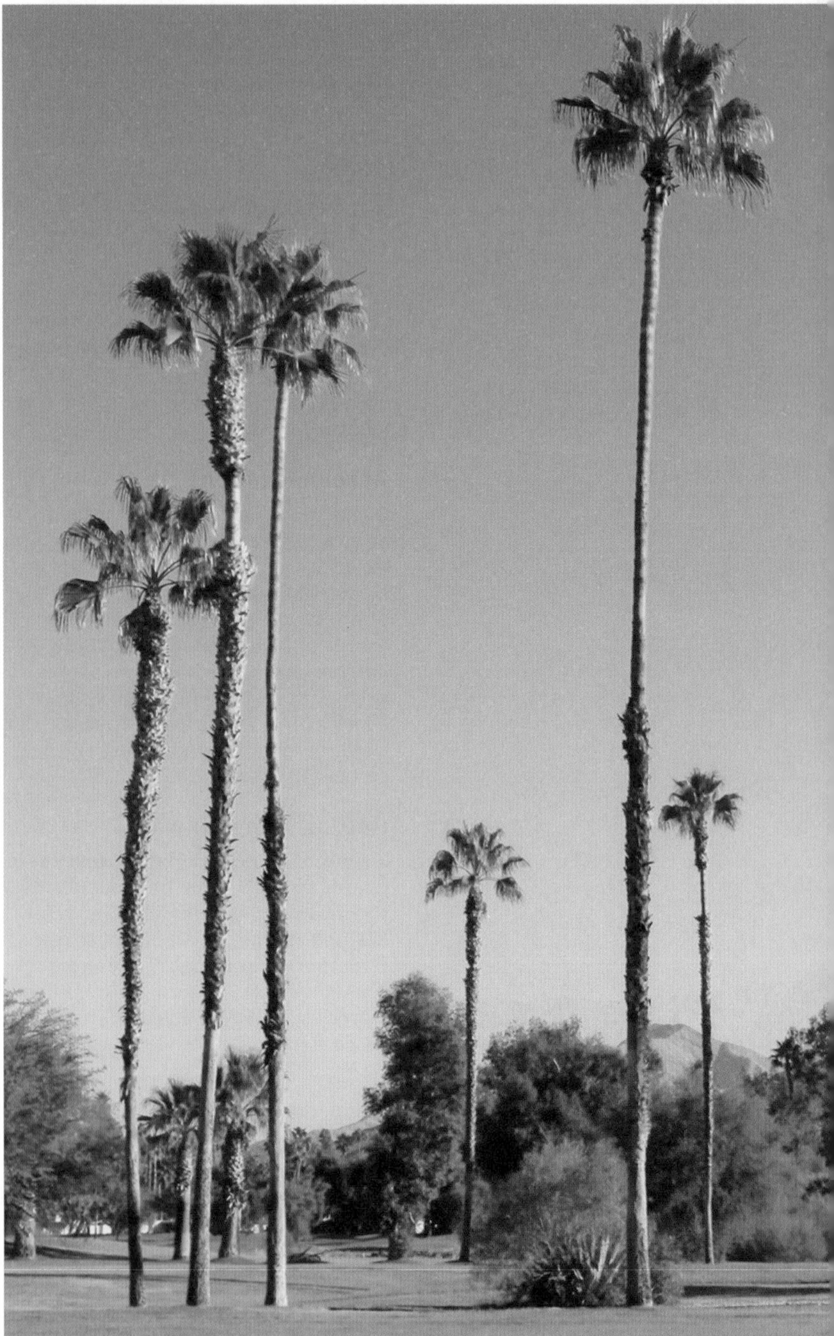

PALM SPRINGS

Palm Springs

The Rat Pack is back, baby, or at least its hangout is. In the 1950s and '60s, Palm Springs, some 100 miles east of LA, was the swinging getaway of Sinatra, Elvis and other Hollywood stars. Once the Rat Pack packed it in, though, Palm Springs surrendered to golfing retirees. In the mid-1990s new generations discovered the city's retro-chic vibe and elegant mid-century modern structures built by famous architects. Today, retirees and snowbirds mix comfortably with hipsters, hikers and a sizeable LGBT community, on getaways from LA or from across the globe.

Palm Springs in Two Days

On day one, head out to explore the mid-century modern **Sunnylands Estate** (p188). With those refined interiors in mind, head back downtown for a spot of shopping, followed by a cocktail at **Bootlegger Tiki** (p191). On day two, take a delightfully dizzying **cable-car ride** (p190) from the desert floor up Mt San Jacinto, then take the afternoon to pamper yourself at the **Estrella Spa** (p190).

Palm Springs in Four Days

Dedicate a good portion of days three and four to exploring the stunning natural beauty of nearby **Joshua Tree National Park** (p184). Scramble among the **Wonderland of Rocks** and stop by the **Noah Purifoy Desert Art Museum** (p187). Tired but happy, head back into Palm Springs for a refined meal at **Workshop Kitchen + Bar** (p191), then a glass of wine at **Counter Reformation** (p191).

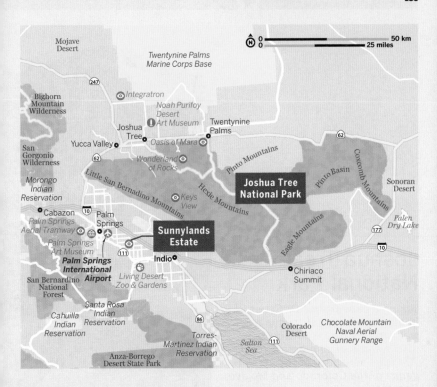

Arriving in Palm Springs

Palm Springs International Airport
Ask if your hotel provides free airport transfers; a taxi downtown costs about $12 to $15.

Car Palm Springs is just over 100 miles east of Los Angeles via I-10 and 140 miles northeast of San Diego via I-15 and I-10.

Train Amtrak's Sunset Limited comes through three times weekly on its route between New Orleans and Los Angeles.

Sleeping

Palm Springs and the Coachella Valley offer an astonishing variety of lodging, including fine vintage-flair boutique hotels, full-on luxury resorts and a huge number of chain motels. Some places don't allow children. Campers should head to Joshua Tree National Park or into the San Jacinto Mountains (via Hwy 74) for a quiet escape.

Joshua Tree National Park

Taking a page from a Dr Seuss book, the whimsical Joshua trees welcome visitors – particularly hikers and rock climbers – to this 794,000-acre park at the convergence of the Colorado and Mojave Deserts.

Great For...

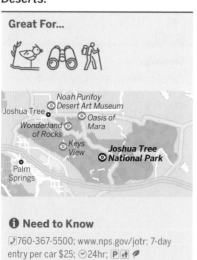

ⓘ Need to Know

☏760-367-5500; www.nps.gov/jotr; 7-day entry per car $25; ⊙24hr; Ⓟ ⓖ ⌀

Don't Miss

Hiking through the magical, eye-popping geological marvel of the Wonderland of Rocks.

It was Mormon settlers who named the Joshua tree, because the branches stretching toward heaven reminded them of the Biblical prophet Joshua pointing the way to the promised land. In springtime, the Joshua trees (actually tree-sized yuccas) send up a huge single cream-colored flower.

Rock climbers know 'JT' as the best place to climb in California, hikers seek out hidden, shady, desert-fan-palm oases fed by natural springs and small streams, and mountain bikers are hypnotized by the desert vistas.

Wonderland of Rocks

This striking rock **labyrinth** (☑760-367-5500; www.nps.gov/jotr; P) extends roughly from Indian Cove in the north to Park Blvd in the south and is predictably a popular rock climbers' haunt. For a quick impression, try the 0.5-mile Indian Cove Trail or the 1-mile Barker Dam Trail. The 7-mile Willow Hole Trail and the 8-mile Boy Scout Trail present more challenging treks and should not be attempted in hot weather.

Oasis of Mara

Behind the park headquarters and Oasis Visitor Center, this natural **oasis** (☑760-367-5500; www.nps.gov/jotr; Utah Trail, Twentynine Palms; P) encompasses the original 29 palm trees that gave Twentynine Palms its name. They were planted by native Serranos who named this 'the place of little springs and much grass.'

Keys View

From Park Blvd, it's an easy 20-minute drive up to **Keys View** (☑760-367-5500;

Rock climbing in Joshua Tree National Park

www.nps.gov/jotr; Keys View Rd; (5185ft), where breathtaking views take in the entire Coachella Valley and extend as far as the Salton Sea. Looming in front of you are Mt San Jacinto (10,834ft) and Mt San Gorgonio (11,500ft), two of Southern California's highest peaks, while below you can spot a section of the San Andreas Fault.

Noah Purifoy Desert Art Museum

The 'Junk Dada' sculptures and instal-lations of African American artist Noah

✗ Take a Break

Stop at **La Copine** (www.lacopinekitchen.com; 848 Old Woman Rd, Flamingo Heights; mains $10-16; ⊘9am-3pm Thu-Sun; P✳) for the signature smoked-salmon salad.

KYLE SPARKS / GETTY IMAGES ©

Purifoy (1917–2004) are collected by the world's finest museums, but some of his coolest works can be seen for free at his former outdoor **desert studio** (www.noahpurifoy.com; 63030 Blair Lane, Joshua Tree; ⊘dawn-dusk; P) FREE north of Joshua Tree. Toilets, tires, monitors, bicycles and beds are among the eclectic castoffs he turned variously into political statements, social criticism or just plain nonsense. Pick up a pamphlet for a self-guided tour.

Integratron

It may look just like a **white-domed structure** (☎760-364-3126; www.integratron.com; 2477 Belfield Blvd, Landers; sound baths weekdays/weekends $30/35; ⊘Wed-Mon; P), but in reality it's an electrostatic generator for time travel and cell rejuvenation. Yup! At least that's what its creator, former aerospace engineer George Van Tassel be-lieved when building the place in the 1950s after receiving telepathic instructions from extraterrestrials. Today, you can pick up on the esoteric vibes during a 60-minute 'sound bath' in the wooden dome, whose special design and location on a geomag-netic vortex generate an extra-strong magnetic field.

Getting There & Away

Joshua Tree has three park entrances. Access the west entrance from the town of Joshua Tree, the north entrance from Twentynine Palms and the south entrance from I-10. From Palm Springs it takes about an hour to reach the park's west entrance.

★ Top Tip

The park's northern half harbors most of the attractions, including all the Joshua trees.

TODD EBERLE / GETTY IMAGES ©

Sunnylands Estate

Sunnylands is the mid-century modern winter retreat of Walter and Leonore Annenberg, one of America's 'first families.' It was here that they entertained US presidents, royalty, Hollywood celebrities and heads of state.

Great For...

Don't Miss

Auguste Rodin's sensual statue *Eve* in the building's foyer.

The House

The masterpiece of designer William Haines and Los Angeles–based architect A Quincy Jones, this estate is a gorgeous example of visionary mid-century design. Harmoniously tied to the surrounding landscape, the building features large overhanging roof lines to shield the interiors from direct sun and huge glass walls to allow the desert brightness to fill the radiant rooms. Stepping into the front room, with Auguste Rodin's twisting statue *Eve* at its center, is unforgettable.

The Gardens

The estate gardens host 70 species of plants from North and South America, the Mediterranean and Africa, all displayed over an exquisitely manicured 9 acres. Hundreds of bird species have been spotted

Gerald Ford Dr *Sunnylands*
⊙*Estate*
Frank Sinatra Dr

RANCHO
MIRAGE

Coachella
Valley
Preserve

ⓘ Need to Know

☏760-202-2222; www.sunnylands.org; 37977 Bob Hope Dr, Rancho Mirage; tours $20-45, center & gardens free; ⊘9am-4pm Thu-Sun, closed early Jun–mid-Sep; Ⓟ

✕ Take a Break

Indulge in a pre-estate-visit breakfast at Cheeky's (p191).

★ Top Tip

Like many modernist buildings, the estate's architectural elements are clearly visible.

here and it is a temporary home to fluttering monarch butterflies, who stop on their annual migration to feast on the milkweed. The planning of the gardens was inspired by the Annenberg's impressive collection of impressionist and post-impressionist paintings.

Visiting the Estate

The only way to get inside the house is on a guided 90-minute tour ($45), which must be booked far in advance via the website. No reservations are required to see the exhibits at the new visitor center. House-tour tickets are released at 9am on the 15th of the preceding month and usually sell out the same day.

Two other types of tours are available: the Open-Air Experience ($20) is a

45-minute first-come, first-served shuttle tour of the grounds and golf course or, with prior reservation, you can join a bird tour ($35; 9:15am Thursdays). Both options run November to April.

What's Nearby?

Living Desert Zoo & Gardens   Zoo

(☏760-346-5694; www.livingdesert.org; 47900 Portola Ave, Palm Desert; adult/child $20/10; ⊘9am-5pm Oct-May, 8am-1:30pm Jun-Sep; Ⓟ👫) ✐ This amazing animal park showcases desert plants and animals alongside exhibits on regional geology and Native American culture. Highlights include a walk-through wildlife hospital and an African-themed village with a fair-trade market and storytelling grove. Camel rides, giraffe feeding, a spin on the endangered species carousel, and a hop-on, hop-off shuttle cost extra. It's educational, fun and worth the 15-mile drive down-valley.

⊙ SIGHTS

Palm Springs
Aerial Tramway
Cable Car

(📞760-325-1391, 888-515-8726; www.pstramway.com; 1 Tram Way, Palm Springs; adult/child $26/17, parking $5; ⏰1st tram up 10am Mon-Fri, 8am Sat & Sun, last tram down 9:45pm daily, varies seasonally; P⛰) This rotating cable car climbs nearly 6000 vertical feet and covers five different vegetation zones, from the Sonoran desert floor to pine-scented Mt San Jacinto State Park, in 10 minutes during its 2.5-mile journey. From the mountain station (8561ft), which is up to 40°F (22°C) cooler than the desert floor, you can enjoy stupendous views, dine in two restaurants (ask about ride 'n' dine passes), explore over 50 miles of trails or visit the natural-history museum.

Palm Springs
Art Museum
Museum

(📞760-322-4800; www.psmuseum.org; 101 Museum Dr, Palm Springs; adult/student $12.50/free, all free 4-8pm Thu; ⏰10am-5pm Sun-Tue & Sat, noon-9pm Thu & Fri; P) Art fans should not miss this museum, which presents changing exhibitions drawn from its stellar collection of international modern and contemporary painting, sculpture, photography and glass art. The permanent collection includes works by Henry Moore, Ed Ruscha, Mark di Suvero, Frederic Remington and many more heavy hitters. Other highlights are glass art by Dale Chihuly and William Morris and a collection of pre-Columbian figurines.

✪ ACTIVITIES

Estrella Spa at
Avalon Palm Springs
Spa

(📞760-318-3000; www.avalon-hotel.com/palm-springs/estrella-spa; 415 S Belardo Rd, Palm Springs; 1hr massage $145; ⏰9am-6pm Sun-Thu, to 10pm Fri & Sat) A tranquil vibe permeates this stylish retreat whose menu includes such holistic treatments as the Desert Rhythms massage or the Milk Y Way manicure/pedicure that starts with a warm fresh-milk soak.

✈ TOURS

Desert Tasty Tours
Tours

(📞760-870-1133; www.deserttastytours.com; tours $65; ⏰11am Mon-Sat) Get the inside

Palm Springs Aerial Tramway

scoop of Palm Springs' rejuvenated dining scene on three-hour walking tours of Palm Canyon Dr. A snack is served at each of the seven stops. Also available along El Paseo in Palm Desert.

Palm Springs Modern Tours   Tours
(760-318-6118; www.palmspringsmoderntours. com; tours $85; ☺9:30am & 1:30pm) Three-hour minivan tour of mid-century modern architectural jewels by such masters as Albert Frey, Richard Neutra and John Lautner. Reservations are required since the group size is restricted to a maximum of six. Private tours available.

EATING
Cheeky's   Californian $
(760-327-7595; www.cheekysps.com; 622 N Palm Canyon Dr, Palm Springs; mains $9-14; ☺8am-2pm Thu-Mon, last seating 1:30pm; ❄) Waits can be long and service only so-so at this breakfast and lunch spot, but the farm-to-table menu dazzles with witty inventiveness. The kitchen tinkers with the menu on a weekly basis but perennial faves, such as custardy scrambled eggs and grass-fed burger with pesto fries, keep making appearances.

Workshop Kitchen + Bar   American $$$
(760-459-3451; www.workshoppalmsprings. com; 800 N Palm Canyon Dr, Palm Springs; mains $26-45; ☺5-10pm Mon-Sun, 10am-2pm Sun; ❄) Hidden away in the back of the ornate 1920s El Paseo building, a large patio with olive trees leads to this starkly beautiful space centered on a lofty concrete tunnel flanked by mood-lit booths. The kitchen crafts American classics reinterpreted with seasonal ingredients for the 21st century and the bar is among the most happening in town.

DRINKING & NIGHTLIFE
Bootlegger Tiki   Cocktail Bar
(760-318-4154; www.bootleggertiki.com; 1101 N Palm Canyon Dr, Palm Springs; ☺4pm-2am)

 Palm Springs in Your Palm

The free Palm Springs Modern app for iPhone and Android covers more than 80 iconic mid-century modern private homes and public buildings on three tours enhanced with videos, audio and photographs.

Mid-century modern architecture in Palm Springs
SOLIDAGO / GETTY IMAGES ©

Crimson light bathes even pasty-faced hipsters into a healthy glow as do the killer cocktails at this teensy speakeasy with blowfish lamps and rattan walls. The entrance is via the Ernest coffee shop.

Counter Reformation   Wine Bar
(760-770-5000; www.theparkerpalmsprings. com/dine/counter-reformation.php; 4200 E Palm Canyon Dr, Palm Springs; ☺3-10pm Mon, Thu & Fri, noon-10pm Sat & Sun) If you worship at the altar of Bacchus (the Roman god of wine), you'll be singing his praises in this dimly lit clandestine boite at the Parker Palm Springs resort. The handpicked menu features just 17 reds, whites and champagne from small vineyards around the world.

INFORMATION
Palm Springs Official Visitors Center
(760-778-8418, 800-347-7746; www. visitpalmsprings.com; 2901 N Palm Canyon Dr, Palm Springs; ☺9am-5pm) Well-stocked and well-staffed visitors center in a 1965 Albert Frey–designed gas station, 3 miles north of downtown.

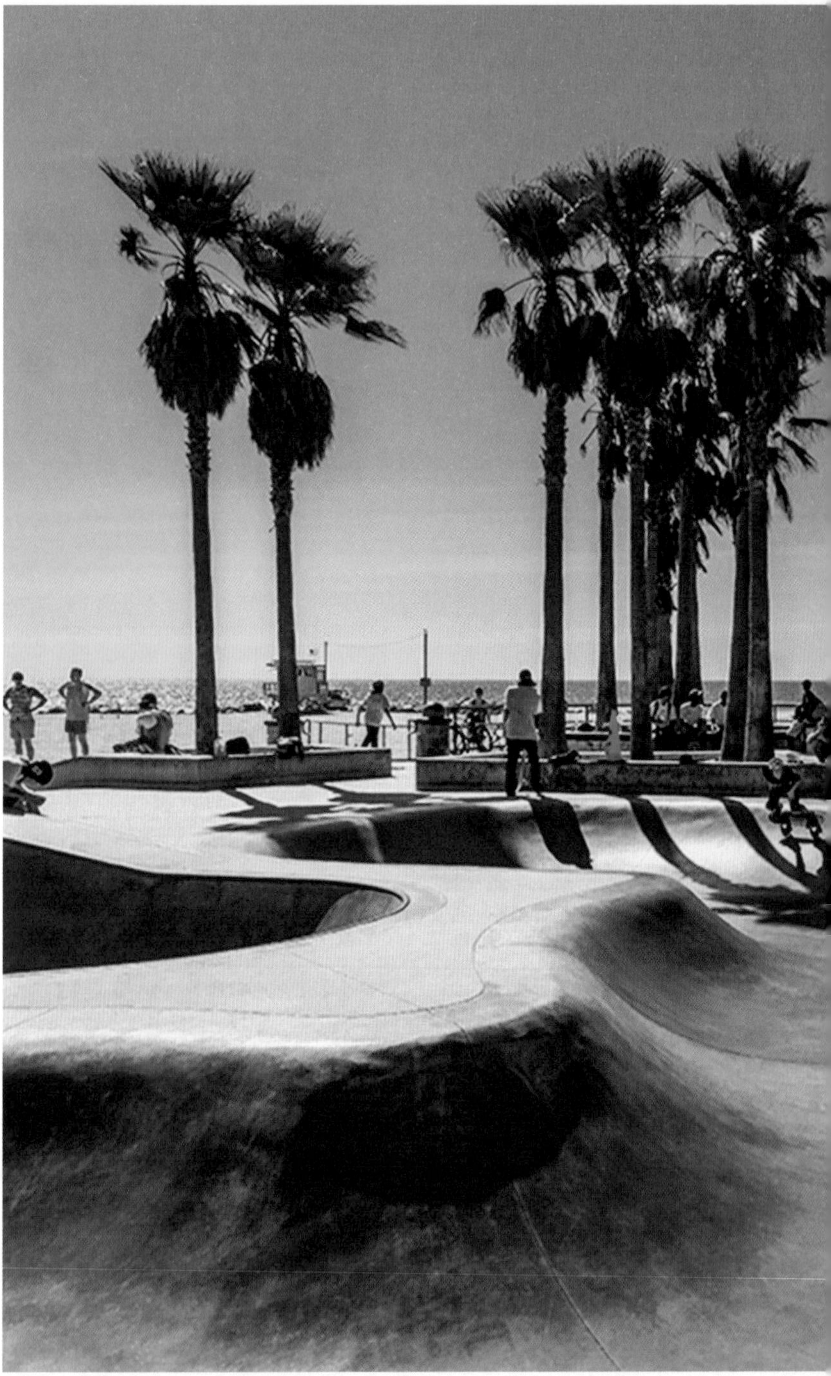

LOS ANGELES

Los Angeles

Ruggedly good looking, deeply creative, with a sunny disposition to boot...if LA were on Tinder, the app would crash. This is a city of incredible energy, architectural riches and some of the best places to eat and drink in the nation. Despite the plastic clichés, LA is one of the world's great cultural cities, home to exceptional art collections, world-shaking architecture and an extraordinary melting pot of cultures. But it's the incomparable beauty of its setting that makes it special. Here, the rat race comes with sweeping beaches, mountain vistas and bewitching sunsets.

Los Angeles in Two Days

Start your LA adventure by finding all your favorite stars and then walking right over them on the **Hollywood Walk of Fame** (p199). Spend the afternoon at the **Griffith Observatory** (p200), then (hopefully) spot more stars over dinner at **Catch LA** (p214). On day two, spend an hour or six discovering modern masterpieces at **Broad** (p204) or **MOCA Grand** (p204). Earmark the evening for craft beers and jazz at **Blue Whale** (p220).

Los Angeles in Four Days

With two more days in town, you'll want to get a taste of beach life – take in all the sights at the **Santa Monica Pier** (p196), then rent a bike and cruise all the way to Venice. Hungry? Pop a few blocks inland to **Gjusta** (p216). On day four, stump up for more incredible art at the **Getty Center** (p208) or join the locals in the great outdoors with a **Runyon Canyon** (p210) hike. Keep up the healthy vibe and dine at vegan restaurant **Crossroads** (p214).

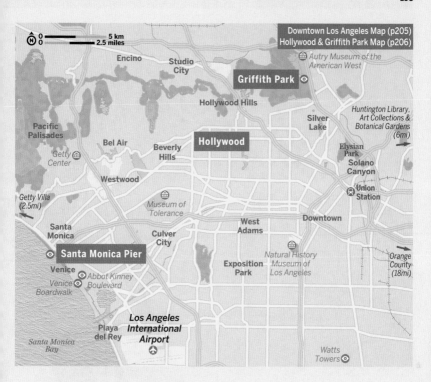

Arriving in Los Angeles

Los Angeles International Airport
LAX FlyAway (www.lawa.org/FlyAway) buses run to Union Station (Downtown), Hollywood, Van Nuys, Westwood Village near UCLA, and Long Beach. A one-way ticket costs $9.75. Flat-rate taxis to Downtown cost $47 (around 30 minutes).

Sleeping

From rock-and-roll Downtown digs to fabled Hollywood hideaways, LA serves up a dizzying array of slumber options. The key is to plan well ahead. Do your research and find out which neighborhood best appeals to your style and interests. For seaside life, base yourself in Santa Monica or Venice; cool-hunters and party people will be happiest in Hollywood or WeHo; culture vultures in Downtown LA.

A ferris wheel, Santa Monica Pier

KENKISTLER / SHUTTERSTOCK ©

Santa Monica Pier

Once the very end of Route 66, Santa Monica Pier dates back to 1908 and is the city's most compelling landmark. Extending almost a quarter-mile over the Pacific, it's all about the view: stroll to the edge and gaze out over the rolling blue-green sea.

Great For...

Don't Miss

The beautiful, hand-painted horses of the 1922 carousel at the entrance to the pier.

Carousel

Near the pier entrance, nostalgic souls and their offspring can giddy up the beautifully hand-painted horses (and one rabbit and one goat) of the 1922 **carousel** (✆310-394-8042; Santa Monica Pier; ☺hours vary; 👪), also featured in the movie *The Sting*.

Aquarium

Peer under the pier – just below the carousel – for Heal the Bay's **Santa Monica Pier Aquarium** (✆310-393-6149; www.healthebay.org; 1600 Ocean Front Walk; adult/child $5/free; ☺2-6pm Tue-Fri, 12:30-6pm Sat & Sun; 👪; Ⓜ Expo Line to Downtown Santa Monica) ✐. Sea stars, crabs, sea urchins and other critters and crustaceans scooped from the bay stand by to be

Aerial view of Santa Monica Pier

FRANCKREPORTER / GETTY IMAGES ©

ⓘ Need to Know

☎310-458-8901; www.santamonicapier.
org; 🚻

✕ Take a Break

Arrive early for excellent coffee and
breakfast burritos at **Dogtown Coffee**
(www.dogtowncoffee.com; 2003 Main St;
⊘5:30am-5pm Mon-Fri, from 6:30am Sat &
Sun).

★ Top Tip

Santa Monica's free Twilight Concert
Series features music to move you at
the pier on Thursdays in summer.

petted – ever so gently – in their adopted
touch-tank homes.

Trapeze School New York

Ever wanted to learn how to fly on the trapeze? In a cordoned-off and netted area on
the pier, **Trapeze School** (☎310-394-5800;
www.trapezeschool.com; 370 Santa Monica Pier;
2hr classes $35-65; ⊘class schedule varies) will
give you the chance. So chalk up and leave
your fear of heights and inhibitions at the
door. The public is watching.

Pacific Park

Kids (and kids at heart) get their kicks at
Pacific Park (☎310-260-8744; www.pacpark.
com; 380 Santa Monica Pier; per ride $5-10, all-
day pass adult/child under 8yr $32/18; ⊘daily,
seasonal hours vary; 🚻; ⓂExpo Line to Down-

town Santa Monica), a small, classic Americana amusement park, with a solar-powered
Ferris wheel, kiddy rides, midway games
and food stands. Check the website for
discount passes.

What's Nearby?

South of the pier is the **Original Muscle
Beach** (www.musclebeach.net; 1800 Ocean
Front Walk; ⊘sunrise-sunset), where the
Southern California exercise craze began
in the mid-20th century. New equipment
now draws a fresh generation of fitness
fanatics. Close by, the search for the next
Bobby Fischer is on at the **International
Chess Park** (☎310-458-8450; www.smgov.
net; Ocean Front Walk at Seaside Tce; ⊘sun-
rise-sunset). Anyone can join in. Following
the **South Bay Bicycle Trail** (⊘sunrise-
sunset; 🚻), a paved bike and walking path,
south for about 1.5 miles takes you straight
to Venice Beach. Bike or in-line skates are
available to rent on the pier and at beachside kiosks.

Hollywood Blvd

Hollywood

No other corner of LA is steeped in as much mythology as Hollywood. You'll find the Walk of Fame, Capitol Records and Grauman's Chinese Theatre, where the entertainment deities have been immortalized in concrete.

Great For...

Don't Miss

Stepping into the shoe prints of your favorite movie star at Grauman's Chinese Theatre.

Grauman's Chinese Theatre

Ever wondered what it's like to be in George Clooney's shoes? Just find his footprints in the forecourt of this world-famous **movie palace** (TCL Chinese Theatres; ☏323-461-3331; www.tclchinesetheatres.com; 6925 Hollywood Blvd; guided tour adult/senior/child $16/13.50/8; 🚹; Ⓜ Red Line to Hollywood/Highland). The exotic pagoda theater – complete with temple bells and stone heaven dogs from China – has shown movies since 1927.

Dolby Theatre

The Academy Awards are handed out at the **Dolby Theatre** (☏323-308-6300; www.dolby theatre.com; 6801 Hollywood Blvd; tours adult/child, senior & student $23/18; 🕙10:30am-4pm; Ⓟ; Ⓜ Red Line to Hollywood/Highland). Guided tours will show you the auditorium, a VIP room and an Oscar statuette.

JOECHO-16 / GETTY IMAGES ©

ⓘ Need to Know

Many of Hollywood's tourist attractions can be found near the intersection of Hollywood Blvd and Highland Ave.

✕ Take a Break

Step right up to Musso & Frank Grill (p214), Hollywood's oldest eatery.

★ Top Tip

The Metro Red Line has three stops along Hollywood Blvd. Hollywood/Vine and Hollywood/Highland stations are especially useful for Hollywood tourist sights.

Hollywood Museum

For a taste of Old Hollywood, do not miss this musty **museum** (☑323-464-7776; www. thehollywoodmuseum.com; 1660 N Highland Ave; adult/child $15/5; ☺10am-5pm Wed-Sun; Ⓜ Red Line to Hollywood/Highland), its four floors crammed with movie and TV costumes and props. The museum is housed inside the 1914 Max Factor Building.

Hollywood Walk of Fame

Big Bird, Bob Hope, Marilyn Monroe and Aretha Franklin are among the stars being sought out, photographed and stepped on along the **Hollywood Walk of Fame** (www. walkoffame.com; Hollywood Blvd; Ⓜ Red Line to Hollywood/Highland). Since 1960 more than 2600 performers have been honored with a pink-marble sidewalk star; check the website for upcoming ceremonies.

Hollywood Forever Cemetery

With paradisiacal landscaping, vain-glorious tombstones and epic mausole-ums this **cemetery** (☑323-469-1181; www. hollywoodforever.com; 6000 Santa Monica Blvd; ☺usually 8:30am-5pm, flower shop 9am-5pm Mon-Fri, to 4pm Sat & Sun; Ⓟ) is an appropri-ate resting place for some of Hollywood's most iconic dearly departed. For a full list of residents, purchase a map ($5) at the flower shop.

Paramount Pictures

Star Trek, Indiana Jones and *Shrek* are among the blockbusters that originated at **Paramount** (☑323-956-1777; www.paramount studiotour.com; 5555 Melrose Ave; tours from $55; ☺tours 9:30am-5pm, last tour 3pm), the country's second-oldest movie studio and the only one still in Hollywood proper. Two-hour tours of the studio complex are offered year-round, taking in the back lots and sound stages.

Hollywood sign

Griffith Park

A gift to the city in 1896 by mining mogul Griffith J Griffith, and five times the size of NY's Central Park, Griffith Park is one of the country's largest urban green spaces, containing a major outdoor theater, a zoo, an observatory, 53 miles of hiking trails and the Hollywood sign.

Great For...

Don't Miss

The sweeping Hollywood Hills views from the observatory roof.

Griffith Observatory

LA's landmark 1935 **observatory** (☏213-473-0890; www.griffithobservatory.org; 2800 E Observatory Rd; admission free, planetarium shows adult/child $7/3; ◷noon-10pm Tue-Fri, from 10am Sat & Sun; 🅿🚼; 🚌DASH Observatory) **FREE** opens a window onto the universe from its perch on the southern slopes of Mt Hollywood. Its planetarium claims the world's most advanced star projector, while its astronomical touch displays explore some mind-bending topics, from the evolution of the telescope and the ultraviolet x-rays used to map our solar system to the cosmos itself. Then, of course, there are the views, which (on clear days) take in the entire LA basin, surrounding mountains and Pacific Ocean.

The public is welcome to peer into the Zeiss Telescope on the east side of the roof

Griffith Observatory

ⓘ Need to Know

☎323-644-2050; www.laparks.org; 4730 Crystal Springs Dr; ⏰5am-10pm, trails sunrise-sunset; P♿ FREE

✕ Take a Break

Fuel up for a Griffith Park hike at walk-up cafe **Trails** (☎323-871-2102; 2333 Fern Dell Dr, Los Feliz; pastries $3-4, meals $5-9; ⏰8am-5pm; 🛜♿).

★ Top Tip

Access to the park is easiest via the Griffith Park Dr or Zoo Dr exits off I-5. Parking is plentiful and free.

where sweeping views of the Hollywood Hills and the gleaming city below are especially spectacular at sunset. After dark, staff wheel additional telescopes out to the front lawn for star gazing.

Downstairs, the Leonard Nimoy Event Horizon Theater screens a fascinating 24-minute documentary about the observatory's history.

Autry Museum of the American West

Established by singing cowboy Gene Autry, this expansive **museum** (☎323-667-2000; www.autrynationalcenter.org; 4700 Western Heritage Way, Griffith Park; adult/senior & student/child $14/10/6, 2nd Tue each month free; ⏰10am-4pm Tue-Fri, to 5pm Sat & Sun; P♿) offers contemporary perspectives on the history and people of the American West,

as well as their links to the region's contemporary culture. Permanent exhibitions explore everything from Native American traditions to the cattle drives of the 19th century and daily frontier life.

Hollywood Sign

LA's most famous landmark first appeared in the hills in 1923 as an advertising gimmick for a real-estate development called 'Hollywoodland.' Each letter is 50ft tall and made of sheet metal. Once aglow with 4000 light bulbs, the sign even had its own caretaker who lived behind the 'L' until 1939.

The last four letters were lopped off in the '40s as the sign started to crumble. In the late '70s Alice Cooper and Hugh Hefner joined forces with fans to save the famous symbol, and Hef was back at it again in 2010 when the hills behind the sign became slated for a housing development.

Architecture Downtown

Filled with amazing buildings, eateries and museums, Downtown LA is one of the most exciting neighborhoods for a stroll.

Start Verve
Distance 2.5 miles
Duration 3 hours

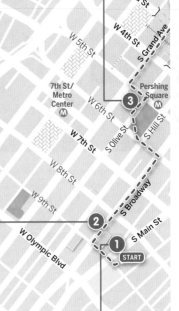

3 The **Millennium Biltmore Hotel** boasts on-screen cameos in *Ghostbusters*, *Fight Club* and *Mad Men*.

2 Architect Claud Beelman's extraordinary 1929 **Eastern Columbia Building** is a masterpiece of art moderne architecture.

1 Start the tour with a perfect cup of joe from microroastery **Verve** (📞213-455-5991; www.vervecoffee. com: 833 S Spring St,Downtown; ⏱7am-7pm Mon-Fri, to 8pm Sat & Sun).

Take a Break See the Damian Hirst mural and sip an extraordinary cocktail at **Otium** (p213).

101

W 1st St

N Broadway

5

4

S Olive St

Ⓜ Civic Center/ Grand Park

S Broadway

E Temple St

E 1st St

6

FINISH

S Main St

E 2nd St

E 3rd St

E 4th St

E 5th St

Classic Photo A selfie outside the glittering facade of Gehry's Walt Disney Concert Hall.

5 Frank Gehry's showstopping masterpiece, the **Walt Disney Concert Hall** (p204), is home to the LA Philharmonic.

6 The beaux-arts **Grand Central Market** (p204) has been satisfying appetites since 1917.

4 Gape in wonder at **Broad** (p204), Downtown's most extraordinary building.

Ⓝ 0   500 m
0   0.25 miles

SIGHTS

Downtown LA

Broad Museum
(213-232-6200; www.thebroad.org; 221 S
Grand Ave; 11am-5pm Tue & Wed, to 8pm Thu
& Fri, 10am-8pm Sat, to 6pm Sun; P; MRed/
Purple Lines to Civic Center/Grand Park) FREE
From the instant it opened in September
2015, the Broad (rhymes with 'road')
became a must-visit for contemporary-art
fans. It houses the world-class collection of
local philanthropist and billionaire real-
estate honcho Eli Broad and his wife
Edythe, with more than 2000 postwar pieces by dozens of heavy hitters,
including Cindy Sherman, Jeff Koons,
Andy Warhol, Roy Lichtenstein, Robert
Rauschenberg, Keith Haring and Kara
Walker.

Grammy Museum Museum
(213-765-6800; www.grammymuseum.
org; 800 W Olympic Blvd; adult/child $13/11;
10:30am-6:30pm Mon-Fri, from 10am Sat
& Sun; P) It's the highlight of LA Live.
Music lovers will get lost in interactive
exhibits, which define, differentiate and
link musical genres. Spanning three levels,
the museum's rotating exhibitions might
include threads worn by the likes of Michael
Jackson, Whitney Houston and Beyonce,
scribbled words from the hands of Count
Basie and Taylor Swift, and instruments
once used by world-renowned rock deities.
Inspired? Interactive sound chambers allow
you to try your own hand at singing, mixing
and remixing.

Grand Central Market Market
(www.grandcentralmarket.com; 317 S Broadway;
8am-10pm; MRed/Purple Lines to Pershing
Sq) LA's Grand Central Market has been
satisfying appetites in this beaux-arts
building since 1917. Originally leased to the
Ville de Paris department store, this was
the city's first fireproof, steel-reinforced
commercial building, designed by prolific
architect John Parkinson and once home to
an office occupied by Frank Lloyd Wright.
Lose yourself in its bustle of neon signs,

stalls and counters, peddling everything
from fresh produce and nuts, to sizzling
Thai street food, hipster egg rolls, artisanal
pasta and specialty coffee.

MOCA Grand Museum
(Museum of Contemporary Art; 213-626-
6222; www.moca.org; 250 S Grand Ave; adult/
child $15/free, 5-8pm Thu free; 11am-6pm
Mon, Wed & Fri, to 8pm Thu, to 5pm Sat & Sun)
MOCA's superlative art collection focuses
mainly on works created from the 1940s
to the present. There's no shortage of
luminaries, among them Mark Rothko,
Dan Flavin, Willem de Kooning, Joseph
Cornell and David Hockney, their creations
housed in a postmodern building by
award-winning Japanese architect Arata
Isozaki. Galleries are below ground, yet
sky-lit bright.

**Walt Disney
Concert Hall** Notable Building
(323-850-2000; www.laphil.org; 111 S Grand
Ave; guided tours usually noon & 1:15pm Thu-
Sat, 10am & 11am Sun; P; MRed/Purple Lines to
Civic Center/Grand Park) FREE A molten blend
of steel, music and psychedelic architecture, this iconic concert venue is the home
base of the Los Angeles Philharmonic,
but has also hosted contemporary bands
such as Phoenix and classic jazz performers such as Sonny Rollins. Frank Gehry
pulled out all the stops: the building is a
gravity-defying sculpture of heaving and
billowing stainless steel.

City Hall Landmark
(213-485-2121; www.lacity.org; 200 N Spring
St; 9am-5pm Mon-Fri) FREE Until 1966 no LA
building stood taller than the 1928 City Hall,
which appeared in the *Superman* TV series
and 1953 sci-fi thriller *War of the Worlds*. On
clear days you'll have views of the city, the
mountains and several decades of Downtown growth from the observation deck.
On the way up, stop off on level three to eye
up City Hall's original main entrance, which
features a breathtaking, Byzantine-inspired
rotunda graced with marble flooring and a
mosaic dome.

Downtown Los Angeles

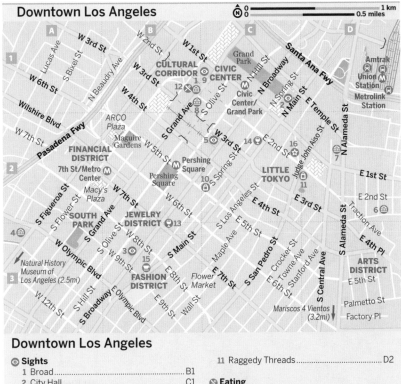

Downtown Los Angeles

Hauser & Wirth
Gallery

(☏213-943-1620; www.hauserwirthlosangeles.com; 901 E 3rd St; ◷11am-6pm Wed & Fri-Sun, to 8pm Thu) **FREE** The LA outpost of internationally acclaimed gallery Hauser & Wirth has art fiends in a flurry with its museum-standard exhibits of modern and contemporary art. It's a huge space, occupying 116,000 sq ft of a converted flour mill complex in the Arts District. Past exhibits have showcased the work of luminaries

such as Louise Bourgeois, Eva Hesse and Jason Rhoades. The complex is also home to a superlative art bookshop.

⊙ West Hollywood & Mid-City

Los Angeles County Museum of Art
Museum

(LACMA; ☏323-857-6000; www.lacma.org; 5905 Wilshire Blvd, Mid-City; adult/child $15/free, 2nd Tue each month free; ◷11am-5pm Mon, Tue & Thu, to 8pm Fri, 10am-7pm Sat &

Hollywood & Griffith Park

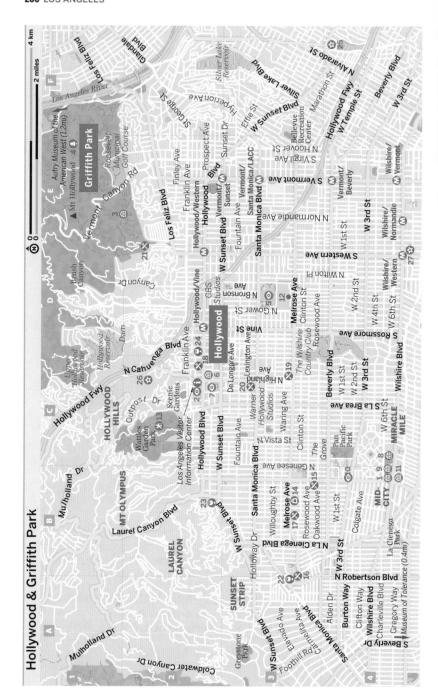

Hollywood & Griffith Park

Sun; P; ◻Metro lines 20, 217, 720, 780 to Wilshire & Fairfax) The depth and wealth of the collection at the largest museum in the western US is stunning. It holds all the major players – Rembrandt, Cézanne, Magritte, Mary Cassat, Ansel Adams – plus millennia worth of Chinese, Japanese, pre-Columbian and ancient Greek, Roman and Egyptian sculpture. Recent acquisitions include massive outdoor installations such as Chris Burden's *Urban Light* (a surreal selfie backdrop of hundreds of vintage LA streetlamps) and Michael Heizer's *Levitated Mass,* a surprisingly inspirational 340-ton boulder perched over a walkway.

Original Farmers Market   Market

(📞323-933-9211; www.farmersmarketla.com; 6333 W 3rd St, Fairfax District; ◷9am-9pm Mon-Fri, to 8pm Sat, 10am-7pm Sun; P👪) Long before the city was flooded with farmers markets, there was the originalfarmers market. Fresh produce, roasted nuts, do-nuts, cheeses, blinis – you'll find them all at this 1934 landmark. Casual and kid-friend-ly, it's a fun place for a browse, a snack or people-watching.

Petersen Automotive Museum   Museum

(📞323-930-2277; www.petersen.org; 6060 Wilshire Blvd, Mid-City; adult/senior & student/child $15/12/7; ◷10am-6pm; P👪; ◻Metro lines 20, 217, 720, 780 to Wilshire & Fairfax) A four-story ode to the auto, the Petersen Automotive Museum is a treat even for those who can't tell a piston from a carburetor. A headlights-to-brake-lights futuristic makeover (by Kohn Pederson Fox) in late 2015 left it fairly gleaming from the outside; the exterior is undulating bands of stainless steel on a hot-rod-red background. The once-dowdy inside is now equally gripping, with floors themed for the history, industry and artistry of motorized transportation.

La Brea Tar Pits & Museum   Museum

(www.tarpits.org; 5801 Wilshire Blvd, Mid-City; adult/student & senior/child $12/9/5, 1st Tue of month Sep-Jun free; ◷9:30am-5pm; P👪) Mammoths, saber-toothed cats and dire wolves used to roam LA's savannah in prehistoric times. We know this because of an archaeological trove of skulls and

Huntington Library, Art Collections & Botanical Gardens

One of the most delightful, inspirational spots in LA, the **Huntington** (☏626-405-2100; www.huntington.org; 1151 Oxford Rd, San Marino; adult weekday/weekend & holidays $23/25, child $10, 1st Thu each month free; ☽10am-5pm Wed-Mon; ℗) is rightly a highlight of any trip to California thanks to a world-class mix of art, literary history and over 120 acres of themed gardens, all set amid stately grounds. There's so much to see and do that it's hard to know where to begin; allow three to four hours for even a basic visit.

You might start with the library. Only a fraction of its six million rare books and related items can possibly go on display to the public, but they're pretty darned impressive: a Gutenberg Bible, a manuscript of *The Canterbury Tales* by Geoffrey Chaucer, and books by Marco Polo and Christopher Columbus.

Nearby, in the galleries of European and American art, you can lose yourself in the brushstrokes of Thomas Gainsborough's *The Blue Boy* and Thomas Lawrence's *Pinkie*, or take in American classics by the likes of Mary Cassatt, Andy Warhol and Frank Stella.

Then there are the gardens – about a dozen – meticulously curated like museums. Among our favorites is the Chinese Garden, with rockeries and a pond; the Japanese Garden, with its precision-pruned pine trees; and the surprisingly full-of-life Desert Garden.

Huntington Library

bones unearthed here at the La Brea Tar Pits, one of the world's most fecund and famous fossil sites. A museum has been built here, where generations of young dino-hunters have come to seek out fossils and learn about paleontology from docents and demonstrations in on-site labs.

◎ Beverly Hills & Around

Getty Center　Museum
(☏310-440-7300; www.getty.edu; 1200 Getty Center Dr, off I-405 Fwy; ☽10am-5:30pm Tue-Fri & Sun, to 9pm Sat; ℗🚼; 🚌734, 234) **FREE** In its billion-dollar, in-the-clouds perch, high above the city grit and grime, the Getty Center presents triple delights: a stellar art collection (everything from medieval triptychs to baroque sculpture and impressionist brushstrokes), Richard Meier's cutting-edge architecture, and the visual splendor of seasonally changing gardens. Admission is free, but parking is $15 ($10 after 3pm).

Museum of Tolerance　Museum
(☏reservations 310-772-2505; www.museumof tolerance.com; 9786 W Pico Blvd; adult/senior/ student $15.50/12.50/11.50, Anne Frank Exhibit adult/senior/student $15.50/13.50/12.50; ☽10am-5pm Sun-Wed & Fri, to 9:30pm Thu, to 3:30pm Fri Nov-Mar; ℗) Run by the Simon Wiesenthal Center, this powerful, deeply moving museum uses interactive technology to engage visitors in discussion and contemplation around racism and bigotry. Particular focus is given to the Holocaust, with a major basement exhibition that examines the social, political and economic conditions that led to the Holocaust as well as the experience of the millions persecuted. On the museum's 2nd floor, another major exhibition offers an intimate look into the life and effect of Anne Frank.

Frederick R Weisman Art Foundation　Museum
(☏310-277-5321; www.weismanfoundation. org; 265 N Carolwood Dr; ☽90min guided tours 10:30am & 2pm Mon-Fri, by appointment only)

Grand Central Market (p204)

FREE The late entrepreneur and philanthropist Frederick R Weisman had an insatiable passion for art, a fact confirmed when touring his former Holmby Hills home. From floor to ceiling, the mansion (and its manicured grounds) bursts with extraordinary works from visionaries such as Picasso, Kandinsky, Miró, Magritte, Rothko, Warhol, Rauschenberg and Ruscha. There's even a motorcycle painted by Keith Haring. Tours should be reserved at least a few days ahead.

◎ Malibu & Pacific Palisades

Getty Villa Museum

(☏310-430-7300; www.getty.edu; 17985 Pacific Coast Hwy, Pacific Palisades; ☉10am-5pm Wed-Mon; ℗♿; ☐line 534 to Coastline Dr) **FREE** Stunningly perched on an ocean-view hillside, this museum in a replica 1st-century Roman villa is an exquisite, 64-acre showcase for Greek, Roman and Etruscan antiquities. Dating back 7000 years, they were amassed by oil tycoon J Paul Getty. Galleries, peristiles, courtyards and lushly landscaped gardens ensconce

all manner of friezes, busts and mosaics, millennia-old cut, blown and colored glass and brain-bending geometric configurations in the Hall of Colored Marbles. Other highlights include the Pompeii fountain and Temple of Herakles.

◎ Venice

Abbot Kinney Boulevard Area

(☐Big Blue Bus line 18) Abbot Kinney, who founded Venice in the early 1900s, would probably be delighted to find that one of Venice's best-loved streets bears his name. Sort of a seaside Melrose with a Venetian flavor, the mile-long stretch of Abbot Kinney Blvd between Venice Blvd and Main St is full of upscale boutiques, galleries, lofts and sensational restaurants. A few years back, GQ named it America's coolest street, and that cachet has only grown since.

Venice Boardwalk Waterfront

(Ocean Front Walk; Venice Pier to Rose Ave) Life in Venice moves to a different rhythm and nowhere more so than on the famous

Venice Boardwalk, officially known as Ocean Front Walk. It's a freak show, a human zoo and a wacky carnival alive with Hula-hoop magicians, old-timey jazz combos, solo distorted garage rockers and artists (good and bad) – as far as LA experiences go, it's a must.

Venice Canals   Area

Even many Angelenos have no idea that just a couple of blocks from the Boardwalk madness is an idyllic neighborhood that preserves 3 miles of Abbot Kinney's canals. The **Venice Canal Walk** threads past eclectic homes, over bridges and along waterways where ducks preen and locals lollygag in little rowboats. It's best accessed from either Venice or Washington Blvds.

◎ Exposition Park & South LA

Watts Towers   Landmark

(📞213-847-4646; www.wattstowers.us; 1761-1765 E 107th St, Watts; adult/child 13-17yr & senior/child under 13yr $7/3/free; ⊙tours 11am-3pm Thu & Fri, 10:30am-3pm Sat, noon-3pm Sun; Ⓟ; ⓂBlue Line to 103rd St) The three Gothic spires of the fabulous Watts Towers rank among the world's greatest monuments of folk art. In 1921 Italian immigrant Simon Rodia set out 'to make something big' and then spent 33 years cobbling together this whimsical free-form sculpture from concrete, steel and a motley assortment of found objects: green 7-Up bottles to sea shells, tiles, rocks and pottery.

✪ ACTIVITIES

Despite spending a lot of time jammed on freeways, Angelenos love to get physical. Theirs is a city made for pace-quickening thrills, with spectacular mountain hikes, one of the country's largest urban nature reserves and surf-pounded beach. Add to this almost 300 days of sunshine and you'll forgive the locals for looking so, so good.

Runyon Canyon   Hiking

(www.runyoncanyonhike.com; 2000 N Fuller Ave; ⊙dawn-dusk) A chaparral-draped cut in the

City Hall (p204)

FLIPHOTO / SHUTTERSTOCK ©

Hollywood Hills, this 130-acre public park is as famous for its buff runners and exercising celebrities as it is for the panoramic views from the upper ridge. Follow the wide, partially paved fire road up, then take the smaller track down to the canyon, where you'll pass the remains of the Runyon estate.

Free morning yoga sessions (bring your own mat) are run daily in the park; click the link on the website for details.

Mishe Mokwa Trail
& Sandstone Peak   Hiking
(www.nps.gov/samo; 12896 Yerba Buena Rd, Malibu) On warm spring mornings, when the snowy blue *ceonothus* perfumes the air with honeysuckle, there's no better place to be than this 6-mile loop trail that winds through a red-rock canyon dotted with climbers, into the oak oasis at **Split Rock** and up to Mt Allen (aka Sandstone Peak), the tallest peak in the Santa Monica Mountains.

Santa Monica Mountains   Hiking
(www.nps.gov/samo/index.htm) A haven for hikers, trekkers and mountain bikers, the northwestern-most stretch of the Santa Monica Mountains is where nature gets bigger and wilder, with jaw-dropping red-rock canyons, and granite outcrops with sublime sea views. The best trails are in Pacific Palisades, Topanga and Malibu.

🅐 SHOPPING

Consider yourself a disciplined shopper? Get back to us after your trip. LA is a pro at luring cards out of wallets. After all, how can you not bag that super-cute vintage-fabric frock? Or that tongue-in-cheek tote? Creativity and whimsy drive this town, right down to its racks and shelves.

Last Bookstore
in Los Angeles   Books
(📞213-488-0599; www.lastbookstorela.com; 453 S Spring St; ⏰10am-10pm Mon-Thu, to 11pm Fri & Sat, to 9pm Sun) What started as a one-man operation out of a Main St storefront

Treasures at the Rose Bowl Flea Market

Every month, rain or shine, since the 1960s, the Rose Bowl football field has hosted 'America's Marketplace of Unusual Items,' with rummaging hordes seeking the next great treasure. Over 2500 vendors and some 20,000 buyers converge on the **market** (www.rgcshows.com; 1001 Rose Bowl Dr, Pasadena; admission from $9; ⏰9am-4:30pm 2nd Sun each month, last entry 3pm, early admission from 5am), and it's always a great time. Street-fair-style refreshments (burgers, dogs, fries, sausages, sushi – this is LA – lemonade, cocktails etc) are on hand to fuel your shopping.

Neon sign at the Rose Bowl entrance
ANGEL DIBILIO / SHUTTERSTOCK ©

is now California's largest new-and-used bookstore, spanning two levels of an old bank building. Eye up the cabinets of rare books before heading upstairs, home to a horror-and-crime book den, a book tunnel and a few art galleries to boot. The store also houses a terrific vinyl collection.

Raggedy Threads   Vintage
(📞213-620-1188; www.raggedythreads.com; 330 E 2nd St; ⏰noon-8pm Mon-Sat, to 6pm Sun; Ⓜ Gold Line to Little Tokyo/Arts District) A tremendous vintage Americana store just off the main Little Tokyo strip. There's plenty of beautifully ragged denim, with a notable collection of pre-1950s workwear from the US, Japan and France. You'll also find a good number of Victorian dresses, soft T-shirts and a wonderful turquoise collection at decent prices.

Fred Segal Fashion & Accessories

(☎323-651-4129; www.fredsegal.com; 8100 Melrose Ave, Mid-City; ☺10am-7pm Mon-Sat, noon-6pm Sun) Celebs and beautiful people circle for the very latest from Babakul, Aviator Nation and Robbi & Nikki at this warren of high-end boutiques under one impossibly chic but slightly snooty roof. The only time you'll see bargains (sort of) is during the two-week blowout sale in September.

Sika Art

(☎323-295-2502; 4330 Degnan Blvd, Leimert Park; ☺noon-6pm) It would be hard to find a better collection of antiques, masks, clothes and jewelry outside of West Africa than those found in this owner-operated treasure chest, a pillar of Leimert Park. It's also known for nose piercings. It co-sponsors a three-day Labor Day Music, Food & Art Festival in the lot next door.

Mystery Pier Books Books

(www.mysterypierbooks.com; 8826 W Sunset Blvd, West Hollywood; ☺11am-7pm Mon-Sat, noon-5pm Sun) An intimate, hidden-away courtyard shop that specializes in selling signed shooting scripts from past block-busters, and first-edition books by writers such as William Shakespeare ($2500 to $4000), JD Salinger ($21,000) and JK Rowling (from $30,000).

 EATING

Bring an appetite. A big one. LA's cross-cultural makeup is reflected at its table, which is an epic global feast. And while there's no shortage of just-like-the-motherland dishes – from Cantonese *xiao long bao* to Ligurian *farinata* – it's the takes on tradition that really thrill. Ever tried Korean-Mexican tacos? Or a vegan cream-cheese donut with jam, basil and balsamic reduction? LA may be many things, but a culinary bore isn't one of them.

⊗ Downtown LA

Mariscos 4 Vientos Mexican $

(☎323-266-4045; www.facebook.com/Mariscos-4Vientos; 3000 E Olympic Blvd; dishes $2.25-14;

From left: Original Farmers Market (p207); Getty Center (p208); Roof detail of Walt Disney Concert Hall (p204); Last Bookstore in Los Angeles (p211)

⊗9am-5:30pm Mon-Thu, to 6pm Fri-Sun) You'll find the greatest shrimp taco of your life at no-frills Mariscos 4 Vientos. Order from the truck (if you're in a hurry) or grab a table inside the bustling dining room. Either way, surrender to corn tortillas folded and stuffed with fresh shrimp, then fried and smothered in *pico de gallo*.

Manuela   Modern American **$$**
(📞323-849-0480; www.manuela-la.com; 907 E 3rd St; ⊗5:30-10pm Sun-Thu, to 11pm Fri & Sat, also 11:30am-3:30pm Wed-Fri & 10am-4pm Sat & Sun; 🛜) Young Texan chef Wes Whitsell heads this deserving it-kid inside the Hauser & Wirth arts complex. The woody warmth of the loft-like space is echoed in the oft-tweaked menu, a beautiful fusion of local ingredients and smokey southern accents. Pique the appetite with a house-pickled appetizer then lose yourself in deceptively simple soul-stirrers like sultry pork ragù over flawless polenta.

Otium   Modern American **$$$**
(📞213-935-8500; http://otiumla.com; 222 S Hope St, Downtown; dishes $15-45; ⊗11:30am-2:30pm & 5:30-10pm Tue-Thu, 11:30am-2:30pm & 5:30-11pm Fri, 11am-2:30pm & 5:30-11pm Sat, 11am-2:30pm & 5:30-10pm Sun; 🛜) In a modernist pavilion beside the Broad is this fun, of-the-moment hot spot helmed by chef Timothy Hollingsworth. Prime ingredients conspire in unexpected ways, from the crunch of wild rice and amaranth in an eye-candy salad of avocado, beets and pomegranate, to a twist of lime and sake in flawlessly al dente wholewheat bucatini with dungeness crab.

⊗ Hollywood

Petit Trois   French **$$**
(📞323-468-8916; http://petittrois.com; mains $14-36; ⊗noon-10pm Sun-Thu, to 11pm Fri & Sat; 🅿) Good things come in small packages...like tiny, no-reservations Petit Trois! Owned by acclaimed TV chef Ludovic Lefebvre, it has two long counters (the place is too small for tables) where food lovers squeeze in for smashing, honest, Gallic-inspired grub, from a ridiculously light Boursin-stuffed omelette to a show-stopping double cheeseburger served with a standout foie gras–infused red-wine Bordelaise.

STEFANO POLITI MARKOVINA / GETTY IMAGES ©

A SAMSON / SHUTTERSTOCK ©

Five Standout Los Angeles Bites

Petit Trois (p213) Decadent Bic Mec double cheeseburger.

Mariscos 4 Vientos (p212). Flawless deep-fried shrimp tacos.

Cassia (p216) Vietnamese *pot au feu* with short ribs, veggies and bone marrow.

Crossroads Vegan artichoke 'oysters.'

Salt & Straw (p216) Almond brittle with salted ganache ice cream.

Double cheeseburger
LISA ROMEREIN / GETTY IMAGES ©

Salt's Cure   Modern American $$

(☏323-465-7258; http://saltscure.com; 1155 N Highland Ave; mains $17-34; ☉11am-11pm Mon-Thu, to midnight Fri, 10am-midnight Sat, 10am-11pm Sun) Wood-paneled, concrete-floored Salt's Cure is an out, proud locavore. From the in-season vegetables to the house-butchered and cured meats, the menu celebrates all things Californian. Expect sophisticated takes on rustic comfort grub, whether it's *capicollo* with chili paste or tender duck breast paired with impressively light oatmeal griddle cakes and blackberry compote.

Musso & Frank Grill   Steak $$

(☏323-467-7788; www.mussoandfrank.com; 6667 Hollywood Blvd; mains $15-52; ☉11am-11pm Tue-Sat, 4-9pm Sun; P; MRed Line to Hollywood/Highland) Hollywood history hangs in the thick air at Musso & Frank Grill, Tinseltown's oldest eatery (since 1919). Charlie Chaplin used to knock back vodka gimlets, Raymond Chandler penned

scripts in the high-backed booths, and movie deals were made on the old phone at the back (the booth closest to the phone is favored by Jack Nicholson and Johnny Depp).

⊗ West Hollywood & Mid-City

Crossroads   Vegan $$

(☏323-782-9245; www.crossroadskitchen. com; 8284 Melrose Ave, Mid-City; brunch mains $7-14; dinner mains $12-22; ☉10am-2pm daily, 5-10pm Sun-Thu, to midnight Fri & Sat; ☑) Tal Ronnen didn't get to be a celebrity chef (Oprah, Ellen) by serving ordinary vegan fare. Instead, seasonal creations include 'crab cakes' made from hearts of palm, artichoke 'oysters,' and porcini-crusted eggplant, alongside pizzas and pastas incorporating innovative 'cheeses' made from nuts. Leave the Birkenstocks at home; this place is sophisticated, with full bar and cool cocktails.

Canter's   Deli $$

(☏323-651-2030; www.cantersdeli.com; 419 N Fairfax Ave, Mid-City; ☉24hr; P) As old school delis go, Canter's is hard to beat. A fixture in the traditionally Jewish Fairfax district since 1931, it serves up the requisite pastrami, corned beef and matzo ball soup with a side of sass by seen-it-all waitresses, in a rangy room with deli and bakery counters up front.

The adjacent Kibitz Room is part-restaurant, part-dive-bar, and has been visited over the decades by rockers from Frank Zappa to Joni Mitchell, Guns 'n' Roses and Jakob Dylan. There are still performances most nights. Who knows? You might catch tomorrow's big star.

Catch LA   Fusion $$$

(☏323-347-6060; http://catchrestaurants. com/catchla; 8715 Melrose Ave, West Hollywood; shared dishes $11-31, dinner mains $28-41; ☉11am-3pm Sat & Sun, 5pm-2am daily; P) An LA-scene extraordinaire. You may well find sidewalk paparazzi stalking celebrity guests and a doorman to check your reservation, but all that's forgotten once you're up in this 3rd-floor rooftop restaurant-bar above WeHo. The Pacific Rim–inspired menu features super-creative cocktails and shared dishes such as truffle sashimi, black-cod lettuce wraps, and scallop and cauliflower with tamarind brown butter.

Santa Monica

Santa Monica Farmers Markets
Market $

(www.smgov.net/portals/farmersmarket; Arizona Ave, btwn 2nd & 3rd Sts; ⊘Arizona Ave 8:30am-1:30pm Wed, 8am-1pm Sat, Main St 8:30am-1:30pm Sun; 👬) 🍴 You haven't really experienced Santa Monica until you've explored one of its weekly outdoor farmers markets stocked with organic fruits, vegetables, flowers, baked goods and freshly shucked oysters. The Mac Daddy is the Wednesday market, around the intersection of 3rd and Arizona – it's the biggest and arguably the best for fresh produce, and is often patrolled by local chefs.

Erven
Vegan $$

(☎310-260-2255; www.ervenrestaurant.com; 514 Santa Monica Blvd; sandwiches $7-15, snacks $5, dinner mains $15-21; 🖥; Ⓜ Expo Line to Downtown Santa Monica) 🍴 In this city that teems with vegetarian and vegan dining, chef Nick Erven's restaurant ticks it up a few notches in this airy, modern space. Lunch and dinner are different experiences – counter service versus refined sit-down, with different menus – and there's a marketplace counter that's open even when the kitchen is closed.

Milo & Olive
Italian $$

(☎310-453-6776; www.miloandolive.com; 2723 Wilshire Blvd; dishes $7-20; ⊘7am-11pm) We love this place for its small-batch wines, incredible pizzas, terrific breakfasts (creamy polenta and poached eggs, anyone?), breads and pastries, all of which you may enjoy at the marble bar or shoulder to shoulder with new friends at one of two common tables. It's a cozy, neighborhood joint so it doesn't take reservations.

Getty Villa (p209)

Take a Tour in Los Angeles

Whatever your pleasure – dark or light, tragic or profane, sweet or salty – LA has a guided tour for you.

Los Angeles Conservancy (☎213-623-2489; www.laconservancy.org; adult/child $15/10) Nonprofit walking tours of architectural pearls in Downtown LA and beyond.

Esotouric (☎213-915-8687; www.esotouric.com; tours $58) Bus tours that explore the city's hypnotic underbelly, from real-life crime stories to the seedy LA of Chandler and Bukowski.

TMZ Celebrity Tour (☎844-869-8687; www.tmz.com/tour; 6925 Hollywood Blvd; adult/child $54/44; ☺tours departing Hard Rock Cafe Hollywood 12:15pm, 3pm & 5:30pm Thu-Tue, 12:15pm & 3pm Wed; Ⓜ Red Line to Hollywood/Highland) Irreverent celeb-culture bus tours of Hollywood, WeHo and Beverly Hills.

Dearly Departed (☎855-600-3323; www.dearlydepartedtours.com; tours $50-85) A bus tour of scandal and blood, because life and Hollywood can be dark and tragic.

Out & About Tours (www.thelavender-effect.org/tours; tours from $30) Closeted heart-throbs, underground bars and brave radicals are all celebrated on these straight-friendly walking tours of LGBT+ Hollywood, WeHo and Downtown.

Cassia　　　Southeast Asian $$$
(☎310-393-6699; 1314 7th St; appetizers $12-24, mains $18-77; ☺5-10pm Sun-Thu, to 11pm Fri & Sat; Ⓟ) Ever since it opened in 2015, open, airy Cassia has made about every local and national 'best' list of LA restaurants. Chef Bryant Ng draws on his Chinese-Singaporean heritage in dishes such as kaya toast (with coconut jam, butter and a slow-cooked egg), 'sun-bathing' prawns, and the encompassing Vietnamese *pot au feu:* short-rib stew, veggies, bone marrow and delectable accompaniments.

Venice

Salt & Straw　　　Ice Cream $
(☎310-310-8429; www.saltandstraw.com; 1537 Abbot Kinney Blvd, Venice; ice cream from $4; ☺10am-11pm) There always seems to be a line out the door at this branch of the hipster-cool Portland-based ice-cream fantasy land. Maybe it's because there's always something new to try: adventurous, seasonal flavors that change monthly – think farmers-market veggies to late-summer harvest. Check the website for current offerings.

Gjusta　　　Californian $$
(☎310-314-0320; www.gjusta.com; 320 Sunset Ave, Venice; mains $7.50-20; ☺7am-9pm; ⓑBig Blue Bus lines 1, 18) The folks behind the standard-setting Gjelina have opened this very casual, very gourmet, very Venice bakery, cafe and deli behind a nondescript storefront on a hidden side street. The menu changes regularly, but if we say lunches of chicken, cabbage and dumpling soup, house-cured charcuterie and fish (such as gravlax, smoked Wagyu brisket and leg of lamb), does that help?

DRINKING & NIGHTLIFE

Abbey　　　Gay & Lesbian
(☎310-289-8410; www.theabbeyweho.com; 692 N Robertson Blvd, West Hollywood; ☺11am-2am Mon-Thu, from 10am Fri, from 9am Sat & Sun) It's been called the best gay bar in the world, and who are we to argue? Once a humble coffee house, the Abbey has expanded into WeHo's bar-club-restaurant

Venice

of record. Always a party, it has so many different flavored martinis and mojitos that you'd think they were invented here, plus there'a full menu of upscale pub food (mains $14 to $21).

Edison
Cocktail Bar

(☏213-613-0000; www.edisondowntown.com; 108 W 2nd St; ☺5pm-2am Wed-Fri, from 7pm Sat; Ⓜ Red/Purple Lines to Civic Center/Grand Park) Accessed through easy-to-miss Harlem Pl alleyway, this extraordinary basement lounge sits in a century-old power plant. It's like a dimly lit, steampunk wonderland, punctuated with vintage generators, handsome leather lounges and secret nooks. Look for celebrity signatures in the original coal furnace and stick around for the live tunes (anything from jazz to folk), burlesque or aerialist performances.

Clifton's Republic
Cocktail Bar

(☏213-627-1673; www.cliftonsla.com; 648 S Broadway; ☺11am-midnight Tue-Thu, to 2am Fri, 10am-2:30am Sat, 10am-midnight Sun; 🛜;

Ⓜ Red/Purple Lines to Pershing Sq) Opened in 1935 and back after a $10-million renovation, multilevel, mixed-crowd Clifton's defies description. You can chow retro-cafeteria classics (meals around $15) by a forest waterfall, order drinks from a Gothic church altar, watch burlesque performers shimmy in the shadow of a 40ft faux redwood, or slip through a glass-paneled door to a luxe tiki paradise where DJs spin in a repurposed speedboat.

Dirty Laundry
Bar

(☏323-462-6531; http://dirtylaundrybarla.com; 1725 N Hudson Ave; ☺10pm-2am Tue-Sat; Ⓜ Red Line to Hollywood/Vine) Under a cotton-candy-pink apartment block of no particular import is this funky den of musty odor, low ceilings, exposed pipes and good times. There's fine whiskey, funkalicious tunes on the turntables and plenty of eye-candy peeps with low inhibitions. Alas, there are also velvet rope politics at work here, so reserve a table to make sure you slip through.

View from behind the Hollywood sign (p201)

Bar Marmont   Bar
(☑323-650-0575; www.chateaumarmont.
com; 8171 Sunset Blvd, Hollywood; ☺6pm-2am)
Elegant, but not stuck up; been around, yet
still cherished. With high ceilings, molded
walls and terrific martinis, the famous and
the wish-they-weres still flock here. If you
time it right, you might see celebs – the
Marmont doesn't share who (or else they'd
stop coming – get it?). Come midweek.
Weekends are for amateurs.

High   Rooftop Bar
(☑424-214-1062; www.highvenice.com; 1697 Pacific Ave, Hotel Erwin, Venice; ☺3-10pm Mon-Thu,
to midnight Fri, noon-midnight Sat, noon-10pm
Sun) Venice's only rooftop bar is quite an
experience, with 360-degree views from the
shore to the Santa Monica Mountains – if
you can take your eyes off the beautiful people. High serves creative seasonal cocktails
(blood-orange julep, lemon apple hot toddy,
Mexican hot chocolate with tequila) and
dishes like beef or lamb sliders, meze plates
and crab dip. Reservations recommended.

La Descarga   Lounge
(☑323-466-1324; www.ladescargala.com;
1159 N Western Ave; ☺8pm-2am Tue-Sat) This
tastefully frayed, reservations-only rum-
and-cigar lounge is a revelation. Behind
the marble bar sit more than 100 types of
rum from Haiti, Guyana, Guatemala and
Venezuela. The bartenders mix specialty
cocktails, but you'd do well to order something aged, and sip it neat as you enjoy the
mambo and *son* sounds and the burlesque
ballerina on the catwalk.

Sayers Club   Club
(☑323-871-8233; www.facebook.com/TheSayers
Club; 1645 Wilcox Ave; cover varies; ☺9pm-2am
Tue & Thu-Sat; Ⓜ Red Line to Hollywood/Vine)
When established stars such as the Black
Keys, and even movie stars such as Joseph
Gordon-Levitt, decide to play secret shows
in intimate environs, they come to the
back room at this brick-house Hollywood
nightspot, where the booths are leather,
the lighting moody and the music always
satisfying.

⚙ ENTERTAINMENT

Geffen Playhouse   Theater
(☎310-208-5454; www.geffenplayhouse.
com; 10886 Le Conte Ave, Westwood)
American magnate and producer David
Geffen forked over $17 million to get his
Mediterranean-style playhouse back into
shape. The center's season includes both
American classics and freshly minted
works, and it's not unusual to see well-
known film and TV actors treading the
boards.

Hollywood Bowl   Concert Venue
(☎323-850-2000; www.hollywoodbowl.com;
2301 N Highland Ave; rehearsals free, performance costs vary; ☺Jun-Sep) Summers in LA
just wouldn't be the same without alfresco
melodies under the stars at the Bowl, a
huge natural amphitheater in the Hollywood Hills. Its annual season, which usually
runs from June to September, includes
symphonies, jazz bands and iconic acts
such as Blondie, Bryan Ferry and Angélique
Kidjo. Bring a sweater or blanket as it gets
cool at night.

Echo   Live Music
(www.attheecho.com; 1822 W Sunset Blvd, Echo
Park; cover varies) Eastsiders hungry for an
eclectic alchemy of sounds flock to this
super-packed dive, basically a sweaty
bar with a stage and a back patio. On the
music front, expect anything from indie and
electronica, to dub reggae and dream and
power pop. Monday nights are dedicated
to up-and-coming local bands, with regular
club nights including Saturday's always-a-
blast Funky Sole party.

Wiltern Theatre   Theater
(☎213-388-1400; www.wiltern.com; 3790
Wilshire Blvd; ⓂPurple Line to Wilshire/Western)
Soaring confidently at the intersection of
Wilshire and Western Blvds (hence the
name), this extraordinary, turquoise-hued
deco landmark started life as a movie
theater (*West Side Story* premiered here).
These days it's an epic venue for live music,

 **Top 10 Los Angeles
Beaches**

Leo Carrillo Families love this summer-
camp-style beach with its tide pools,
cliff caves, nature trails and great
swimming.

El Matador Arguably Malibu's most
stunning beach, this intimate, remote
hideaway has sandstone spires that rise
from the swirling azure sea.

Zuma Two miles of pearly sand. Mellow
swells make for perfect bodysurfing.

Westward Beach Malibu locals favor
this wide, blonde beach for crystal-clear
water, resident dolphin pods and sea
lion colonies.

Santa Monica Wide slab of sand where
beach-umbrella-toting families descend
like butterfly swarms on weekends to
escape the inland heat.

Venice Beach The wide beaches south
of the Venice Pier are an oft-ignored
gem with excellent bodysurfing.

Manhattan Beach A brassy SoCal
beach with a high flirt factor and hardcore surfers hanging by the pier.

Hermosa Beach LA's libidinous, seemingly never-ending beach party with
hormone-crazed hard bodies getting
their game on.

Malaga Cove This crescent-shaped,
cliff-backed shoreline is the only sandy
Palos Verdes beach easily accessible by
the hoi polloi.

Abalone Cove Hunt for starfish, anem-
ones and other tide-pool critters in and
around this rock-strewn eco-preserve.

Santa Monica Beach
LIANG ZOU / SHUTTERSTOCK ©

From left: Surfer at Santa Monica Beach (p219); Hollywood Theatre sign, Hollywood Blvd; Highway overpasses, Los Angeles

comedy and occasional screenings of cult-status movies: recent live acts included Passenger, David Crosby and comic Adam Devine of *Modern Family* fame.

Blue Whale
Jazz

(☎213-620-0908; www.bluewhalemusic. com; 123 Onizuka St, Suite 301; cover $5-20; ⊘8pm-2am, closed 1st Sun of month; ⓂGold Line to Little Tokyo/Arts District) An intimate, concrete-floored space on the top floor of Weller Court in Little Tokyo, Blue Whale serves top-notch jazz nightly from 9pm. The crowd is eclectic, the beers craft and the bar bites decent. Acts range from emerging and edgy to established, and the acoustics are excellent. Note: bring cash for the cover charge.

Saturdays Off the 405
Live Music

(www.getty.edu; Getty Center; ⊘6-9pm Sat May-Sep) From May to September, the Getty Center courtyard fills with evening crowds for a delicious collision of art, brilliant live acts and beat-pumping DJ sets.

Los Angeles Philharmonic
Classical Music

(☎323-850-2000; www.laphil.org; 111 S Grand Ave) The world-class LA Phil performs classics and cutting-edge works at the Walt Disney Concert Hall (p115), under the baton of Venezuelan phenom Gustavo Dudamel.

Upright Citizens Brigade Theatre
Comedy

(☎323-908-8702; http://franklin.ucbtheatre. com; 5919 Franklin Ave; tickets $5-12) Founded in New York by *Saturday Night Live* alums Amy Poehler and Ian Roberts along with Matt Besser and Matt Walsh, this sketch-comedy group cloned itself in Hollywood in 2005. Its numerous nightly shows feature anything from stand-up comedy to improv and sketch; it's arguably the best comedy hub in town. Valet parking costs $7.

ℹ INFORMATION

Los Angeles Visitor Information Center
(☎323-467-6412; www.discoverlosangeles.com;

Hollywood & Highland, 6801 Hollywood Blvd; ⊙8am-10pm Mon-Sat, 9am-7pm Sun; Ⓜ️Red Line to Hollywood/Highland) The main tourist office for Los Angeles, located in Hollywood. Maps, brochures and lodging information, plus tickets to theme parks and attractions.

❶ GETTING THERE & AWAY

The main LA gateway is Los Angeles International Airport (p309). Its nine terminals are linked by the free LAX Shuttle A, leaving from the lower (arrival) level of each terminal. Cabs and hotel and car-rental shuttles stop here as well. A free minibus for travelers with disabilities can be ordered by calling ☏310-646-6402. Ticketing and check-in are on the upper (departure) level.

❶ GETTING AROUND

CAR & MOTORCYCLE

Unless time is short – or money is extremely tight – you will probably want to spend some time behind the wheel, although this means contending with some of the worst traffic in the country. Avoid rush hour (7am to 9am and 3:30pm to 6pm).

Parking at motels and cheaper hotels is usually free, while fancier ones charge anywhere from $8 to around $45 for the privilege. Valet parking at nicer restaurants and hotels is commonplace, with rates ranging from $3.50 to $10.

PUBLIC TRANSPORTATION

Most public transportation, including buses, metro lines and light rail, is handled by **Metro** (☏323-466-3876; www.metro.net), which offers maps, schedules and trip-planning help through its website.

To ride Metro trains and buses, buy a reusable TAP card. Available from TAP vending machines at Metro stations with a $1 surcharge, the cards allow you to add a preset cash value or day passes.

ORANGE COUNTY

Orange County

LA and Orange County are the closest of neighbors, but in some ways they couldn't be more different. If LA is about stars, the OC is about surfers. LA, ever more urban; OC, proudly suburban, built around cars, freeways and shopping malls. If LA is SoCal's seat of liberal thinking, the OC's heritage is of mega-churches and ultraconservative firebrands. If LA is Hollywood glam, the OC is Real Housewives.

Tourism is dominated by Disneyland in Anaheim in northern OC, and beach communities promising endless summer – and very different lifestyles – as you progress down the coast.

Orange County in Two Days

Spend one day at **Disneyland Park** (p226), meeting Mickey, screaming your head off on Hyperspace Mountain and ensuring "it's a small world" is stuck in your head forevermore. On day two, head south for a classic California day at the beach. Aim for **Huntington Beach** (p240), where you can end the night with a bonfire after a day of killer waves.

Orange County in Four Days

With a couple more days, you'll probably want to add **Disney California Adventure** (p228) to your Disneyland Resort experience, or sample a stretch of sand (or three) in **Laguna Beach** (p234). On day four, prepare to be awed by Spanish colonial history at the beautiful **Mission San Juan Capistrano** (p233), the jewel of the missions.

Huntington Beach Map (p242)

Arriving in Orange County

Orange County has its own airport, John Wayne Airport, although if you're flying into Los Angeles International Airport (LAX) it's usually not worth the time and expense to catch a connecting flight; shuttle vans to the OC and direct buses to Disneyland will get you here in an hour, give or take, depending on distance and traffic.

Sleeping

Accommodation along Orange County's beaches ranges from midrange to very expensive indeed (and probably worth it). The further you go inland, say to Costa Mesa or Anaheim, the cheaper your stay. Anaheim makes a convenient base to explore Disneyland Resort and the region. Disneyland hotels can be part of the experience, but add to the cost, when there are less expensive options just outside the parks' gates.

Disneyland Resort

Welcome to the 'Happiest Place on Earth,' a magical 'imagineered' hyper-reality where the streets are always clean, employees – called 'cast members' – are always upbeat and there are parades every day.

Great For...

Don't Miss

Tomorrowland's Autopia – one of the original rides from 1955.

Since opening his Disneyland home in 1955, Mickey has been a thoughtful host to millions of guests. In 2001 a second theme park, Disney's California Adventure (DCA), designed to salute the state's most famous natural landmarks and cultural history, was added. Downtown Disney, an outdoor pedestrian mall packed with shops, restaurants, bars, hotels and entertainment venues, makes up the Disneyland Resort triumvirate.

Disneyland Park

Spotless, wholesome Disneyland is still laid out according to Walt's original plans. It's here you'll find plenty of rides and some of the attractions most associated with the Disney name – Main Street, U.S.A., Sleeping Beauty Castle and Tomorrowland.

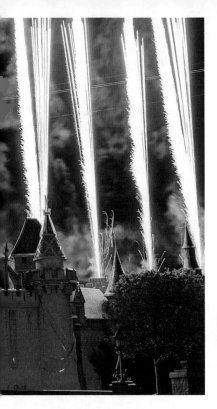

ⓘ Need to Know

☏714-781-4636; www.disneyland.com; 1313 Harbor Blvd; adult/child 3-9yr 1-day pass from $97/91, 2-day park-hopper pass $244/232; ⊙open daily, seasonal hr vary

✕ Take a Break

Make a booking for refined dining at **Napa Rose** (☏714-300-7170; https://disneyland.disney.go.com/dining; Grand Californian Hotel & Spa; mains $38-48, 4-course prix-fixe dinner from $100; ⊙5:30-10pm; 🚗).

★ Top Tip

The Disneyland mobile app lets you purchase tickets, make reservations, view wait times and locate characters.

Main Street, U.S.A., gateway to the park, is a pretty thoroughfare lined with old-fashioned Americana ice-cream parlors and shops. Though kids will make a beeline for the rides, adults may enjoy lingering on Main Street for the antique photos and history exhibit.

At the far end of the street is Sleeping Beauty Castle, an obligatory photo op and a central landmark worth noting – its towering blue turrets are visible from many areas of the park. The different sections of Disneyland radiate from here like spokes on a wheel.

Tomorrowland

How did 1950s imagineers envision the future? As a galaxy-minded community filled with monorails, rockets and Googie-style architecture, apparently. In 1998 this 'land' was revamped to honor three timeless futurists: Jules Verne, HG Wells and Leonardo da Vinci. These days, though, the *Star Wars* franchise gets top billing. Hyperspace Mountain, Tomorrowland's signature attraction and one of the USA's best roller coasters, hurtles you into complete darkness at frightening speed, and Star Wars Launch Bay shows movie props and memorabilia.

Just outside the Tomorrowland monorail station, children (and their grown-ups) will want to drive their own miniature cars in the classic Autopia ride.

Fantasyland

Fantasyland is filled with the characters of classic children's stories. If you only see one attraction here, visit "it's a small world," a boat ride past hundreds of Audio-Animatronics dolls of children from different cultures all singing an earworm of a theme song.

Another classic, the Matterhorn Bobsleds is a steel-frame roller coaster that mimics a bobsled ride down a mountain.

Frontierland

This Disney 'land' is a salute to old Americana: the Mississippi-style paddle-wheel Mark Twain Riverboat, the 18th-century replica Sailing Ship Columbia, a rip-roarin' Old West town with a shooting gallery and the Big Thunder Mountain Railroad, a mining-themed roller coaster.

Adventureland

Loosely deriving its jungle theme from Southeast Asia and Africa, Adventureland has a number of attractions, but the hands-down highlight is the safari-style Indiana Jones Adventure. Nearby, little ones love climbing the stairways of Tarzan's Treehouse.

Adventureland's Pirates of the Caribbean is the longest ride in Disneyland (17 minutes) and provided 'inspiration' for the popular movies.

Disney California Adventure

Across the plaza from Disneyland Park, this ode to California's geography, history and culture – or at least a sanitized G-rated version – covers more acres than Disneyland and feels less crowded, and it has more modern rides and attractions inspired by coastal amusement parks, the inland mountains and redwood forests, the magic of Hollywood, and car culture by way of the movie *Cars*.

Cars Land

This land gets kudos for its incredibly detailed design based on the popular Disney•Pixar *Cars* movies. Top billing goes to the wacky Radiator Springs Racers, a race-car ride that bumps and jumps around a track painstakingly decked out like the Great American West.

Grizzly Peak

Grizzly Peak is broken into sections high-lighting California's natural and human

achievements. Its main attraction, Soarin' Around the World, is a virtual hang-gliding ride using Omnimax technology that 'flies' you over famous landmarks. Enjoy the light breeze as you soar, keeping your nostrils open for aromas blowing in the wind.

Grizzly River Run takes you 'rafting' down a faux Sierra Nevada river – you will get wet, so come when it's warm.

Paradise Pier

If you like carnival rides, you'll love Paradise Pier, designed to look like a combination of all the beachside amusement piers in California. The state-of-the-art California Screamin' roller coaster resembles an old wooden coaster, but it's got a smooth-as-silk steel track: it feels like you're being shot out of a cannon. Just as popular is Toy Story Midway Mania! – a 4D ride where you earn points by shooting at targets while your carnival car swivels and careens through an oversize, old-fashioned game arcade.

Downtown Disney

Downtown Disney is a triumph of market-ing. Once in this open-air pedestrian mall, sandwiched between the two parks and the hotels, it may be hard to extract yourself. There are plenty of opportunities to drop cash in stores (not just Disney stuff either), restaurants and entertainment venues. Apart from the Disney merch, a lot of it is shops you can find elsewhere, but in the moment it's still hard to resist. Most shops here open and close with the parks.

Tickets

There is a multitude of Disneyland Resort ticket options. Single-day ticket prices vary daily, but on low traffic days one-day

★ Top Tip

For information or help inside the parks, just ask any cast member or visit Disneyland's **City Hall** (☎714-781-4565; Main Street, U.S.A.) or Disney California Adventure's guest relations lobby.

tickets start at $97/91 per adult/child for either Disneyland or DCA, and a variety of multiday and 'park-hopper' passes are available. Children's tickets apply to kids aged from three to nine.

FASTPASS

Disneyland and Disney California Adventure's FASTPASS system can significantly cut your wait times.

○ Walk up to a FASTPASS ticket machine – located near the entrance to select theme-park rides – and insert your park entrance ticket or annual passport. You'll receive a slip of paper showing the 'return time' for boarding (it's always at least 40 minutes later).

○ Show up within the window of time on the ticket and join the ride's FASTPASS line. There will still be a wait, but it's shorter (typically 15 minutes or less). Hang on to your FASTPASS ticket until you board the ride.

○ If you're running late and miss the time window printed on your FASTPASS ticket, you can still try joining the FASTPASS line, although showing up before your FAST-PASS time window is a no-no.

You're thinking, what's the catch, right? When you get a FASTPASS, you will have to wait at least two hours before getting another one (check the 'next available' time printed at the bottom of your ticket).

So, make it count. Before getting a FASTPASS, check the display above the machine, which will tell you what the 'return time' for boarding is. If it's much later in the day, or doesn't fit your schedule, a FAST-PASS may not be worth it. Ditto if the ride's current wait time is just 15 to 30 minutes.

Disney Dining

From stroll-and-eat Mickey-shaped pretzels ($4) and jumbo turkey legs ($10) to deluxe, gourmet dinners (sky's the limit), there's no shortage of eating options, though they are mostly pretty expensive and targeted to mainstream tastes. Phone **Disney Dining** (☑714-781-3463; http://disneyland.disney. go.com/dining) to make reservations up to

60 days in advance. Restaurant hours vary seasonally, sometimes daily. Check the Disneyland app or Disney Dining website for same-day hours.

Outside the parks proper, Downtown Disney has a number of dining and drinking options.

Disney Accommodation

For the full-on Disney experience, there are three different hotels within Disneyland Resort, though there are less-expensive options just beyond the Disney gates in Anaheim. In the resort, choose from **Disney's Grand Californian Hotel & Spa** (☑info 714-635-2300, reservations 714-956-6425; https://disneyland.disney.go.com/grand-californian-hotel; 1600 S Disneyland Dr; d from $360; P❋@☎☜), Disney's homage to the arts-and-crafts architectural movement;

Disneyland Hotel (☑714-778-6600; www. disneyland.com; 1150 Magic Way, Anaheim; r $210-395; P@중종), built in 1955, but rejuvenated with a dash of bibbidi-bobbidi-boo; or **Disney's Paradise Pier Hotel** (☑info 714-999-0990, reservations 714-956-6425; http://disneyland.disney.go.com/paradise-pier-hotel; 1717 S Disneyland Dr, Anaheim; d from $240; P❄@중종), with beachy decor and a games arcade.

Each of the resort's hotels has a swimming pool with a waterslide, kids' activity programs, a fitness center, restaurants and bars, a business center, and valet parking or complimentary self-parking for registered guests.

Getting There & Away

Disneyland and Anaheim can be reached by car (off the I-5 Fwy) or Amtrak or Metrolink trains at Anaheim's ARTIC (p247) transit center. From here it's a short taxi, ride share or **Anaheim Resort Transportation** (ART; ☑888-364-2787; www.rideart.org; adult/child fare $3/1, day pass $5.50/2, multiple-day passes available) shuttle to Disneyland proper.

★ Top Tip

To beat the crowds, arrive when parking lots and ticket booths open, an hour before the theme parks' official opening times.

★ Local Knowledge

Disneyland may be the happiest place on earth, but it ain't because of alcohol; no booze is allowed or served in the park. For that you have to go to DCA, Downtown Disney or one of the Disneyland hotels.

AHMET27 / SHUTTERSTOCK ©

California's Missions

California's gracious Spanish missions stand as quiet reminders of the state's tumultuous past. Founded by Spanish missionaries almost 200 years ago, they still offer a chance to step into California's complex history.

Great For...

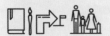

Don't Miss

The whitewashed Serra Chapel, believed to be the oldest standing building in the state.

From California's first mission at San Diego de Alcalá, which was founded in 1769, to the state's last, the 1823 Mission San Francisco Solano, the 21 California missions were built as the first European effort to colonize the Pacific Coast. These military and religious fortresses gave Spain a foothold in the New World, and signaled the downfall of California's once-thriving indigenous population. Indeed, legend has it that ghosts still pace the cloisters of many missions, built by Native Californian conscripts, many of whom didn't survive to see their completion.

Mission San Juan Capistrano

Famous for its swallows that fly back to town every year on March 19 (though sometimes they're just a bit early), San

Serra Chapel, Mission San Juan Capistrano

SUPANNEE HICKMAN / SHUTTERSTOCK ©

ℹ Need to Know

California's missions are a key part of California's State Park system. Hours and fees vary.

✕ Take a Break

Before exploring Mission San Juan Capistrano, fuel up with breakfast at **Ramos House Café** (☑949-443-1342; www.ramoshouse.com; 31752 Los Rios St; weekday mains $17-21, weekend brunch $44; ☺8:30am-3pm).

★ Top Tip

San Juan Cap and Mission San Juan Capistrano are usually visited as a day trip from beach cities like Laguna.

erful earthquake on December 8, 1812. The **Serra Chapel** (1782) – whitewashed outside with restored frescoes inside – is believed to be the oldest existing building in California. It's certainly the only one still standing in which Junípero Serra gave Mass.

Admission includes a worthwhile free audio tour with interesting stories narrated by locals. For the elementary-school set, there's a special audio tour called Saved by the Mission Bell.

California Mission Trail

California's 21 missions are strung like pearls along the well-marked Historic Mission Trail. They are all located on or near Hwy 101 and roughly trace 'El Camino Real,' named in honor of the Spanish monarchy that financed their construction as a way to expand their empire. If you're traveling through California today, the missions make an excellent detour, and you'll find stunningly renovated buildings from San Diego in the south to Solano in the north.

Juan Capistrano is home to its eponymous **mission** (☑949-234-1300; www.missionsjc.com; 26801 Ortega Hwy; adult/child $9/6; ☺9am-5pm; 🚻), nicknamed the 'jewel of the California missions.' Founded by peripatetic priest Junípero Serra in 1776, and built around a series of 18th-century arcades, the mission complex encloses stone arcades, bubbling fountains and flowery gardens. Archaeologists, engineers and restoration artists have done an exquisite job of keeping the mission alive, and you can plan on spending at least an hour or two poking around the sprawling grounds and stately buildings – including the padre's quarters, soldiers' barracks and cemetery.

Particularly moving are the towering remains of the **Great Stone Church**, almost completely destroyed by a pow-

Main Beach (p237) as seen from Heisler Park (p236)

Laguna Beach

It's easy to love Laguna: secluded coves, romantic cliffs, azure waves and waterfront parks imbue the city with a classic Riviera-like feel. But nature isn't the only draw. From public sculptures and art festivals to free summer shuttles, the city has taken thoughtful steps to promote tourism while discreetly maintaining its moneyed quality of life.

Great For...

❶ Need to Know

The Visit Laguna Beach app (www. visitlagunabeach.com/app) has tons of information, from sights and restaurants to the next bus arrival times.

★ **Top Tip**

Stop by the **visitor center** (☎949-497-9229; www.lagunabeachinfo.com; 381 Forest Ave; ☉10am-5pm; ☎) **to pick up brochures detailing self-guided tours on foot and by public bus.**

One of the earliest incorporated cities in California, Laguna has a strong tradition in the arts, starting with the plein air impressionists who lived and worked here in the early 1900s. Today it's the home of renowned arts festivals, galleries, a well-known museum and exquisitely preserved arts-and-crafts cottages and bungalows that come as a relief after seeing endless miles of suburban beige-box architecture. It's also the OC's most prominent gay enclave (even if the gay nightlife scene is a shadow of its former self).

Separated from the inland flatlands by a long steep canyon, Laguna stretches about 7 miles along Pacific Coast Hwy. Shops, restaurants and bars are concentrated along a walkable stretch of downtown's 'village,' along three parallel streets: Broadway, Ocean Ave and Forest Ave.

Laguna Art Museum

This breezy **museum** (✆949-494-8971; www. lagunaartmuseum.org; 307 Cliff Dr; adult/student & senior/child under 13yr $7/5/free, 5-9pm 1st Thu of month free; ⊗11am-5pm Fri-Tue, to 9pm Thu) has changing exhibitions featuring contemporary California artists, and a permanent collection heavy on California landscapes, vintage photographs and works by early Laguna bohemians.

Beaches

With 30 public beaches sprawling along 7 miles of coastline, Laguna Beach is perfect for do-it-yourself exploring. There's always another stunning view or hidden cove just around the bend. For a bird's-eye view of the shoreline, head to the grassy, bluff-top **Heisler Park** (375 Cliff Dr), where

Shaw's Cove

you'll find vistas of craggy coves and deep-blue sea.

Near downtown's village, **Main Beach** has volleyball and basketball courts, a playground and restrooms. It's the first beach you see as you come down Laguna Canyon Blvd from the 405 Fwy, and it's Laguna's best beach for swimming. Just north of Main Beach, **Picnic Beach** is too rocky to surf but has excellent tide pooling.

South of downtown, locals' favorite **Aliso Beach County Park** (☑949-923-2280; http://ocparks.com/beaches/aliso; 31131 S

Pacific Coast Hwy; parking per hr $1; ⏱6am-10pm; P🚻) is popular with surfers, boogie boarders and skimboarders. With picnic tables, fire pits and a play area, it's also good for families.

South again, **West Street Beach** (West St) has long been a hangout for Laguna's (and the OC's) LGBT community (with an emphasis on the G).

Less than a mile down the road, and jealously guarded by locals, **Thousand Steps Beach** (off 9th Ave) is hidden off Hwy 1 just south of Mission Hospital. At the south end of 9th St, more than 200 steps (way less than 1000) lead down to the sand. Though rocky, the beach is great for sunbathing, surfing and bodysurfing.

Diving & Snorkeling

With its coves, reefs and rocky outcroppings, Laguna is one of the best SoCal beaches for diving and snorkeling. One of the most famous spots is **Divers Cove** just below Heisler Park. It's part of the **Glenn E Vedder Ecological Reserve**, an underwater park stretching to the northern border of Main Beach. Also popular is **Shaw's Cove**. Check weather and surf conditions with the city's **marine safety forecast line** (☑949-494-6573) beforehand, as drownings have happened. The visitors bureau has tide charts.

Kayaking

Take a guided kayaking tour of the craggy coves of Laguna's coast with **La Vida Laguna** (☑949-275-7544; www.lavidalaguna. com; 1257 S Coast Hwy; 2hr guided tour from $85) and you might just see a colony of sea lions. Reservations required.

TRACEROUDA / GETTY IMAGES ©

Old Towne Orange

The city of Orange, 7 miles southeast of Disneyland, retains its charming historical center, called Old Towne Orange. Visitors will find it well worth the detour for antiques and vintage clothing shops, smart restaurants and pure SoCal nostalgia.

Great For...

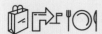

Don't Miss

The attractively landscaped traffic circle of Plaza Square Park, the crossroads of Old Towne Orange.

Orange was originally laid out by Alfred Chapman and Andrew Glassell, who in 1869 received the 1-sq-mile piece of real estate in lieu of legal fees. Orange became California's only city laid out around a central plaza, a traffic circle where present-day Glassell St and Chapman Ave meet, and it remains pleasantly walkable today.

Classic Eats

Stroll around Old Towne Orange's traffic circle, then along Glassell St to take your pick of more than a dozen atmospheric cafes, restaurants, wine bars and brewpubs, including some quietly gourmet spots. Many of the restaurants around the circle have bar scenes that go late into the evening.

Make sure to stop by the **Watson Soda Fountain Café** (714-202-2899; www.

can find the OC's most concentrated collection of antiques, collectibles and vintage and consignment shops. It's fun to browse and some of the shops are particularly well curated.

A hipster's love affair, **Elsewhere Vintage** (☏714-771-2116; www.elsewherevintage.com; 105 W Chapman Ave; ⊙11am-7pm) has gorgeous sundresses, hats, leather handbags and fabulous costume jewelry, all with a special emphasis on the 1920s to the '60s. Its brother shop, **Joy Ride** (☏714-771-7118; www.joyridevintage.com; 109 W Chapman Ave; ⊙11am-7pm), has a similar vibe, only with men's clothing: from 1950s bowling shirts to immaculately maintained wool blazers, plus vintage cameras, straight-edge razors and other manly pursuits. It even has a hat-repair clinic.

watsonscafe.com; 116 E Chapman Ave; mains $8-18; ⊙7am-9pm Sun-Wed, to 10pm Thu, to midnight Fri & Sat). Established in 1899, this former drugstore has been refurbished to a period design (check out the old safe, apothecary cabinets and telephone switchboard). It offers old-fashioned soda-fountain treats such as malts, milkshakes and sundaes, as well as burgers, fries, fried pickle chips and breakfast all day. Bonus: check out the beer and wine list and very tall cakes in the adjacent **Rockwell Bakery**.

Vintage Finds

Alongside its dining scene, Old Towne Orange is also a great place for shopping. Independent boutiques line up primarily north and south, and to a lesser extent east and west, of Old Towne's plaza, where you

Antiques Emporium

Among the many antique malls in Old Towne Orange, the **Orange Circle Antique Mall** (☏714-538-8160; www.orangeantiquemall.com; 118 S Glassell St; ⊙10am-4:45pm Mon, to 5:45pm Tue-Sat, 11am-5:45pm Sun) stands out for its 125 vendors over two floors, selling everything from estate jewelry and fine china to vintage clothing, pinup art, album covers and decades worth of *Life* magazine.

Huntington Beach

'No worries' is the phrase you'll hear over and over in Huntington Beach, the town that goes by the trademarked nickname 'Surf City USA.' In 1910, real-estate developer and railroad magnate Henry Huntington hired Hawaiian-Irish surfing star George Freeth to give demonstrations. When legendary surfer Duke Kahanamoku moved here in 1925 the town's status as a surf destination was set.

HB remains a quintessential spot to celebrate the hang-loose SoCal coastal lifestyle: consistently good waves, surf shops, a surf museum, bonfires on the sand, a canine-friendly beach and hotels and restaurants with killer views.

◎ SIGHTS

Bolsa Chica Ecological Reserve   Nature Reserve
(☎714-846-1114; http://bolsachica.org; 18000 Pacific Coast Hwy; ☺sunrise-sunset; P) You'd be forgiven for overlooking Bolsa Chica, at least on first glance. Against a backdrop of nodding oil derricks, this flat expanse of wetlands doesn't exactly promise the unspoiled splendors of nature. However, more than 200 bird species aren't so aesthetically prejudiced, either making the wetlands their home throughout the year, or dropping by mid-migration. Simply put, the restored salt marsh is an environmental success story.

Bolsa Chica State Beach   Beach
(www.parks.ca.gov; Pacific Coast Hwy, btwn Seapoint & Warner Aves; parking $15; ☺6am-10pm; P) A 3-mile-long strip of sand favored by surfers, volleyball players and fishers, Bolsa Chica State Beach stretches alongside Pacific Coast Hwy between **Huntington Dog Beach** (www.dogbeach.org; 100 Goldenwest Street; ☺5am-10pm; P) to the south and Sunset Beach to the north. Even though it faces a monstrous offshore oil rig, Bolsa Chica (meaning 'little pocket' in Spanish) gets mobbed on summer weekends. You'll find picnic tables, fire rings and beach showers, plus a bike path running north to Anderson Ave in Sunset Beach and south to Huntington State Beach.

Huntington Beach Pier

Huntington City Beach Beach

(www.huntingtonbeachca.gov; ⊙5am-10pm; P♿) One of SoCal's best beaches, the sand surrounding the pier at the foot of Main St gets packed on summer weekends with surfers, volleyball players, swimmers and families. Bathrooms and showers are located north of the pier at the back of the snack-bar complex. In the evening, volleyball games give way to beach bonfires.

Huntington Beach Pier Historic Site

(cnr Main St & Pacific Coast Hwy; ⊙5am-midnight) The 1853ft Huntington Pier is one of the West Coast's longest. It has been here – in one form or another – since 1904, though the mighty Pacific has damaged giant sections or completely demolished it multiple times since then. The current concrete structure was built in 1983 to withstand 31ft waves or a 7.0 magnitude earthquake, whichever hits HB first. On the pier you can rent fishing gear from **Let's Go Fishing** (📞714-960-1392; 21 Main Street, Huntington Beach Pier; fishing sets per hour/day $6/15; ⊙hours vary) bait and tackle shop.

➕ ACTIVITIES

Dwight's Beach Concession Surfing

(📞714-536-8083; www.dwightsbeachconcession.com; 201 Pacific Coast Hwy; surfboard rentals per hour/day $10/40, bicycle rentals from $10/30; ⊙9am-5pm Mon-Fri, to 6pm Sat & Sun) Rents surfboards, bodyboards, bikes and other beach gear at competitive rates. It's HB's oldest longest running business, since 1932.

Zack's Surfing

(📞714-536-0215; www.zackssurfcity.com; 405 Pacific Coast Hwy; group lessons $85, surfboard rentals per hour/day $12/35, wet suits $5/15) This well-established outfit by the pier offers surfing lessons and rents all sorts of beach equipment. Lessons include equipment rental for the day.

Huntington Beach Festivals

Every Tuesday brings **Surf City Nights** (www.surfcitynights.com; 1st 3 blocks Main St; ⊙5-9pm Tue), a street fair with a petting zoo and bounce house for the kids, about 90 vendors doing sidewalk sales for the grown-ups, and live music and farmers-market goodies for everyone.

Car buffs get up early on Saturday mornings for the **Donut Derelicts Car Show** (www.donutderelicts.com; cnr Magnolia St & Adams Ave; ⊙Sat mornings), a weekly gathering of woodies, beach cruisers and pimped-out street rods.

Street entertainers at Huntington Beach Pier
DOUGLAS SACHA / GETTY IMAGES ©

Vans Off the Wall Skatepark Outdoors

(📞714-379-6666; 7471 Center Dr; helmet & pad set rentals $5; ⊙9am-8pm daily) **FREE** This custom-built facility by the OC-based sneaker and skatewear company has plenty of ramps, bowls, dips, boxes and rails for boarders to catch air. It's BYOB (board). Helmets and pads required for visitors under 18 years – they can be rented here for $4.

🛍 SHOPPING

Katin Surf Shop Sports & Outdoors

(📞562-592-2052; www.katinsurf.com; 16250 Pacific Coast Hwy; ⊙9am-6pm) A local icon since 1959, Katin Surf Shop is known for its handmade canvas board shorts, but nowadays it sells all kinds of surfwear, swimsuits and beach gear.

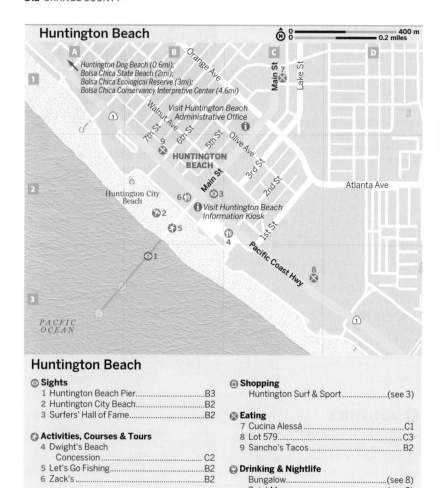

Huntington Beach

400 m
0.2 miles

Huntington Dog Beach (0.6mi);
Bolsa Chica State Beach (2mi);
Bolsa Chica Ecological Reserve (3mi);
Bolsa Chica Conservancy Interpretive Center (4.6mi)

Visit Huntington Beach
Administrative Office

HUNTINGTON
BEACH

Huntington City
Beach

Atlanta Ave

Visit Huntington Beach
Information Kiosk

Pacific Coast Hwy

PACIFIC
OCEAN

Huntington Beach

Huntington Surf & Sport
Sports & Outdoors

(www.hsssurf.com; 300 Pacific Coast Hwy;
⊘8am-9pm Sun-Thu, to 10pm Fri & Sat) Towering behind the statue of surf hero Duke
Kahanamoku at the corner of Pacific Coast
Hwy and Main St, this massive store sup-
ports the Surf City vibe with vintage surf
photos, the **Surfers' Hall of Fame** (www.
hsssurf.com/shof) and lots of tiki-themed
decor. You'll also find rows of surfboards,
beachwear and surfing accessories.

✖ EATING

Lot 579
Food Hall

(www.gopacificcity.com/lot-579; Pacific City,
21010 Pacific Coast Hwy; ⊘hours vary; P🅿🛜♿)
The food court at HB's stunning new
ocean-view mall offers some unique and
fun restaurants for pressed sandwiches
(Burnt Crumbs – the spaghetti grilled
cheese is so Instagrammable), Aussie
meat pies (Pie Not), coffee (Portola)
and ice cream (Han's). For best views,
take your takeout to the deck, or eat at

American Dream (brew pub) or Bear Flag Fish Company.

Sancho's Tacos — Mexican $
(☏714-536-8226; www.sanchostacos.com; 602 Pacific Coast Hwy; mains $3-10; ⏱8am-9pm Mon-Sat, to 8pm Sun; P) There's no shortage of taco stands in HB, but locals are fiercely dedicated to Sancho's, across from the beach. This two-room shack with patio grills flounder, shrimp and tri-tip to order. Trippy Mexican-meets-skater art.

Cucina Alessá — Italian $$
(☏714-969-2148; http://cucinaalessarestaurants.com; 520 Main St; mains lunch $9-13, dinner $12-25; ⏱11am-10pm) Every beach town needs its favorite go-to Italian kitchen. Alessá wins hearts and stomachs with classics like Neapolitan lasagna, butternut-squash ravioli and chicken masala. Lunch brings out panini, pizzas and pastas, plus breakfasts including frittata and 'famous' French toast. Get sidewalk seating, or sit behind big glass windows.

DRINKING & NIGHTLIFE

Bungalow — Club
(☏714-374-0399; www.thebungalow.com/hb; Pacific City, 21058 Pacific Coast Hwy, Suite 240; ⏱5pm-2am Mon-Fri, noon-2am Sat, noon-10pm Sun) This Santa Monica landmark of cool has opened a second location here in Pacific City, and with its combination of lounge spaces, outdoor patio, cozy, rustic-vintage design, specialty cocktails, DJs who know how to get the crowd going and – let's not forget – ocean views, it's already setting new standards for the OC. The food menu's pretty great too.

Don the Beachcomber — Bar
(☏562-592-1321; www.donthebeachcomber.com; 16278 Pacific Coast Hwy; ⏱3pm-9pm Mon & Tue, to 10pm Wed & Thu, 11am-midnight Fri & Sat, to 9pm Sun) This been-there-forever, seriously kitschy tiki bar spreads over numerous rooms for dining, dancing, drinking or all three. The 'Vicious Virgin' and 'Missionary's Downfall' drinks may knock you off your head. And there are Polynesian *pupu*, like sticky ribs and ahi *poke* tacos, to snack on. Zombie cocktail limit: two.

Saint Marc — Bar
(☏714-374-1101; www.saintmarcusa.com; Pacific City, 21058 Pacific Coast Hwy; ⏱11am-midnight Mon-Wed, to 2am Thu & Fri, 10am-2am Sat, to 10pm Sun) Indoor-outdoor Saint Marc is technically a restaurant, but it's just so darn much fun as a bar: giant beer pong table, beer bombers, wine on draft, infused vodkas, red Solo cup cocktails and, um, jello shots! Should you get hungry, they serve cheese boards to New Orleans–inflected meals, or just go for bacon by the slice from the bacon bar.

ℹ INFORMATION

Visit Huntington Beach operates a hard-to-spot **administrative office** (☏800-729-6232, 714-969-3492; www.surfcityusa.com; 301 Main St, Suite 212; ⏱9am-5pm Mon-Fri), but the **Pier Plaza kiosk** (☏714-969-3492, 800-729-6232; www.surfcityusa.com; Pier Plaza, 325 Pacific Coast Hwy; ⏱10:30am-7pm Mon-Fri, from 10am Sat & Sun, shorter hours in winter) is more convenient and is open weekends.

ℹ GETTING THERE & AWAY

Pacific Coast Hwy (PCH) runs alongside the beach. Main St intersects PCH at the pier. Heading inland, Main St ends at Hwy 39 (Beach Blvd), which connects north to I-405.

Public parking lots by the pier and beach – when you can get a spot – are 'pay and display' for $1.50 per hour, $15 daily maximum. On-street parking meters cost $1 per 40 minutes.

OCTA (www.octa.net) bus 1 connects HB with the rest of OC's beach towns every hour; one-way/day pass $2/5, payable on board (exact change). When we passed through, a free Surf City USA Shuttle (www.surfcityusashuttle.com) was operating from 10am to 10pm on Fridays and Saturdays and 8pm on Sundays during summer, making a loop around beach and inland areas.

San Clemente

Just before reaching San Diego County, PCH slows down and rolls past the laid-back surf town of San Clemente. Home to surfing legends, top-notch surfboard companies, a surfing museum and the dearly departed *Surfing* magazine (1964–2017), this unpretentious enclave may be one of the last spots in the OC where you can authentically live the surf lifestyle.

⊙ SIGHTS

San Clemente Pier Pier

(611 Avenida Victoria; ⊘4am-midnight; Ⓟ) San Clemente City Beach stretches alongside this historic 1296ft-long, wood-built pier. The original 1928 pier, where Prohibition-era bootleggers once brought liquor ashore, was rebuilt most recently in 1985. Surfers go north of the pier, while swimmers and bodysurfers take the south side.

**Surfing Heritage
& Culture Center** Museum

(☎949-388-0313; www.surfingheritage.org; 110 Calle Iglesia; suggested donation $5; ⊘11am-4pm Mon-Sat; Ⓟ) FREE This foundation gives a timeline of surfing history by exhibiting surfboards ridden by the greats from Duke Kahanamoku to Kelly Slater, and its photo archive has some 100,000 photos (a tiny fraction may be on display at any one time). Temporary exhibits (photos, skateboarding, and more) change out approximately every three months.

🔒 SHOPPING

Rocket Fizz Food & Drinks

(☎949-492-0099; www.rocketfizz.com; 107 Avenida del Mar; ⊘11am-8:30pm Mon-Wed, 10:30am-9pm Thu & Sun, 10:30am-9:30pm Fri & Sat) This 'soda pop and candy shop' fits perfectly in picturesque San Clemente. Rocket Fizz sells old-timey American penny candy like saltwater taffy and Jolly Ranch-

Vans Off the Wall Skatepark (p241), Huntington Beach

ers, plus treats from around the world (German Ritter Sport to Japanese Pocky). Then there are the unusually flavored sodas from the sublime (strawberry shortcake) to the ridiculous (peanut butter and jelly).

EATING

Riders Club Cafe Burgers $

(🖉949-338-3858; www.ridersclubcafe.com; 1701 N El Camino Real; burgers from $10, hot dog sets from $7; ⏱11:30am-9pm Tue-Sun) Locals adore this tiny roadhouse where they grill juicy, messy, hand-packed, quality burgers (served with *ka-runchy* potato chips and tangy pickled beets), generous chef's salads and carnitas sandwiches. There's simple indoor-outdoor seating and (mostly) craft beers on tap.

Pierside
Kitchen & Bar American $$

(🖉949-218-0980; www.piersidesc.com; 610 Avenida Victoria; mains $14-28; ⏱11am-11pm Mon-Thu, 11am-1am Fri, 9am-1am Sat, 9am-11pm Sun) The name really says it all at this urbane spot across from the water. Get a table by the window for the best ocean views as you chomp on a modern California menu (kale Caesar salad, bacon-wrapped dates, braised short ribs, ginger soy scallops) with some crazy-cat twists like chowder fries. Weekend brunch gets rocking with live music.

Fisherman's
Restaurant & Bar Seafood $$$

(🖉949-498-6390; www.thefishermans restaurant.com; 611 Avenida Victoria; mains lunch $11-21, dinner $14-54; ⏱8am-9:30pm Sun-Thu, to 10pm Fri & Sat) Right on the pier, Fisherman's chowders, fish and chips and mesquite-grilled fresh catches come with a side of incomparable ocean views. Generous four-course Fisherman's Feasts ($29 to $62 per person, two or more guests) offer clams, chowder, salad and your choice of fish. Sure, you'll be with tourists (see 'right on the pier'), but hey, you're a tourist too, right? Embrace it.

🍴 Packing House Food Hall

Anaheim's 1919 former Sunkist orange **packing house** (🖉714-533-7225; www.anaheimpackingdistrict.com; 440 S Anaheim St; ⏱opens 9am, closing hours vary) has a fabulous new life. Over 20 stalls and restaurants sell both sit-down and stroll-around eats and drinks: from fish dinners to ramen, cocktails to shaved ice, adventurous ice-cream pops to entire meals based on waffles. It's all airy and modern on the inside, with lots of spaces to hang out.

Watermelon shaved ice
JANUVA / SHUTTERSTOCK ©

ℹ GETTING THERE & AWAY

OCTA (www.octa.net) bus 1 heads south from Dana Point every 30 to 60 minutes. At San Clemente's Metrolink station, transfer to OCTA bus 191, which runs hourly to San Clemente Pier. Unless you have a bus pass, you'll need to pay the one-way fare ($2, exact change) twice.

San Clemente is about 6 miles southeast of Dana Point via PCH. Pay-and-display parking at the pier costs $1 per hour, though good luck finding a space at peak times.

Anaheim

You can't really talk about Anaheim without mentioning Disneyland – but if that's all you talk about, you're missing out. Anaheim has grown into Orange County's largest city and, particularly in the last decade, has developed some surprising pockets of cool that have nothing to do with the Mouse House.

California's Classic Seal Beach

The OC's first beach town driving south from LA County, 'Seal' is one of the last great California beach towns and a refreshing alternative to the more crowded coast further south. Its 1.5 miles of pristine beach sparkle like a crown, and that's without mentioning three-block Main St, a stoplight-free zone with mom-and-pop restaurants and indie shops that are low on 'tude and high on charm.

Although the town's east side is dominated by the sprawling retirement community Leisure World and the huge US Naval Weapons Station (look for grass-covered bunkers), all that fades away along the charming Main St and the oceanfront.

Seal Beach at sunset
JON BILOUS / SHUTTERSTOCK ©

⊙ SIGHTS

Anaheim Packing District   Area

(www.anaheimpackingdistrict.com; S Anaheim Bl) The Anaheim Packing District launched in 2013 around a long shuttered 1925 Packard dealership and the 1919 orange packing house a couple of miles from Disneyland, near the city's actual downtown. There's an ineffably cool collection of shops and restaurants.

Center Street Anaheim   Area

(www.centerstreetanaheim.com; W Center St) A quietly splashy redeveloped neighborhood. There's a futuristic **ice rink** (☏714-535-7465; www.anaheimice.com; 300 W Lincoln Ave;

adult/child $11/9, rentals $4; ⊙11:30am-1:30pm & 3:30-5:30pm Mon-Fri, 11am-3pm Sat & Sun, additional evening hours; 🖶) and a couple of blocks packed with hipster-friendly shops selling everything from casual clothing and accessories to comic books. At **Barbeer** (☏714-533-3737; www.facebook.com/barbeer-anaheim; 165 Center St Promenade; ⊙10am-7pm Mon-Fri, to 6pm Sat, to 4pm Sun) you can get a trim and a brewski, or check out the writerly **Ink & Bean** (☏714-635-2326; www.inkand-beancoffee.com; 115 W Center St Promenade; ⊙7:30am-5pm Mon, to 7:30pm Tue-Fri, 8am-9pm Sat, to 5pm Sun) coffee saloon.

⊗ EATING & DRINKING

Pour Vida   Mexican $

(☏657-208-3889; www.pourvidalatinflavor.com; 185 W Center St Promenade; tacos $2-8; ⊙10am-7pm Mon, to 9pm Tue-Thu, to 10pm Fri, 9am-10pm Sat, 9am-7pm Sun) Chef Jimmy has worked in some of LA's top kitchens but returned to his Mexican roots to make some of the most gourmet tacos we've ever seen: pineapple skirt steak, tempura oyster, heirloom cauliflower...*caramba*! Even the tortillas are special, made with squid ink, spinach and a secret recipe. It's deliberately informal, all brick and concrete with chalkboard walls.

Olive Tree   Middle Eastern $$

(☏714-535-2878; 512 S Brookhurst St; mains $8-16; ⊙10am-9pm Mon-Sat, to 8pm Sun) In Little Arabia, this simple restaurant in a nondescript strip mall ringed by flags of Arab nations has earned accolades from local papers as well as *Saveur* magazine. You *could* get standards like falafel and kebabs, but daily specials are where it's at; Saturday's *kabseh* is righteous, fall-off-the-bone lamb shank over spiced rice with currants and onions.

Blind Rabbit   Cocktail Bar

(www.theblindrabbit.com; Anaheim Packing House, 440 S Anaheim Blvd; ⊙reservations 5pm-10:30pm Mon-Fri, from noon Sat & Sun) This chill, dimly lit, atmospheric speak-

San Clemente Pier (p244)

easy carves its own ice, makes its own juice, does regularly changing (but always creative) cocktails and has live music four nights a week. Reserve online (until 2pm on the same day) and they'll tell you where to show up. A dress code means no flip-flops, shorts or ball caps.

Unsung Brewing Company
Microbrewery

(714-706-3098; www.unsungbrewing.com; 500 S Anaheim Bl; ⊙4-10pm Mon-Thu, 1-11pm Fri, 11am-11pm Sat, noon-7pm Sun) Beer with a comic-book aesthetic? Unsung calls its Buzzman light lager a mutant ale, while Anthia has mango, pineapple and banana overtones and nutty Propeller-Head is brewed with coffee. Speaking of coffee, they also do cold brews. Buy a growler, and take home a comic book too.

ℹ INFORMATION

Visit Anaheim (☑855-405-5020; http://visit anaheim.org; 800 W Katella Ave, Anaheim

Convention Center) Phone or go online for information.

ℹ GETTING THERE & AWAY

Anaheim's sparkling new transit center, **ARTIC** (Anaheim Regional Transportation Intermodal Center; 2150 E Katella Ave, Anaheim), connects trains and buses from out of town with local transport. ARTIC is about 3 miles east of the Disney Resort area.

Greyhound (www.greyhound.com) has several daily buses between ARTIC and Downtown LA (from $10, 40 minutes) and San Diego (from $14, 2¼ hours).

Amtrak (www.amtrak.com) has almost a dozen daily trains to/from LA's Union Station ($15, 40 minutes) and San Diego ($28, 2¼ hours). Less frequent Metrolink (www.metrolinktrains.com) commuter trains connect Anaheim to LA's Union Station ($8.75, 50 minutes), Orange ($2.50, six minutes), San Juan Capistrano ($8.50, 40 minutes) and San Clemente ($10, 50 minutes).

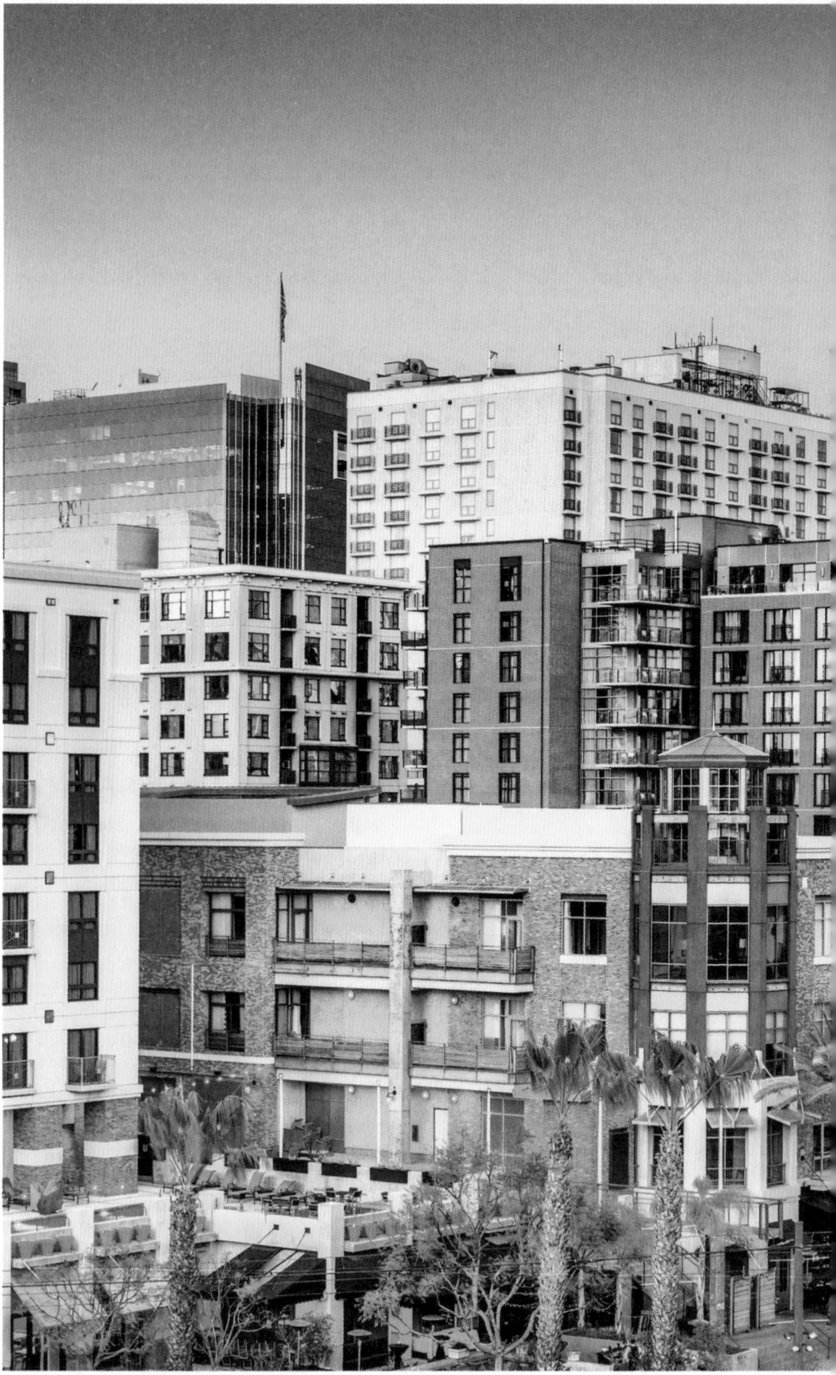

SAN DIEGO

San Diego

San Diego bursts with world-famous attractions for the entire family, including the zoo, Legoland and the museums of Balboa Park, plus a bubbling Downtown, beautiful hikes for all, more than 60 beaches and America's most perfect weather. Indeed, San Diego calls itself 'America's Finest City' and its breezy confidence filters down to folks you encounter every day on the street. It feels like a collection of villages each with their own personality, but it's the nation's eighth-largest city and we're hard-pressed to think of a place that's more laid-back.

San Diego in Two Days

Fill your belly (for the whole day) with breakfast at **Hash House a Go Go** (p262), then make tracks for Balboa Park and the **San Diego Zoo** (p253). If you manage to tear yourself away from the animals, check out the fascinating exhibits at the **San Diego Museum of Man** (p254). Spend day two rambling around the **Old Town San Diego State Historic Park** (p256) and hit **Prohibition Lounge** (p264) for some jazz in the evening.

San Diego in Four Days

Day three is beach day – head to **Mission and Pacific Beaches** (p256) for a spot of people-watching and be seduced by the sand till sunset. Back in town, seek out **Bang Bang** (p263) for tasty eats and delicious cocktails. If you've kids in tow, spend day four among the bricks at **Legoland** (p257). Otherwise, grab supplies from **Liberty Public Market** (p262), then get out of town and join the locals hiking **Los Penasquitos Canyon Trail** (p259).

 San Diego Zoo

Balboa Park

San Diego Map (p258)

Arriving in San Diego

San Diego International Airport

Bus 992 (the Flyer, $2.25) operates at 10- to 15-minute intervals between the airport and Downtown, with stops along Broadway. The route takes roughly 20 minutes. A taxi to Downtown typically costs between $12 and $18 and takes 10 minutes. Airport shuttle services (from about $10 per person to Downtown, more to other destinations) include Super Shuttle (www.supershuttle.com).

Where to Stay

Downtown is San Diego's most convenient place to stay, for its wealth of restaurants and hotels and its easy access to transit. Base yourself in San Diego's Old Town, and you may not need a car; many lodgings offer free airport shuttles and there are convenient transit links on the other side of the state park. A stay in Coronado Village puts you close to the beach, shops and restaurants.

SAM ANTONIO PHOTOGRAPHY / GETTY IMAGES ©

Balboa Park & San Diego Zoo

San Diego Zoo is a highlight of any trip to California and essential for first-time visitors. The zoo is at the heart of Balboa Park, a 1200-acre space with 17 museums and cultural institutions, and expansive gardens.

Great For...

Don't Miss

The adorable baby animals at the zoo's heart-melting nursery. It's best in spring.

Balboa Park History

Early plans for San Diego included a 1400-acre city park at the northeastern corner of what was to become Downtown, in what was then all bare hilltops and deep arroyos. Enter Kate O Sessions, a UC Berkeley botany graduate who in 1892 started a nursery on the site to landscape fashionable gardens for the city's emerging elite. The city granted her 30 acres of land in return for planting 100 trees a year in the park and donating 300 more for placement throughout the city. By the early 20th century, Balboa Park had become a well-loved part of San Diego.

Balboa Park Gardens

Balboa Park includes a number of gardens, reflecting different horticultural styles and environments, including Alcazar Garden, a

Caribbean flamingo at San Diego Zoo

STUART WESTMORLAND / GETTY IMAGES ©

ⓘ Need to Know

Balboa Park Visitors Center (☏619-239-0512; www.balboapark.org; House of Hospitality, 1549 El Prado; ⏱9:30am-4:30pm)

✕ Take a Break

Get a civilized lunch, afternoon cocktails or appetizers in the bar at **Prado** (☏619-557-9441; www.pradobalboa.com; 1549 El Prado; lunch $8-19, dinner $8-37; ⏱11:30am-3pm Mon, 11am-10pm Tue-Thu, 11:30am-9:30pm Sat, 11am-9pm Sun; ♿).

★ Top Tip

Balboa Park is easily reached from Downtown on bus 7 along Park Blvd.

formal, Spanish-style garden; Palm Canyon, with more than 50 species of palms; Japanese Friendship Garden; Australian Garden; Rose Garden; and Desert Garden. Florida Canyon gives an idea of the San Diego landscape before Spanish settlement.

San Diego Zoo

Located in the northern part of Balboa Park, this justifiably famous **zoo** (☏619-231-1515; http://zoo.sandiego.org; 2920 Zoo Dr; 1-day pass adult/child from $52/42, 2-visit pass to zoo & safari park adult/child $83.25/73.25; ⏱9am-9pm mid-Jun–early Sep, to 5pm or 6pm early Sep–mid-Jun; ℗♿) ♪ is one of SoCal's biggest attractions. It hosts more than 3000 animals representing more than 650 species in a beautifully landscaped setting. Its sister park is San Diego Zoo Safari Park in northern San Diego County.

The zoo's bioclimatic environments include the Conrad Prebys Australian Outback exhibit, with the largest colony of koalas outside Australia; the 7.5-acre Elephant Odyssey; the Tiger Trail; and the Sun Bear Trail, where the Asian bears are famously playful. Get a close-up view of polar bears swimming at the Northern Frontier, and hippos grazing in the water through thick panes of glass on the Hippo Trail.

The Monkey Trail takes you on an elevated path into the tree canopy, where you can see capuchin, colobus and spot-nosed monkeys swinging around, while the large, impressive Scripps Aviary has well-placed feeders to allow some close-up viewing. Finally, don't miss Africa Rocks, an 8-acre exhibit for African plants and animals.

To get a grip on all of this, there's a guided double-decker bus tour that gives a good overview of the zoo, with informative commentary: sitting downstairs puts you closer to the animals. The Skyfari cable car goes right across the park and can save you some walking time, though there may be a line to get on it.

Key Balboa Park Museums

San Diego Museum of Man (☏619-239-2001; www.museumofman.org; Plaza de California, 1350 El Prado; adult/child/teen $13/6/8; ☉10am-5pm; 🖈) This is the county's only anthropological museum, with exhibits spanning ancient Egypt, the Mayans and local indigenous Kumeyaay people as well as human evolution and the human life cycle. The basket and pottery collections are especially fine.

San Diego Museum of Art (SDMA; ☏619-232-7931; www.sdmart.org; 1450 El Prado; adult/child $15/free; ☉10am-5pm Mon, Tue & Thu-Sat, from noon Sun) The SDMA is the city's largest art museum. The permanent collection has works by a number of European masters from the renaissance to the modernist eras, American landscape paintings and several fantastic pieces in the Asian galleries.

Timken Museum of Art (☏619-239-5548; www.timkenmuseum.org; 1500 El Prado; ☉10am-4:30pm Tue-Sat, from noon Sun) **FREE** Don't skip the Timken, home of the small but impressive Putnam collection, featuring works by Rembrandt, Rubens, El Greco, Cézanne and Pissarro, plus a wonderful selection of Russian icons.

San Diego Natural History Museum (☏877-946-7797; www.sdnhm.org; 1788 El Prado; adult/youth 3-17yr/child under 2yr $19/12/free; ☉10am-5pm; 🖈) The 'Nat' houses 7.5 million specimens, including rocks, fossils and taxidermied animals, as well as an impressive dinosaur skeleton and a California fault-line exhibit, all in beautiful spaces.

Balboa Park

Reuben H Fleet Science Center (📞619-238-1233; www.rhfleet.org; 1875 El Prado; adult/child 3-12yr incl IMAX $20/17; ⏲10am-5pm Mon-Thu, to 6pm Fri-Sun; 👶) One of Balboa Park's most popular venues, this hands-on science museum features interactive displays and a toddler room. The biggest draw is the Giant Dome Theater, which screens several different films each day.

San Diego History Center (📞619-232-6203; www.sandiegohistory.org; 1649 El Prado, Suite 3; donation recommended; ⏲10am-5pm Tue-Sun) **FREE** The San Diego Historical Society operates this center, with permanent and temporary exhibitions on the city's history.

Mingei International Museum (📞619-239-0003; www.mingei.org; 1439 El Prado; adult/youth/child $10/7/free; ⏲10am-5pm Tue-Sun; 👶) A diverse collection of folk art, costumes, toys, jewelry, utensils and other handmade objects of traditional cultures from around the world, plus changing exhibitions on everything from beads to surfboards. Check the website to find out what's on.

San Diego Air & Space Museum (📞619-234-8291; www.sandiegoairandspace.org; 2001 Pan American Plaza; adult/youth/child under 2yr $19.75/$10.75/free; ⏲10am-4:30pm; 👶) The round building at the southern end of the plaza houses an excellent museum with extensive displays of aircraft throughout history – originals, replicas, models – plus memorabilia from legendary aviators, including Charles Lindbergh and astronaut John Glenn.

Spreckels Organ Pavilion

Going south from Plaza de Panama, you can't miss this **pavilion** (📞619-702-8138; http://spreckelsorgan.org; Balboa Park) **FREE**, with its circle of seating and curved colonnade, in front of the band shell housing the organ said to be the world's largest outdoor pipe organ. Donated by the Spreckels family of sugar fortune and fame, the pipe organ came with the stipulation that San Diego must always have an official organist. Make a point of attending the free concerts, held throughout the year at 2pm Sundays and on Monday evenings in summer (7.30pm to 9.30pm).

> ### ★ Top Tip
> Free tours of Balboa Park depart from the visitor center each week, covering various themes from botany to architecture; see www.balboapark.org/explore/tours for details.

F11PHOTO / GETTY IMAGES ©

> ### ❶ Need to Know
> The multiday explorer pass (adult/child $97/62) covers admission to Balboa Park's 17 museums and one day at the zoo; it's valid for seven days.

⊙ SIGHTS

San Diego's Downtown is the region's main business, financial and convention district. Whatever intense urban energy Downtown generally lacks, it makes up for in spirited shopping, dining and nightlife in the historic Gaslamp Quarter, while the East Village and North Park are hipster havens. The waterfront Embarcadero is good for a stroll, and in the northwestern corner of Downtown, vibrant Little Italy is full of good eats, and Old Town is the seat of local history.

The city of Coronado – with its landmark **Hotel del Coronado** (⏹619-435-6611; www.hoteldel.com; 1500 Orange Ave, Coronado; Ⓟ⏹), built in 1888, and top-rated **beach** (www.coronado.ca.us; Ⓟ⏹) – sits across San Diego Bay from Downtown. At the entrance to the bay, Point Loma has sweeping views across sea and city from the Cabrillo National Monument (p260). The coast to the northwest, including Ocean, Mission and Pacific Beaches, epitomizes the SoCal beach scene.

Mission & Pacific Beaches   Beach

ꜰʀᴇᴇ Central San Diego's best beach scene is concentrated in a narrow strip of land between the ocean and Mission Bay. There's amazing people-watching on the Ocean Front Walk, the boardwalk that connects the two beaches. From South Mission Jetty to Pacific Beach Point, it's crowded with joggers, inline skaters and cyclists anytime of the year. On warm summer weekends, oiled bodies, packed like sardines, cover the beach from end to end and cheer the setting sun.

**Old Town San Diego
State Historic Park**   Historic Site

(⏹619-220-5422; www.parks.ca.gov; 4002 Wallace St; ⊙visitor center & museums 10am-5pm daily; Ⓟ⏹) ꜰʀᴇᴇ This park has an excellent history museum in the Robinson-Rose House at the southern end of the plaza. You'll also find a diorama depicting the original pueblo at the park's visitor center, where you can pick up a copy of the *Old Town San Diego State Historic Park Tour Guide & Brief History* ($3), or join a presentation tour (free) at 11am and 2pm

San Diego skyline

daily. Personal tours cost $10 and depart at 11:30am and 1pm.

Across from the visitors center, the restored La Casa de Estudillo is filled with authentic period furniture. Other buildings around the plaza include the first San Diego Courthouse/jail and the Fiesta de Reyes, just off the plaza's northwestern corner, is a colorful collection of import shops and restaurants – great for Mexican souvenirs without the trip to Tijuana. Along San Diego Ave, on the southern side of the plaza, small, historical-looking buildings (only one is authentic) house more souvenir and gift shops.

California Surf Museum   Museum

(☑760-721-6876; www.surfmuseum.org; 312 Pier View Way; adult/child/student $5/free/3, first Tue of month free; ☺10am-4pm Fri-Wed, to 8pm Thu; ⚑) It's easy to spend an hour in this heartfelt museum of surf artifacts, which has a timeline of surfing history, surf-themed art and a radical collection of boards, including the one chomped by a shark when it ate the arm of surfer Bethany Hamilton. Special exhibits change frequently along different themes (eg Women of Surfing and Surfers of the Vietnam War).

Maritime Museum   Museum

(☑619-234-9153; www.sdmaritime.org; 1492 N Harbor Dr; adult/child $16/8; ☺9am-9pm late May-early Sep, to 8pm early Sep-late May; ⚑) This museum is easy to find: look for the 100ft-high masts of the iron-hulled square-rigger *Star of India*. Built on the Isle of Man and launched in 1863, the tall ship plied the England–India trade route, carried immigrants to New Zealand, became a trading ship based in Hawaii and, finally, ferried cargo in Alaska. It's a handsome vessel, but don't expect anything romantic or glamorous on board.

New Children's Museum   Museum

(☑619-233-8792; www.thinkplaycreate.org; 200 W Island Ave; $13; ☺10am-4pm Mon, Wed, Thu & Sat, 9.30am-4pm Fri, noon-4pm Sun; ⚑) This interactive children's museum offers interactive art meant for kids. Installations are

⇱ Legoland California Resort

This **amusement park** (☑760-918-5346; www.legoland.com/california; 1 Legoland Dr; adult/child 3-12yr from $95/89; ☺hours vary, at least 10am-5pm year-round; [P]⚑) is a fantasy environment built largely of those wonderful little plastic blocks from Denmark. Many of the rides and attractions are targeted to elementary schoolers: a junior 'driving school,' a jungle cruise lined with Lego animals, and fairy-tale-, princess-, pirate-, adventurer- and dino-themed escapades. The whole family will probably get a kick out of Miniland USA, re-creating the skylines of New York, San Francisco, Las Vegas and Washington, DC entirely of Lego blocks, alongside many world monuments.

From I-5, take the Legoland and Cannon Rd exit and follow the signage. Parking is $17.

Legoland cruise
IMAGE COURTESY OF LEGOLAND® CALIFORNIA RESORT

designed by artists, so children can learn theprinciples of movement and physics while simultaneously being exposed to art and working out the ants in their pants. Exhibits change roughly every 18 months, so there's always something new.

USS Midway Museum   Museum

(☑619-544-9600; www.midway.org; 910 N Harbor Dr; adult/child $20/$10; ☺10am-5pm, last admission 4pm; [P]⚑) The giant aircraft carrier USS *Midway* was one of the navy's flagships from 1945 to 1991, last playing

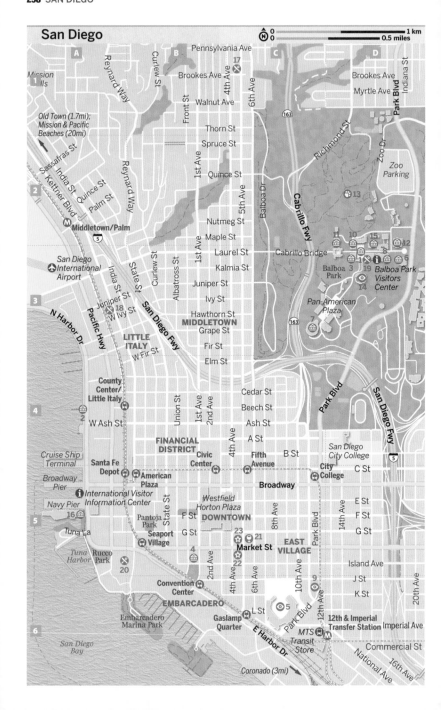

San Diego

Pennsylvania Ave

Brookes Ave

Walnut Ave

Thorn St

Spruce St

Quince St

Nutmeg St

Maple St

Laurel St

Kalmia St

Juniper St

Ivy St

Hawthorn St

MIDDLETOWN

Grape St

Fir St

Elm St

Cedar St

Beech St

Ash St

A St

FINANCIAL DISTRICT

Civic Center

B St

Fifth Avenue

San Diego City College

City College

C St

Broadway

E St

F St

G St

DOWNTOWN

Westfield Horton Plaza

Market St

EAST VILLAGE

Island Ave

J St

K St

L St

EMBARCADERO

Gaslamp Quarter

12th & Imperial Transfer Station Imperial Ave

MTS Transit Store

Commercial St

Coronado (3mi)

National Ave

Brookes Ave

Myrtle Ave

Indiana St

Park Blvd

Zoo Dr

Zoo Parking

Richmond St

Balboa Dr

Cabrillo Fwy

Cabrillo Bridge

Balboa Park

Balboa Park Visitors Center

Pan-American Plaza

Park Blvd

San Diego Fwy

Reynard Way

Curlew St

Front St

4th Ave

6th Ave

Mission Hills

Old Town (1.7mi); Mission & Pacific Beaches (20mi)

Sassafras St

India St

Kettner Blvd

Quince St

Palm St

Reynard Way

Middletown/Palm

San Diego International Airport

India St

State St

Curlew St

Albatross St

1st Ave

5th Ave

1st Ave

Juniper St

W Ivy St

LITTLE ITALY

W Fir St

San Diego Fwy

N Harbor Dr

Pacific Hwy

County Center/ Little Italy

W Ash St

Union St

1st Ave

2nd Ave

4th Ave

Cruise Ship Terminal

Broadway Pier

Santa Fe Depot

American Plaza

International Visitor Information Center

Navy Pier

Tuna La

State St

Pantoja Park

F St

G St

8th Ave

Park Blvd

14th Ave

E St

F St

G St

Tuna Harbor

Ruocco Park

Seaport Village

2nd Ave

4th Ave

6th Ave

10th Ave

Market St

Convention Center

Embarcadero Marina Park

San Diego Bay

E Harbor Dr

Park Blvd

12th Ave

16th Ave

20th Ave

N 0 1 km
0 0.5 miles

a combat role in the first Gulf War. On the flight deck of the hulking vessel, walk right up to some 29 restored aircraft, including an F-14 Tomcat and F-4 Phantom jet fighter. Admission includes an audio tour, along the narrow confines of the upper decks to the bridge, admiral's war room, brig and 'pri-fly' (primary flight control; the carrier's equivalent of a control tower). Parking costs $10.

San Diego Main Library Library
(☑619-236-5800; www.sandiego.gov/public-library; 330 Park Blvd; ⊙9:30am-7pm Mon-Thu, 9.30am-6pm Fri & Sat, noon-6pm Sun) FREE A couple of blocks east of **Petco Park** (☑619-795-5011; www.padres.com; 100 Park Blvd; tours adult/child/senior $15/10/10; ⊙10:30am & 12:30pm Sun-Fri, 3pm Sat; ♿), the city's recent landmark is a beauty. Crowned by a steel-and-mesh dome, the futuristic, nine-story library features art-filled public spaces and plenty of learning opportunities – it has the second largest collection of baseball memorabilia in the US. The library is fully open to the public for a wander and you can even access the free wi-fi. The architect? Rob Wellington Quigley, who also designed the New Children's Museum.

🜨 ACTIVITIES

There are plenty of hikes in San Diego, but most outdoor activities involve the ocean.

These waters are a dream for surfers, paddle boarders, kayakers and boaters.

Los Penasquitos Canyon Trail
Hiking
(☑county ranger 858-538-8066; www.sandiego.gov/park-and-recreation/parks/osp/lospenasquitos; entry via Park Village Rd & Celome Way; ⊙sunrise-sunset) FREE A 20-minute drive inland is a series of wonderful, mostly flat, shady and sunny paths snaking through a lush valley and past a cascading waterfall surrounded by volcanic rock. The main 7-mile pathway is moderately trafficked with runners, walkers and mountain bikers. Look out for butterflies, mule deers and bobcats. Stay alert when exploring – rattlesnakes also favor these arid pathways.

Torrey Pines State Natural Reserve
Hiking
(☑858-755-2063; https://torreypine.org/parks/trails.html; 12600 North Torrey Pines Rd; ⊙7:15am-sunset, visitor center 9am-6pm) FREE Walkers and hikers explore eight miles of **trails** in 2000 acres of well-trodden coastal state park. Choose from routes of varying difficulties including the 0.7 mile Guy Fleming Trail, with panoramic sea views and paths through wildflowers, ferns and cacti, or the 1.4-mile Razor Point Trail with a good whale-spotting lookout during winter months.

San Diego

🔭 Whale-Watching in San Diego

Gray whales pass San Diego from mid-December to late February on their way south to Baja California, and again in mid-March on their way back up to Alaskan waters. Their 12,000-mile round-trip journey is the longest migration of any mammal on earth.

Cabrillo National Monument (☏619-557-5450; www.nps.gov/cabr; 1800 Cabrillo Memorial Dr; per car $10; ⊙9am-5pm; 🅿🎦) 🐋 is the best place to see the whales from land, where you'll also find exhibits, whale-related ranger programs and a shelter from which to watch the whales breach (bring binoculars).

Half-day whale-watching boat trips are offered by most of the companies that run daily fishing trips, including **Seaforth Sportfishing** (☏619-224-3383; www.seaforthlanding.com; 1717 Quivira Rd, Mission Bay; trips $24-300). The trips generally cost $24 per adult excursion, sometimes with a guaranteed sighting or a ticket refu.

Cabrillo National Monument
DAVID H. CARRIERE / GETTY IMAGES ©

San Diego-La Jolla Underwater Park   Snorkeling, Diving

Some of California's best and most accessible diving is in this reserve, accessible from La Jolla Cove. With an average depth of 20ft, the 6000 acres of look-but-don't-touch underwater real estate is great for snorkeling, too. Ever-present are the spectacular, bright orange Garibaldi

fish – California's official state fish and a protected species (there's a hefty fine for poaching one).

🛍 SHOPPING

San Diego is chock-full of shops selling everything from local-pride souvenirs, Mexican gifts, adventure goods, beachwear and interesting antiques. Keep your eyes peeled in neighborhood streets for independent shops and boutiques trading in local wares. Farmers markets are also a big hit around town.

Pangaea Outpost   Fashion & Accessories

(☏858-224-3195; http://pangaeaoutpost.com; 909 Garnet Ave, Pacific Beach; ⊙10am-7pm Sun-Thu, to 8pm Fri-Sat) Like a miniworld unto themselves, the 70-plus merchants here offer a supremely eclectic selection of clothing, jewelry, wraps, handbags and semiprecious stones (just for starters!) from all around the world.

Adams Avenue   Antiques

(www.adamsaveonline.com; Adams Ave) This is San Diego's main 'antique row,' featuring dozens of shops selling furniture, art and antiques from around the world; it cuts across some of San Diego's less-visited neighborhoods. Take a rest from all the shopping at the Blind Lady Ale House (p264), serving pizzas and craft beers.

🍽 EATING

San Diego has a thriving dining culture, with an emphasis on Mexican, Californian and seafood. San Diegans eat dinner early, usually around 6pm or 7pm, and most restaurants are ready to close by 10pm. Breakfast is a big affair, and there's a growing locavore and gourmet scene, especially in North Park.

Dirty Birds   American $

(www.dirtybirdsbarandgrill.com; 4656 Mission Blvd; 5 wings for $7.50/20 for $26; ⊙11am-12pm Sun-Wed, 11am-2am Thu-Sat) Come to

The *Star of India* at the Maritime Museum (p257)

this sports bar and surf hangout for its award-winning chicken wings. On the menu are 37 different flavors, including classic buffalo, plus weird and wonderful concoctions like salt and vinegar, apple bourbon chipotle, and chicken enchilada. Wash them down with 10 rotating draft brews.

Fig Tree Cafe
Cafe $

(☑858-274-2233; http://figtreeeatery.com; 5119 Cass Street, Pacific Beach; mains from $9; ⊙8am to 4pm Mon-Fri, to 3pm Sat & Sun) You'll queue at the weekends for this laid-back outdoor cafe housed in an old cottage. Eat breakfast, brunch and lunch in the leafy garden area or patio, with heaters for cooler months. Our favorites are the stacked pancakes with strawberry, banana or orange, and melt-in-the-mouth Benedicts – accompanied by smoked turkey and avo, Canadian bacon, or with sun-dried tomato, spinach and basil.

Carnitas' Snack Shack
Californian, Mexican $

(☑619-294-7665; http://carnitassnackshack. com; 2632 University Ave; mains $8-13; ⊙11am-midnight; 🖩) Eat honestly priced, pork-inspired slow food in a cute outdoor patio with natural wooden features. Wash dishes like the triple-threat pork sandwich (with schnitzel, bacon, pepperoncini, pickle relish, shack aioli and an Amish bun) down with local craft ales. Happy hour runs from 3pm to 6pm Monday to Friday with $5 tacos, $5 drafts and $6 wines.

Nomad Donuts
Desserts $

(☑619-431-5000; https://nomaddonuts.com; 4504 30th St; doughnuts from $4; ⊙6am-2pm Mon-Fri, 8am-2pm Sat & Sun) 🍩 If you think you know doughnuts, think again. This artisanal doughnut shop is headed up by pastry chef Kristianna Zabala, who handcrafts every batch using cage-free, organic eggs and other ingredients from farmers markets. The menu changes daily, and when they're gone, they're gone. Our faves include bacon flavor, charred blueberry–cream cheese, and the *ube taro* coconut doughnut.

Liberty Public Market Market $

(☏619-487-9346; http://libertypublicmarket.
com; 2820 Historic Decatur Rd; ⊘7am-10pm)
What the Ferry Building Marketplace is to
San Francisco, the newly opened Liberty
Public Market is to San Diego. Inside this
converted old navy building are more than
30 hip artisan vendors such as Baker
& Olive, Wicked Maine Lobster, Paraná
Empanadas, Mastiff Sausage Company,
Mama Made Thai, Le Parfait Paris, Cecilia's
Taqueria and FishBone Kitchen.

Urban Solace Californian $$

(☏619-295-6464; www.urbansolace.net; 3823
30th St, North Park; mains lunch $12-22, dinner
$14-27; ⊘11am-9pm Mon-Tue, to 9:30pm Wed-
Thu, to 10:30pm Fri, 10:30am-10:30pm Sat,
9:30am-2:30pm & 4-9pm Sun) North Park's
young hip gourmets revel in creative com-
fort food here: quinoa-veg burger; 'not your
mama's' meatloaf of ground lamb, fig, pine
nuts and feta; 'duckaroni' (mac 'n' cheese
with duck confit); and pulled chicken and
dumplings. The setting's surprisingly chill
for such great eats, maybe because of the
creative cocktails.

Hash House a Go Go American $$

(☏619-298-4646; www.hashhouseagogo.com;
3628 5th Ave, Hillcrest; breakfast $10-22, dinner
mains $15-29; ⊘7.30am-2.30pm Mon, 7:30am-
2pm & 5:30-9pm Tue-Thu, to 2:30pm & 9:30pm
Fri-Sun; ⓲) This buzzing bungalow makes
biscuits and gravy straight outta Indiana,
towering Benedicts, large-as-your-head
pancakes and – wait for it – hash seven
different ways. Eat your whole breakfast,
and you won't need to eat the rest of the
day. It's worth coming back for the equally
massive burgers, sage-fried chicken and
award-winning meatloaf sandwich. No
wonder it's called 'twisted farm food.'

Puesto at the
Headquarters Mexican $$

(☏610-233-8880; www.eatpuesto.com; 789
W Harbor Dr, The Headquarters; mains $11-19;
⊘11am-10pm) This eatery serves Mexican
street food that knocked our *zapatos* off:
innovative takes on traditional tacos like
chicken (with hibiscus, chipotle, pineapple
and avocado) and some out-there fillings
like zucchini and cactus. Other highlights:
crab guacamole, the lime-marinated

Seals at San Diego-La Jolla Underwater Park (p260)

DANIEL M SILVA / SHUTTERSTOCK ©

shrimp ceviche and the grilled Baja striped bass.

Juniper & Ivy
Californian $$$

(🎫619-269-9036; www.juniperandivy.com; 2228 Kettner Blvd; small plates $10-23, mains $19-45; ⏰5-10pm Sun-Thu, to 11pm Fri & Sat) The menu changes daily at chef Richard Blais' highly rated San Diego restaurant, opened in 2014. The molecular gastronomy includes dishes in the vein of lobster congee, Hawaiian snapper with Valencia Pride mango, ahi tuna with creamed black trumpets, and pig-trotter *totelloni*. It's in a rockin' refurbished warehouse.

🍷 DRINKING & NIGHTLIFE

Bang Bang
Bar

(🎫619-677-2264; www.bangbangsd.com; 526 Market St; cocktails $14-26; ⏰5-10:30pm Wed-Thu, to 2am Fri & Sat) Beneath lantern light, the Gaslamp's hottest new spot brings in local and world-renowned DJs and serves sushi and Asian small plates like dumplings and panko-crusted shrimp to nurse the imaginative cocktails (some in giant goblets meant for sharing with your posse). Plus, the bathrooms are shrines to Ryan Gosling and Hello Kitty: in a word, awesome.

Coin-Op Game Room
Bar, Game Room

(🎫619-255-8523; www.coinopsd.com; 3926 30th St, North Park; ⏰4pm-1am Mon-Fri, noon-1am Sat & Sun) Dozens of classic arcade games – pinball to Mortal Kombat, Pac-Man and Big Buck Safari to Master Beer Bong – line the walls of this hipster bar in North Park. All the better to quaff craft beers and cocktails like The Dorothy Mantooth (gin, Giffard Violette, lime, cucumber, Champagne) and chow on truffle-parm tots, fried-chicken sandwiches or fried oreos.

Polite Provisions
Cocktail Bar

(🎫619-677-3784; www.politeprovisions.com; 4696 30th St, North Park; ⏰3pm-2am Mon-Thu, 11:30am-2am Fri-Sun) This place has a French bistro feel and plenty of old-world charm; hip clientele sip cocktails at the marble bar,

🔜 **Traveling Over the Border to Tijuana**

A passport is required to cross the border, and to re-enter the United States. By public transport from San Diego, the San Diego Trolley runs from Downtown to **San Ysidro border crossing** (🎫619-690-8900; www. cbp.gov; 720 E San Ysidro Blvd; ⏰24hr). By car, take I-5 south and look for either signs to Mexico or for the last US exit, where you can park at one of the many lots in the area (from $10 for five hours, from $20 for 24 hours). To cross the border on foot, follow the signs to Mexico, and a turnstile, which you walk through into Mexico. Follow signs reading 'Centro Downtown.'

Mexico side of San Ysidro border crossing
JOHNGK / SHUTTERSTOCK ©

under a glass ceiling, and in a beautifully designed space, complete with vintage cash register, wood-paneled walls and tiled floors. Many cocktail ingredients, syrups, sodas and infusions, are homemade and displayed in apothecary-esque bottles.

The Grass Skirt
Cocktail Bar

(🎫858-412-5237; http://thegrassskirt.com; 910 Grand Ave; ⏰5pm-2am) Through a secret doorway, disguised as a refrigerator in the next door **Good Time Poke** cafe, you'll step into a lost Hawaiian world with Polynesian wood carvings, thatched verandahs, fire features and tiki-girl figurines made into lamps. Sipping on your daiquiri or pina colada, there are more surprises to come... listen out for immersive weather sounds and lighting effects.

From left: Lifeguard tower, Pacific Beach (p256); Old Town San Diego State Historic Park (p256); Torrey Pines State Natural Reserve (p259)

Blind Lady Ale House   Pub

(☑619-225-2491; http://blindlady.blogspot.com; 3416 Adams Ave; ⊘5pm-midnight Mon-Thu, from 11:30am Fri-Sun) A superb neighborhood pub, with creative decor like beer cans piled floor to ceiling and longboard skateboards attached to the walls. It sells craft ales on pump and prepares fresh pizza (from $7). Vegetarians should try the meat-free Mondays offering pies with inventive flavors like the 'crows pass butternut squash' – shiitake mushrooms, sage, fontina, bechamel and lemon zest.

⊛ ENTERTAINMENT

Check out the San Diego *City Beat* or *UT San Diego* for the latest movies, theater, galleries and music gigs around town.

Prohibition Lounge   Live Music

(http://prohibitionsd.com; 548 5th Avenue; ⊘8:00pm-1:30am Wed-Sat) Find the unassuming doorway on 5th Ave with 'Eddie O'Hare's Law Office' on it, then flip the light switch on to alert the doorman, who'll guide you into a dimly lit basement serving craft cocktails, where patrons enjoy live jazz (music from 9:30pm). Come early as it gets busy fast; at weekends expect to put your name on a list.

Shout House   Live Music

(☑619-231-6700; www.theshouthouse.com; 655 4th Ave; cover free-$10) Good, clean fun at this cavernous Gaslamp bar with dueling pianos. Talented players have an amazing repertoire, including classics, rock and more. We once heard a dirty version of 'Part of Your World' from *The Little Mermaid* (OK, maybe the fun's not so clean). The lively crowd ranges from college age to conventioneers.

ⓘ INFORMATION

DISCOUNT CARDS

The Go San Diego card offers up to 55% off big-ticket attractions. The three-day pass (adult/child $189/169) includes San Diego Zoo, many of Balboa Park's museums, SeaWorld, Legoland,

the USS Midway Museum and San Diego Zoo Safari Park.

TOURIST INFORMATION

International Visitor Information Center

(📞619-236-1242; www.sandiego.org; 1140 N Harbor Dr; ⏰9am-5pm Jun-Sep, to 4pm Oct-May) Across from the B St Cruise Ship Terminal, helpful staff offer very detailed neighborhood maps, sell discounted tickets to attractions and maintain a hotel-reservation hotline.

ℹ **GETTING THERE & AWAY**

Most flights to **San Diego International Airport** (SAN; 📞619-400-2404; www.san.org; 3325 N Harbor Dr; 📶) are domestic. The airfield sits just 3 miles west of Downtown.

Allow at least two hours to reach San Diego from LA in nonpeak traffic. With traffic, it's anybody's guess. If there are two or more passengers in your car, you can use the high-occupancy vehicle lanes, which will shave off a fair amount of time in heavy traffic.

Amtrak runs the Pacific Surfliner several times daily to Anaheim (two hours), Los Angeles (2¾ hours) and Santa Barbara (6½ hours) from the historic Union Station. Fares start from around $30 and the coastal views are enjoyable.

Greyhound serves San Diego from cities across North America from its Downtown location.

ℹ **GETTING AROUND**

While most people get around San Diego by car, it's possible to have an entire vacation here using municipal buses and trolleys run by the **Metropolitan Transit System** (📞619-233-3004; www.sdmts.com) and your own two feet. Most buses/trolleys cost $2.25/2.50 per ride. The **MTS Transit Store** (📞619-234-1060; www.sdmts.com; 1255 Imperial Ave; ⏰8am-5pm Mon-Fri) is one-stop shopping for route maps, tickets and one-/two-/three-/four-day passes ($5/9/12/15). Same-day passes are also available from bus drivers. At trolley stations, purchase tickets from vending machines.

ABLOKHIN / GETTY IMAGES ©

Los Angeles downtown

In Focus

Golden Gate Bridge (p38), San Francisco

California Today

California has surged ahead of France to become the world's sixth-largest economy and taken a leading role on global issues like environmental standards, marriage equality and immigrant rights. But the rapid growth has come with its share of hassles, including housing shortages, traffic gridlock and rising costs of living. Escapism, though, is always an option here, thanks to Hollywood blockbusters and legalized marijuana dispensaries.

Environmental Roots

California's culture of conspicuous consumption is world famous, but the state is equally famous for Californians who have long sought out a more sustainable way of life. In the midst of lumber and oil booms, Californians kick-started the world's conservation movement with trailblazing laws curbing industrial dumping, establishing urban green space and protecting wilderness.

The state has also become fertile ground for radical new ecological schemes. California's eco-activists have declared nuclear-free zones, held tree-sitting vigils to preserve old-growth forests, and established the USA's biggest market for hybrid vehicles. But ordinary Californians have also taken green initiatives home, becoming early adopters of organic farming, green construction, plastic-bag bans and mandatory composting.

Fast Companies, Slow Food

Perhaps you've heard of PCs, iPhones, Google and the internet? California's technological innovations need no introduction. Between Silicon Valley and biotech, Northern California is rapidly overtaking Southern California's gargantuan entertainment industry as California's economic engine.

Less than 10% of Californians live in rural areas, but they sustain California's other powerhouse industry: agriculture. Each year, 80,000 Californian farms raise $42 billion worth of food. Climate change and drought are top of mind for many Californians, especially farmers and foodies.

Local menus reflect values close to many Californians' hearts: organic and non-GMO farming, protections against animal cruelty and support for small local businesses. Californians coined the term 'locavore' – people who eat food grown locally – and once you've tasted the difference, you may become California's newest convert.

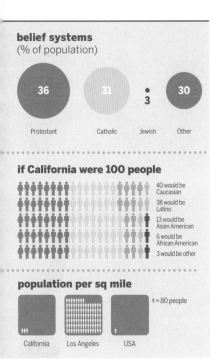

belief systems
(% of population)

36 Protestant 31 Catholic 3 Jewish 30 Other

if California were 100 people

40 would be Caucasian
38 would be Latino
13 would be Asian American
6 would be African American
3 would be other

population per sq mile

= 80 people

California Los Angeles USA

California Dreams versus Reality

Even after you've seen it 1000 times on movies and TV, California still comes as a shock to the system. Venice Beach skateboarders, Santa Cruz hippies, Rodeo Dr posers and Silicon Valley billionaires aren't on different channels here – this is their natural habitat. California is all over the map politically, by turns liberal and conservative. A long track record of conspiracy theories and fringe movements can only partly be explained by the state's legendary fondness for marijuana, legalized here in 2017.

California's trailblazing support for LGBT rights was instrumental in securing marriage equality in 2013. With first- and second-generation immigrants making up more than half the state's population, Californians vocally opposed federal immigration bans by nationality and religion in 2017. Even under threat of federal defunding, Californians continue to march, file lawsuits and support passing a statewide sanctuary law to ensure that all are welcome here.

New World Religions

Though they may not have many followers outside their yurt villages, California's alternative religions and utopian communities have long captivated the imagination. Since its inception California has been a magnet for spiritual seekers, from modern-day pagans to new-age healers. But California is better known for making sensational headlines in the 1960s and '70s with hippie spiritualism and the hype-heavy self-help movement. Founded in 1954, the controversial Church of Scientology has attracted celebrity endorsements from the likes of Tom Cruise and John Travolta. Californian doomsday cults caused commotions in the 1990s with the Heaven's Gate UFO cult in San Diego, and again when Oakland radio minister Harold Camping proselytized that the Rapture was imminent. That was back in 2011 – perhaps it's a miracle we survived.

Mission San Diego de Alcalá (p272)

History

Native American nations called this land home for millennia before European arrivals gave it a new name: California. Spanish conquistadors and priests came here for gold and god, but soon relinquished their flea-plagued missions to Mexico. The unruly territory was handed off to the US mere months before gold was discovered in 1848. Generations of dreamers continue to make the trek for gold, glory and self-determination.

13,000–6000 BC	AD 1542–43	1769
Native communities settle this land, from Yurok redwood houses in the north to Kumeyaay thatch-domed dwellings in the south.	Portuguese navigator Juan Rodríguez Cabrillo and his Spanish crew are among the first Europeans to sail California's coast.	Franciscan friar Junípero Serra and Captain Gaspar de Portolá lead an expedition to establish missions.

Mammoth skeleton excavated from La Brea Tar Pits (p207), Los Angeles

ZUMA PRESS, INC. / ALAMY STOCK PHOTO ©

Native Californians

Humans were settling California as early as 19,000 years ago, leaving behind traces of early California cuisine in large middens of seashells along the beaches and campfire sites on the Channel Islands.

Native Californians spoke at least 100 distinct languages, and passed knowledge of hunting grounds and turf boundaries from generation to generation in song. Northern coastal fishing communities such as the Ohlone, Miwok and Pomo built subterranean roundhouses and sweat lodges, where they held ceremonies and told stories. Northern hunting communities, including the Hupa, Karok and Wiyot, constructed big houses and redwood dugout canoes, while the Modoc lived in summer tipis and winter dugouts – but all their paths converged during California's seasonal salmon runs. Kumeyaay and Chumash villages dotted the central coast, where they fished and paddled canoes as far out into the Pacific as the Channel Islands. Southern Mojave, Yuma and Cahuilla nations made sophisticated pottery and developed irrigation systems for farming in the desert.

1781	1821	1835
Spanish governor Felipe de Neve and a tiny band of settlers set down stakes at the future Los Angeles.	Mexican independence ends Spanish colonization of California. Mexico inherits 21 missions.	An emissary of Andrew Jackson offers to buy Alta California, but Mexico tries to unsuccessfully sell it to Britain instead.

Maritime National Historical Park (p52), San Francisco

PACK SHOT / SHUTTERSTOCK ©

★ **Best Historical Sites**

Autry Museum of the American West
(p201), Los Angeles

Mission Santa Barbara (p160),
Santa Barbara

Maritime National Historical Park
(p52), San Francisco

La Brea Tar Pits & Museum (p207),
Los Angeles

When English sea captain Sir Francis Drake harbored briefly on Miwok land north of San Francisco in 1579, the English were taken to be the dead returned from the afterworld, and shamans saw the arrival as a warning of apocalypse. The omens weren't far wrong: within a century of the arrival of Spanish colonists in 1769, California's indigenous population would plunge by between 80 and 90%, falling to just 20,000 due to foreign diseases, conscripted labor, violence, marginalization and hunger in their own fertile lands.

The Spanish Mission Period

In the 18th century, when Russian and English trappers began trading valuable pelts from Alta California, Spain concocted a plan for colonization. For the glory of God and the tax coffers of Spain, missions would be built across California. According to plan, these missions would be going concerns run by local converts within 10 years. This venture was approved by quixotic Spanish colonial official José de Gálvez of Mexico, who was full of grand schemes, including controlling Baja California with a trained army of apes.

Almost immediately after Spain's missionizing plan was approved in 1769, it began to fail. When Franciscan friar Junípero Serra and Captain Gaspar de Portolá made the overland journey to establish Mission San Diego de Alcalá in 1769, only half the sailors on their supply ships survived. Portolá had heard of a fabled cove to the north, but failing to recognize Monterey Bay in the fog, he gave up and turned back.

Portolá reported to Gálvez that if the Russians or English wanted California, they were welcome to it. But Serra wouldn't give up, and secured support to set up presidios (forts) alongside missions. In exchange for their forced labor, Native Californians were promised one meal a day and a place in God's kingdom – which came much sooner than expected, due to diseases such as smallpox and syphilis that the Spanish introduced.

California's indigenous tribes often rebelled against the Spanish colonists, and the missions barely managed to become self-sufficient. Spanish colonists gave up, other foreigners moved in, and more Native Californians died than were converted.

1848	1850	1869
Gold is discovered near Placerville by mill employees, a San Francisco tabloid spreads the news and the gold rush is on.	With hopes of solid-gold tax revenues, the US declares California the 31st state.	On May 10 the 'golden spike' is nailed in place at Promontory, Utah, completing the first transcontinental railroad.

California Under Mexican Rule

Spain wasn't sorry to lose California to Mexico in the 1810–21 Mexican War of Independence – and Californian settlers known as *rancheros* (ranchers) saw an opportunity. The Spanish, Mexican and American ranchers who had intermarried with Native Californians had become a sizable constituency known as 'Californios,' but the best grazing land was still reserved for the missions. So in 1834 Californios convinced Mexico to secularize the missions.

Californios quickly snapped up deeds to privatized mission property, and capitalized on the growing market for cowhides and tallow (a key ingredient in soap). Only a few dozen Californios were literate in the entire state, so boundary disputes that arose were settled with muscle, not paper. By law, half the lands were supposed to go to Native Californians who worked at the missions, but few actually received their entitlements.

Through marriage and other mergers, most of the land and wealth in California was held by just 46 *ranchero* families by 1846. The average *rancho* (ranch) was now 16,000 acres, having grown from cramped shanties to elegant haciendas where women were ordered to stay confined to quarters at night. But *rancheras* (ranch women) weren't so easily bossed around: women owned some Californian ranches, rode horses as hard as men and caused romantic scandals worthy of modern *telenovelas* (soap operas).

Still, the US saw potential in California. When US president Andrew Jackson offered the financially strapped Mexican government $500,000 for the territory in 1835, the offer was tersely rejected. The Mexican–American War was declared in 1846, lasting two years with very little fighting in California. Hostilities ended with the Treaty of Guadalupe Hidalgo, in which Mexico ceded much of its northern territory (including Alta California) to the US. Just a few weeks after the US took possession of California, gold was discovered.

Fierce Queen Calafía, California's Namesake

Have you heard the one about the sunny island of Amazon women armed with gold weapons, who flew griffins fed with their own sons? This isn't a twisted *Wonder Woman* remake. It's the plot of Garci Rodríguez de Montalvo's 16th-century novel *Las Sergas de Esplandían* – the legend that inspired explorer Hernán Cortés, who claimed in a 1524 letter that he hoped to find the island northwest of Mexico.

Montalvo and Cortés weren't entirely wrong. Across the water from mainland Mexico was a peninsula Spanish colonists called Baja (Lower) California after Queen Calafía, Montalvo's legendary queen of the Amazons. Above it was Alta (Upper) California, where gold was discovered 50 years after the Spaniards gave up their search.

1882	1906	1928
The US Chinese Exclusion Act suspends new immigration from China and denies citizenship to those already in the country.	An earthquake levels entire blocks of San Francisco in 42 seconds, setting off fires that rage for three days.	*The Jazz Singer* premieres – as the first feature-length 'talkie' movie, it kicks off Hollywood's Golden Age.

The Gold Rush

The gold rush era in California began with a bluff. Real-estate speculator, lapsed Mormon and wily tabloid publisher Sam Brannan was looking to unload some California swampland in 1848 when he heard rumors of gold flakes found near Sutter's Mill in the Sierra Nevada foothills. Figuring this news should sell some newspapers and raise real-estate values, Brannan published the rumor as fact.

At first Brannan's story didn't generate much excitement – gold flake had surfaced in southern California as far back as 1775. So he ran another story, this time verified by Mormon employees at Sutter's Mill who had sworn him to secrecy. Brannan kept his word until he reached San Francisco, where he legendarily ran through Portsmouth Sq brandishing gold entrusted to him as tithes for the Mormon church, shouting, 'Gold on the American River!'

Other newspapers around the world weren't scrupulous about the facts either, hastily publishing stories of gold near San Francisco. By 1850 – the year California was fast-tracked for admission as the 31st US state – California's non-native population had ballooned from 15,000 to 93,000.

With each wave of new arrivals, profits dropped and gold became harder to find. In 1848 each prospector earned an average of about $300,000 in today's terms. By 1849 earnings were less than half that, and by 1865 they had dipped to $35,000. When surface gold became scarce, miners picked, shoveled and dynamited through mountains. The work was grueling and dangerous and, with few doctors around, injuries often proved lethal. The cost of living in cold, filthy mining camps was sky-high – and with only one woman for every 400 men in some camps, many turned to paid company, booze and opium for consolation.

Vigilantes, Robber Barons & Railroads

Gold prospectors who did best arrived early and got out quick, while those who stayed too long either lost fortunes searching for the next nugget or became targets of resentment. Native Californian laborers who helped miners strike it rich were denied the right to hold claims. Successful Peruvians and Chileans were harassed and denied renewals to their mining claims, and most left California by 1855. The 'Chilecito' neighborhood they established in San Francisco is now called Jackson Sq, but you can still order the drink these early settlers brought to San Francisco circa 1848: Pisco punch.

As mining became industrialized, fewer miners were needed, and jobless prospectors turned anger toward a convenient target: Chinese workers. Frozen out of mining claims, many Chinese opened service-based businesses that survived when mining ventures went bust. By 1860 enough Chinese pioneers had endured to become the second-most populous group in California after Mexicans, but this hard-won resilience met with irrational resentment. Discriminatory Californian laws restricting housing, employment and citizenship for anyone born in China were passed and extended with the 1882 US Chinese Exclusion Act, which remained law until 1943.

1942	1955	1965
Executive Order 9066 sends nearly 120,000 Japanese Americans to internment camps.	Disneyland opens in Anaheim on July 17. As crowds swarm the park, plumbing breaks and Fantasyland springs a gas leak.	The National Guard suppresses the Watts civil unrest in LA. Six days of clashes result in death, devastation and $40 million in damage.

Inter-ethnic rivalries obscured the real competitive threat posed not by fellow workers, but by those who controlled the means of production: California's 'robber barons.' These Californian speculators hoarded the capital and industrial machinery necessary for deep-mining operations. Laws limiting work options for Chinese arrivals served the needs of robber barons, who needed cheap labor to build railroads to their mining claims and reach East Coast markets.

To blast tunnels through the Sierra Nevada, workers were lowered down sheer mountain faces in wicker baskets, planted lit dynamite sticks in rock crevices then urgently tugged the rope to be hoisted out of harm's way. With little other choice of legitimate employment, an estimated 12,000 Chinese laborers blasted through the Sierra Nevada, meeting the westbound end of the transcontinental railroad in 1869.

The Bear Flag Republic

In June 1846, American settlers tanked up on liquid courage declared independence in the northern town of Sonoma. Not a shot was fired – instead, they captured the nearest Mexican official and hoisted a hastily made flag. Locals awoke to discover they were living in the independent 'Bear Republic,' under a flag painted with a grizzly that looked like a drunken dog. The Bear Flag Republic lasted only a month before US orders telling settlers to stand down arrived.

Oil & Water

During the US Civil War (1861–65), California couldn't count on food shipments from the East Coast, and started growing its own. California recruited Midwestern homesteaders to farm the Central Valley with shameless propaganda. The hype worked: more than 120,000 homesteaders came to California in the 1870s and '80s.

These homesteaders soon discovered that California's gold rush had left the state badly tarnished. Hills were stripped bare, vegetation wiped out, streams silted up and mercury washed into water supplies. Cholera spread through open sewers of poorly drained camps, claiming many lives. Smaller mineral finds in Southern California mountains diverted streams, turning the green valleys below into deserts. Recognizing at last that water, not gold, was the state's most precious resource, Californians passed a pioneering law preventing dumping into rivers in 1884.

With the support of budding agribusiness and real-estate concerns, Southern Californians passed bond measures to build aqueducts and dams that made large-scale farming and real-estate development possible. By the 20th century, the lower one-third of the state claimed two-thirds of available water supplies, inspiring Northern California's calls for secession.

While pastoral Southern California was urbanizing, Northern Californians who had witnessed mining and logging devastation firsthand were jump-starting the nation's first

1966
Ronald Reagan is elected governor of California, setting a career precedent for fading entertainment figures.

1967
The Summer of Love kicks off in Golden Gate Park, where draft cards are used as rolling papers.

1968
Presidential candidate and civil-rights ally Robert Kennedy is fatally shot in Los Angeles.

★ **Best for California History**

Slouching Towards Bethlehem (Joan Didion; 1968)

Alice: Memoirs of a Barbary Coast Prostitute (Ivy Anderson and Devon Angus; 2016)

California: A History (Kevin Starr; 1980)

City Lights Books (p57), San Francisco

conservation movement. Scottish immigrant John Muir moved to San Francisco to make his living, but found his true calling as a naturalist on a week-long trip to the Yosemite Valley. Muir founded the Sierra Club in 1892 and devoted his life to defending Yosemite and vast tracts of California's wilderness against the encroachments of dams and pipelines to urban centers.

Reforming the Wild West

When a massive earthquake struck San Francisco in 1906, it unearthed a terrible truth. The earthquake sparked fires across town, but there was no water to put them out. In a city surrounded by water on three sides, there were only two functioning water mains: a fountain donated by opera star Lotta Crabtree at Market and Kearny Sts, and a Mission hydrant atop Dolores Park (still painted gold today, in honor of its service). For three days, fires swept across the city. When the smoke lifted, one thing was clear from this unnatural disaster: it was time for the Wild West to change its ways.

While San Francisco was rebuilt at a rate of 15 buildings a day, political reformers set to work on city, state and national policies, one plank at a time. Californians concerned about public health and the trafficking of women pushed for the passage of the 1914 Red Light Abatement Act, which shut down brothels statewide.

California's Civil Rights Movement

Before the 1963 march on Washington, DC, the civil rights movement was well under way in California. When almost 120,000 Japanese Americans living along the West Coast were ordered into internment camps by President Roosevelt in 1942, the Japanese American Citizens League immediately filed suits that advanced all the way to the US Supreme Court. These lawsuits established groundbreaking civil rights legal precedents, and in 1992 internees received reparations and an official letter of apology signed by President George HW Bush.

1969	1977	1989
Native American activists symbolically reclaim Alcatraz until ousted by the FBI in 1971.	San Francisco Supervisor Harvey Milk becomes the first openly gay man elected to public office in California.	The Loma Prieta Earthquake collapses a two-level section of Interstate 880 and results in 63 deaths and 4000 injuries.

Adopting the nonviolent resistance practices of Mahatma Gandhi and Martin Luther King Jr, labor leaders César Chávez and Dolores Huerta formed United Farm Workers in 1962 to champion the rights of immigrant laborers. Four years later Chávez and Californian grape pickers marched on Sacramento, bringing the issue of fair wages and the health risks of pesticides to the nation's attention. When Bobby Kennedy was sent to investigate, he sided with Chávez, bringing Latinos into the US political fold.

California was again on the front lines during the fight for marriage equality. In open defiance of the 1996 US Defense of Marriage Act (DOMA) that defined marriage as between opposite-sex partners, San Francisco mayor Gavin Newsom began issuing marriage certificates to same-sex couples in 2004. The issue went to the courts, which found DOMA in conflict with California's constitution. Opponents of marriage equality rallied around Proposition 8, a ballot measure that proposed to change California's constitution to invalidate same-sex marriage. Proposition 8 passed by a narrow margin, but was found unconstitutional in 2008 and on appeal in 2013. With this key legal precedent established, the US Supreme Court declared DOMA unconstitutional the same day, and marriage equality was established nationwide.

Today civil rights remains top of mind in California, where new Americans represent over half the population, including 26.9% foreign-born immigrants, and 30.7% naturalized citizens or US-born children of immigrants. A dozen California cities have passed sanctuary statutes, including Berkeley's pioneering 1971 sanctuary resolution and San Francisco's 1989 citywide sanctuary law. These laws protect local police stations, schools and hospitals from having to detain undocumented people not charged with any crime for deportation by federal authorities. Under threat of the removal of federal funds by the Trump administration in 2017, San Francisco and Berkeley reaffirmed their sanctuary policies, and California legislators are considering measures that would extend sanctuary statewide.

Hollywood & California Counterculture

By the 1920s California's greatest export was the sunny, wholesome image it projected to the world through its homegrown film and TV industry. With consistent sunlight and versatile locations, Southern California proved to be an ideal movie location. Early in its career, SoCal was a stand-in for more exotic locales, and got dressed up for period-piece productions such as Charlie Chaplin's *Gold Rush* (1925). But with its beach sunsets and palm-lined drives, California soon stole the scene in Technicolor movies and iconic TV shows. California shed its bad-boy Wild West reputation to become a movie star, dominating the screen behind squeaky-clean beach boys and bikini-clad blondes.

But Northern Californians didn't picture themselves as extras in *Beach Blanket Bingo* (1965). The Navy discharged WWII sailors for insubordination and homosexuality in San Francisco, as though that would teach them a lesson. Instead they found themselves at home in North Beach's jazz clubs, bohemian coffeehouses and City Lights Bookstore.

1992	1994	2003
Four white police officers charged with assaulting Rodney King are acquitted, sparking violent clashes with police in Los Angeles.	The 6.7-magnitude Northridge earthquake strikes LA on January 17, killing 72 and causing $20 billion in property damage.	Republican Arnold Schwarzenegger is elected governor of California.

The final button of convention was popped not by San Francisco artists, but by the CIA. To test psychoactive drugs intended to create the ultimate soldier, the CIA gave LSD to writer Ken Kesey. He saw the potential not for war but for a wild party, and spiked the punch at the 1966 Trips Festival organized by Stewart Brand. The psychedelic era hit an all-time high at the January 14, 1967 Human Be-In in Golden Gate Park, where trip-master Timothy Leary urged a crowd of 20,000 hippies to dream a new American dream and 'turn on, tune in, drop out.'

Northern California had the more attention-grabbing counterculture from the 1940s to '60s, but nonconformity in sunny SoCal shook the country to the core. In 1947, when Senator Joseph McCarthy attempted to root out suspected communists in the film industry, 10 writers and directors refused to admit to communist alliances or to name names. The 'Hollywood Ten' were charged with contempt of Congress and barred from working in Hollywood, but their impassioned defenses of the US Constitution were heard nationwide. Major Hollywood players boldly voiced dissent and hired blacklisted talent until lawsuits finally curbed McCarthyism in the late 1950s.

Geeking Out

When Silicon Valley introduced the first personal computer in 1968, advertisements breathlessly gushed that Hewlett-Packard's new 'light' (40lb) machine could 'take on roots of a fifth-degree polynomial, Bessel functions, elliptic integrals and regression analysis' – all for just $4900 (over $33,000 today). Consumers didn't know quite what to do with such computers, but Trips Festival organizer Stewart Brand had a totally psychedelic idea: what if all that technology could fit into the palm of your hand? Maybe then, the technology governments used to run countries could empower ordinary people.

By the mid-1990s an entire dot-com start-up industry boomed in Silicon Valley, and suddenly people were getting everything – mail, news, pet food and, yes, sex – online. But when dot-com profits weren't forthcoming, venture-capital funding evaporated. Fortunes in stock options disappeared when the Nasdaq plummeted on March 10, 2000, popping the dot-com bubble. Overnight, 26-year-old vice-presidents and Bay Area service-sector employees alike found themselves jobless.

In the years since, California's biotech industry has been quietly booming. An upstart company called Genentech was founded in a San Francisco bar in 1976, and quickly got to work cloning human insulin and introducing the Hepatitis B vaccine. In 2004 California voters approved a $3-billion bond measure for stem-cell research, and by 2008 California had become the USA's biggest funder of stem-cell research, as well as the focus of Nasdaq's new Biotechnology Index. With cloud computing to store and access data, machine learning is now able to make rapid advancements in medical imaging and diagnostics.

So will machines save us all, or surpass us? Dude, that sounds like a good subject for a Hollywood movie – or at least a far-out conversation in a California marijuana dispensary (legal as of 2017, in case you're wondering). No matter what happens next, you can say you saw it coming in California.

2005	**2007**	**2017**
Antonio Villaraigosa is elected mayor of LA, becoming the first Latino to hold that office since 1872.	Wildfires sweep drought-stricken Southern California, forcing one million people to evacuate their homes.	Threatened with defunding from the federal government, over a dozen California cities reinforce their sanctuary statutes.

Surfer, Venice Beach (p219), Los Angeles

BRITTANYNY / SHUTTERSTOCK ©

The Way of Life

In a California dreamworld, you wake up with an espresso and a side of wheatgrass and roll down to the beach while the surf's up. You skateboard down the boardwalk to your yoga class, where everyone admires your downward dog. A food truck pulls up serving sustainable fish tacos topped with organic mango chipotle salsa...and then you wake up.

Living the Dream

What's that you say? You're not ready for this dream to end? OK, let's hit the snooze button and see how far this California dream takes you.

Snoozing on the beach after yoga class, you awake to find a casting agent hovering over you, blocking your sunlight, imploring you to star in a movie based on a best-selling graphic novel. You say you'll have your lawyer look over the papers, and by your lawyer you mean your roommate who plays one on TV. The conversation is cut short when you get a text to meet up with some friends at a bar.

That casting agent was a stress case – she was, like, all business, dude – so you swing by your medical marijuana dispensary and a tattoo parlor to get 'Peace' inscribed on your bicep in Tibetan script as a reminder to yourself to stay chill. At the bar you're called onstage to guest DJ, and afterwards you tell the bartender how the casting agent harshed your mellow. She recommends a wine country getaway, but you're already doing that Big Sur primal scream chakra-cleansing retreat this weekend. Maybe next time.

You head back to your beach house to update your status on your social-networking profile, alerting your one million online friends to the major events of the day: 'Killer taco, solid downward dog, major tattoo, random movie offer thingy, sick beats.' Then you repeat your nightly self-affirmations: 'I am a child of the universe...I am blessed, or at least not a New Yorker...tomorrow will bring sunshine and possibility...om.'

Regional Identity

Now for the reality check. Any Northern Californian hearing your California dream is bound to get huffy. What, political protests and Silicon Valley start-ups don't factor in your dreams? But Southern Californians will also roll their eyes at these stereotypes: they didn't create NASA's Jet Propulsion Lab and almost half of the world's movies by slacking off.

But there is some truth to your California dreamscape. Some 80% of Californians live near the coast rather than inland, even though California beaches aren't always sunny or swimmable. Self-help, fitness and body modification are major industries throughout California, successfully marketed since the 1970s as 'lite' versions of religious experience – all the agony and ecstasy of the major religions, without all those heavy commandments. Exercise and healthy food help keep Californians among the fittest in the nation.

At least Northern and Southern Californians do have one thing in common: they're all baffled by New Yorkers' delusion that the world revolves around them. Whatever, dudes. We'll just be over here on the Best Coast, building your technology, growing your food and providing your entertainment. No need to thank us, really.

Lifestyle

The charmed existence you dreamed about is a stretch, even in California. Few Californians can afford to spend entire days tanning and networking, what with all the aging UVA rays and sky-high rents out here. Eight of the 10 most expensive US housing markets are in California, and in the two most expensive areas, Newport Beach and Palo Alto, the average house price is over $2.5 million. Only multi-millionaires can afford a beach dream-home here. With a modest median household income of $64,500 per year, most Californians rent rather than own their own home.

As for those roommates you dreamed about: if you're a Californian aged 18 to 24, there's a 50-50 possibility that your roomies are your parents. Among adult Californians, one in four live alone, and about half are unmarried. If you're not impressed with your dating options in California, stick around: of those who are currently married, about a third won't be in 10 years. Increasingly Californians are shacking up together: the number of unmarried cohabiting couples has increased 40% since 1990.

If you're like most Californians, you effectively live in your car. Californians commute an average of 29 minutes each way to work and spend at least $1 out of every $5 earned on car-related expenses. Small wonder that six of the US cities with the highest air-pollution levels are in California. But Californians are zooming ahead of the national energy-use curve in their smog-checked cars, buying more hybrid and fuel-efficient cars than any other state. With all these statewide efforts to spare the air, two of the 25 US cities with the cleanest air are now in California (kudos, Redding and Salinas!).

Almost half of all Californians reside in cities, but most of the other half live in the suburbs, where the cost of living is just as high – only without all the cultural perks of city living. The Silicon Valley hub of San Jose has been ranked the most overpriced city in America, yet other Californian cities (especially San Francisco and San Diego) consistently top national quality-of-life indexes, with a sunny outlook dubbed the 'Golden State of Mind.' According to a recent Cambridge University study, creativity, imagination, intellectualism and mellowness are all defining characteristics of Californians, compared with inhabitants of other US states.

Californian Languages

More than 200 different languages are spoken in California, with Spanish, Chinese, Tagalog, Russian, Hindi and Arabic in the top 10. Around 44% of state residents speak a language other than English at home.

Homelessness is not part of the California dream, but it's a reality for at least 115,000 Californians, representing more than 20% of the total US homeless population. Some are teens who have run away or been kicked out by their families, but the largest contingent of homeless are US military veterans – 25% of the nation's homeless vets are in California. What's more, in the 1970s mental-health programs were cut, and state-funded drug treatment programs were dropped in the 1980s, leaving many Californians with mental illnesses and substance-abuse problems no place to go.

Also standing in line at homeless shelters are the working poor, unable to afford to rent even a small apartment on minimum-wage salaries. Recent California minimum-wage increases still don't cover the cost of living here – you'd need to earn $33 an hour to pay the average rent in Los Angeles. Rather than addressing the underlying causes of homelessness, some California cities have criminalized loitering, panhandling and even sitting on sidewalks. More than three out of every 1000 Californians already sit in the state's notoriously overcrowded jails, mostly for minor drug-related offenses.

Population & Religion

With more than 39 million residents, California has more people than any other state. One in every eight Americans lives here. It's also one of the fastest-growing states, with three of America's 10 biggest cities (Los Angeles, San Diego and San Jose) and more than 300,000 newcomers each year. Although the high Sierras and southern deserts are sparsely populated, California's overall population density is 251 people per square mile – almost triple the national average.

If you were the average Californian, you'd be statistically likely to be Latina, aged about 36 and living in densely populated LA, Orange or San Diego Counties. You'd speak more than one language, and there's a one-in-four chance you were born outside the US. If you were born in the US, the odds are 50-50 you moved here recently from another state.

California is one of the most religiously diverse US states, but also one of the least religious. Less than half of Californians consider religion very important, and a quarter of all Californians profess no religion at all. Of those Californians who do practice a religion, a third identify as Protestant and about a quarter are Catholic. California is home to most of the nation's practicing Hindus, the biggest Jewish community outside New York, a sizable Muslim community and the largest number of Buddhists anywhere outside Asia. Californians have also established their own spiritual practices, including the Church of Satan, EST self-help movement and UFO cults.

Hollywood movie set, Universal Studios, Los Angeles

On Location: Film & TV

Pitcure Orson Welles whispering 'Rosebud,' Judy Garland clicking her ruby-red heels, or the Terminator threatening 'I'll be back': California is where iconic film images come to life. Shakespeare claimed 'all the world's a stage,' but in California, it's actually more of a movie set. With over 40 TV shows and scores of movies shot here annually, every palm-lined boulevard or beach seems to come with its own IMDB.com resume.

The Industry

You might know it as the TV and movie business, but to Southern Californians it's simply 'the Industry.' It all began in the humble orchards of Hollywoodland, a residential suburb of Los Angeles where entrepreneurial moviemakers established studios in the early 20th century. Within a few years, immigrants turned a humble orchard into Hollywood. In 1915 Polish immigrant Samuel Goldwyn joined with Cecil B DeMille to form Paramount Studios, while German-born Carl Laemmle opened nearby Universal Studios, selling lunch to curious guests to help underwrite his moving pictures. A few years later, a family of Polish immigrants arrived from Canada, and Jack Warner and his brothers soon set up a movie studio of their own.

With perpetually balmy weather and more than 315 days of sunshine a year, SoCal proved an ideal shooting location, and moviemaking flourished. In those early Wild West movie-making days, patent holders such as Thomas Edison sent agents to collect payments, or repossess movie equipment. Fledgling filmmakers saw them coming, and made runs for the Mexican border with their equipment. Palm Springs became a favorite weekend hideaway for Hollywood stars, partly because its distance from LA (just under 100 miles) was as far as they could travel under restrictive studio contracts.

Seemingly overnight, Hollywood studios made movie magic. Fans lined up for premieres in LA movie palaces for red-carpet glimpses of early silent-film stars such as Charlie Chaplin and Harold Lloyd. Moviegoers nationwide celebrated the first big Hollywood wedding in 1920, when swashbuckler Douglas Fairbanks married 'America's sweetheart' Mary Pickford. Years later, their divorce would be one of Hollywood's biggest scandals, but the United Artists studio they founded with Charlie Chaplin endures today. When the silent-movie era gave way to 'talkies' with the 1927 musical *The Jazz Singer*, the world hummed along.

The Art of Animation

In 1923 a young cartoonist named Walt Disney arrived in LA, and within five years he had a hit called *Steamboat Willie* and a breakout star called Mickey Mouse. That film spawned the entire Disney empire, and dozens of other California animation studios have followed with films and TV programs. Among the most beloved are Warner Bros (Bugs Bunny et al in *Looney Tunes*), Hanna-Barbera (*The Flintstones, The Jetsons, Yogi Bear* and *Scooby-Doo*), DreamWorks (*Shrek, Madagascar, Kung-Fu Panda*), Pixar Animation Studios (*Toy Story, Finding Dory, Inside Out*) and Film Roman (*The Simpsons*). Even if much of the hands-on work takes place overseas (in places such as South Korea), concept and supervision still takes place in LA and the San Francisco Bay Area.

Hollywood & Beyond

By the 1920s Hollywood became the Industry's social and financial hub, but it's a myth that most movie production took place there. Of the major studios, only Paramount Pictures is in Hollywood proper, surrounded by block after block of production-related businesses, such as lighting and post-production. Most movies have long been shot elsewhere around LA, in Culver City (at MGM, now Sony Pictures), Studio City (at Universal Studios) and Burbank (at Warner Bros and later Disney).

Moviemaking hasn't been limited to LA either. Founded in 1910, the American Film Manufacturing Company (aka Flying 'A' Studios) churned out box-office hits in San Diego and then Santa Barbara. Balboa Studios in Long Beach was another major silent-era dream factory. Contemporary movie production companies based in the San Francisco Bay Area include Francis Ford Coppola's American Zoetrope, Pixar animation studios and George Lucas' Industrial Light & Magic. Both San Francisco and LA remain major hubs for independent filmmakers and documentarians.

But not every Californian you meet is in the Industry, even in Tinseltown. The high cost of filming has sent location scouts far beyond LA's San Fernando Valley (where most of California's movie and TV studios are found) to Vancouver, Toronto and Montreal, where film production crews are welcomed with open arms (and sweet deals) to 'Hollywood North.' California recently passed a $330 tax credit to lure filmmakers back to Cali, and it seems to be working – more 2016 TV pilots were shot in here than in any other location.

Paramount Pictures (p199), Los Angeles

★ **Top California Film Festivals**

AFI Fest (www.afi.com/afifest)

LA Film Fest (www.lafilmfest.com)

Palm Springs Film Fest (www.psfilmfest.org)

San Francisco Film Fest (www.sffs.org)

Frameline LGBT (www.frameline.org)

Still, for Hollywood dreamers and movie buffs, LA remains *the* place for a pilgrimage. You can tour major movie studios, be part of a live TV studio audience, line up alongside the red carpet for an awards ceremony, catch movie premieres at film festivals, wander the Hollywood Walk of Fame and discover what it's like to live, dine and party with the stars.

California on Celluloid

California is a sneaky scene-stealer in many Hollywood films, stepping out of the background to become a main topic and character in its own right. From sunny capers to moody film-noir mysteries, California has proved its versatility in movie classics ranging from *The Maltese Falcon* (1941) to *Blade Runner* (1982) to *The Big Lebowski* (1998).

The Small Screen

After a year of tinkering, San Francisco inventor Philo Farnsworth transmitted the first television broadcast in 1927 of...a straight line. Giving viewers something actually interesting to watch would take a few more years. The first TV station began broadcasting in Los Angeles in 1931, beaming iconic images of California into living rooms across America and around the world with *Dragnet* (1950s), *The Beverly Hillbillies* (1960s), *The Brady Bunch* and *Charlie's Angels* (1970s), *LA Law* (1980s), and *Baywatch, Buffy the Vampire Slayer* and *The Fresh Prince of Bel-Air* (1990s). *Beverly Hills 90210* (1990s) made that LA zip code into a status symbol, while *The OC* (2000s) glamorized Orange County and *Silicon Valley* (2014–now) satirizes NorCal start-ups. Reality-TV fans will recognize Southern California locations from *Top Chef*, *Real Housewives of Orange County* and *Keeping Up with the Kardashians*.

A suburban San Francisco start-up changed the TV game in 2005, launching a streaming video on a platform called YouTube. With on-demand streaming services competing with cable channels to launch original series, we have entered a new golden age of California television. Netflix Studios (in Silicon Valley and LA), Amazon Studios (Santa Monica) and Hulu Studios (Santa Monica) are churning out original series, satisfying binge-watching cravings with futuristic dystopias such as *Stranger Things, Man in the High Castle* and *The Handmaid's Tale*. Only time will tell if streaming services will also yield breakthrough Californian comedies to compare with Showtime's sharp-witted suburban pot-growing dramedy *Weeds*, Showtime's *Californication* adventures of a successful New York novelist gone Hollywood, or HBO's *Curb Your Enthusiasm,* an insider satire of the industry featuring *Seinfeld* co-creator Larry David and Hollywood celebrities playing themselves.

Broad (p204), Los Angeles

Music & the Arts

Go ahead and mock, but when Californians thank their lucky stars – or good karma, or the goddess – they don't live in New York, they're not just talking about beach weather. This place has long supported thriving music and arts scenes that aren't afraid to be completely independent, even outlandish. In the US' most racially and ethnically diverse state, expect eclectic playlists, involving performances and vivid shows of pride and individuality.

Music

In your California dream, you're a DJ – so what kind of music do you play? Beach Boys covers, West Coast rap, bluegrass, original punk, classic soul, hard bop, heavy-metal riffs on opera? To please Californian crowds, try all of the above. To hear the world's most eclectic playlist, just walk down a city street in California.

Much of the traditional recording industry is based in LA, and SoCal's film and TV industries have produced many pop princesses and airbrushed boy bands. But NorCal DIY tech approach is launching YouTube artists daily, and encouraging Californians to make strange sounds in their garages with Moog machines and keytars. None of this would be possible without California's decades of innovation, musical oddities and wild dance parties.

Swing, Jazz, Blues & Soul

As California's African American community grew with the 'Great Migration' during the WWII shipping and manufacturing boom, the West Coast blues sound was born. Texas-born bluesman T-Bone Walker worked in LA's Central Ave clubs before making hit records of his electric guitar stylings for Capitol Records. Throughout the 1940s and '50s, West Coast blues were nurtured in San Francisco and Oakland by guitarists such as Pee Wee Crayton and Oklahoma-born Lowell Fulson.

With Beat poets riffing over improvised bass lines and audiences finger-snapping their approval, the cool West Coast jazz of Chet Baker and Bay Area–born Dave Brubeck emerged from San Francisco's North Beach neighborhood in the 1950s. Meanwhile, in the African American cultural hub along LA's Central Ave, the hard bop of Charlie Parker and Charles Mingus kept SoCal's jazz scene alive and swinging.

In the 1950s and '60s, doo-wop, rhythm and blues, and soul music were all in steady rotation at nightclubs in South Central LA, considered the 'Harlem of the West.' Soulful singer Sam Cooke ran his own hit-making record label, attracting soul and gospel talent to LA.

Rockin' Out

The first homegrown rock-and-roll talent to make it big in the 1950s was San Fernando Valley–born Richie Valens, whose 'La Bamba' was a rockified version of a Mexican folk song. Dick Dale experimented with reverb effects in Orange County in the 1950s, becoming known as 'the King of the Surf Guitar.' He topped the charts with his band the Del-Tones in the early '60s, influencing everyone from the Beach Boys to Jimi Hendrix – you might recognize his recording of 'Miserlou' from the movie *Pulp Fiction*.

Guitar got psychedelic in 1960s California. When Joan Baez and Bob Dylan had their Northern California fling in the early 1960s, Dylan plugged in his guitar and pioneered folk rock. Janis Joplin and Big Brother & the Holding Company developed their own shambling musical stylings in San Francisco, splintering folk rock into psychedelia. Emerging from the same San Francisco Fillmore scene, Jefferson Airplane turned Lewis Carroll's children's classic *Alice's Adventures in Wonderland* into the psychedelic hit 'White Rabbit.' For many 1960s Fillmore headliners, the show ended too soon with drug overdoses – though for the original jam band, the Grateful Dead, the song remained the same until guitarist Jerry Garcia died in rehab in 1995.

On LA's famous Sunset Strip, LA bands were also blowing minds at the legendary Whisky a Go-Go nightclub – especially the Byrds and the Doors. But the California sound also got down and funky with iconic funk bands War from Long Beach, Tower of Power from Oakland, and San Francisco's Sly and the Family Stone.

Post-Punk to Pop

The 1980s saw the rise of such influential LA crossover bands as Bad Religion (punk) and Suicidal Tendencies (hardcore/thrash), while more mainstream all-female bands the Bangles and the Go-Gos, new wavers Oingo Boingo, and California rockers Jane's Addiction and Red Hot Chili Peppers took the world by storm. Hollywood's Guns N' Roses set the '80s standard for arena rock, while San Francisco's Metallica showed the world how to head bang with a vengeance. Avant-garde rocker Frank Zappa earned a cult following and a rare hit with the 1982 single 'Valley Girl', in which his 14-year-old daughter Moon Unit taught the rest of America to say 'Omigo-o-od!' like an LA teenager.

By the 1990s California's alternative rock acts took the national stage, including songwriter Beck, political rockers Rage Against the Machine and Orange County's ska-rockers No Doubt, fronted by Gwen Stefani. Hailing from East LA, Los Lobos was king of the Chicano (Mexican American) bands, an honor that has since passed to Ozomatli.

Berkeley's 924 Gilman Street club revived punk in the 1990s, launching the career of Grammy Award–winning Green Day. Riding the wave were Berkley ska-punk band Rancid, surf-punk Sublime from Long Beach, San Diego–based pop-punksters Blink 182, and Orange County's resident loudmouths, the Offspring.

Rap & Hip-Hop

Since the 1980s, West Coast rap and hip-hop have spoken truth and hit the beat. When the NWA album *Straight Outta Compton* was released in 1989, it launched the careers of Eazy E, Ice Cube and Dr Dre, and established gangsta rap. Dre cofounded Death Row Records, which helped launched megawatt talents such as Long Beach bad boys Snoop Dogg, Warren G and the late Tupac Shakur. The son of a Black Panther leader who'd fallen on hard times, Tupac combined party songs and hard truths learned on Oakland streets until his untimely shooting in 1996 in a suspected East Coast/West Coast rap feud. Feuds also checkered the musical career of LA rapper Game, whose 2009 *R.E.D Album* brought together an all-star lineup of Diddy, Dr Dre, Snoop Dogg and more.

Punk's Not Dead in California

In the 1970s American airwaves were jammed with commercial arena rock that record companies paid DJs to shill like laundry soap. California teens bored with prepackaged anthems started making their own with secondhand guitars, three chords and crappy amps that added a loud buzz to unleashed fury.

LA punk paralleled the scrappy local skate scene with the hardcore grind of Black Flag from Hermosa Beach and LA's the Germs. LA band X bridged punk and new wave from 1977 to 1987 with John Doe's rockabilly guitar, Exene Cervenka's angsty wail, and disappointed-romantic lyrics inspired by Charles Bukowski and Raymond Chandler.

San Francisco's punk scene was arty and absurdist, in rare form with Dead Kennedys singer (and future San Francisco mayoral candidate) Jello Biafra mocking Golden State complacency in 'California Uber Alles.'

Throughout the 1980s and '90s, California maintained a grassroots hip-hop scene in Oakland and LA. Reacting against the increasing commercialization of hip-hop in the late 1990s, the Bay Area scene produced underground 'hyphy' (short for hyperactive) artists such as E-40. Political commentary and funk hooks have become signatures of East Bay groups Blackalicious, the Coup and Michael Franti & Spearhead.

Architecture

There's more to California than beach houses and boardwalks. Californians have adapted imported styles to the climate and available materials, building cool, adobe-inspired houses in San Diego and fog-resistant redwood-shingle houses in Mendocino. After a century and a half of Californians grafting on inspired influences and eccentric details as the mood strikes them, the element of the unexpected is everywhere: tiled Maya deco facades in Oakland, Shinto-inspired archways in LA, English thatched roofs in Carmel and Chinoiserie streetlamps in San Francisco. California's architecture was postmodern before the word even existed.

Spanish Missions & Victorian Queens

The first Spanish missions were built around courtyards, using materials that Native Californians and Spaniards found on hand: adobe, limestone and grass. Many missions crumbled into disrepair as the church's influence waned, but the style remained practical

Interior, Sunnylands Estate (p188), Palm Springs

TODD EBERLE / GETTY IMAGES ©

★ **Architectural Icons**

Golden Gate Bridge (p38), SF

Getty Center (p208), LA

Sunnylands Estate (p188), Palm Springs

California Academy of Sciences (p59), SF

Bixby Bridge (p148), Big Sur

for the climate. Early California settlers later adapted it into the rancho adobe style, as seen in Downtown LA's El Pueblo de Los Angeles and San Diego's Old Town.

Once the mid-19th-century gold rush was on, California's nouveau riche imported materials to construct grand mansions matching European fashions. Many millionaires favored the gilded Queen Anne style, raising the stakes with ornamental excess. Outrageous examples of colorful, gingerbread-swagged Victorian 'Painted Ladies' can be found in San Francisco, Ferndale and Eureka.

But Californian architecture has always had its contrarian streak. Many turn-of-the-20th-century architects rejected frilly Victorian styles in favor of the simpler, classical lines of Spanish designs. Spanish Colonial Revival architecture (also known as Mission Revival style) recalls early California missions with their restrained functional details: arched doors and windows, long covered porches, fountain courtyards, solid walls and red-tile roofs. Downtown Santa Barbara showcases this revival style, as do stately buildings in San Diego's Balboa Park, Scotty's Castle in Death Valley and several SoCal train depots, including those in Downtown LA, San Diego and Santa Barbara.

Arts & Crafts to Art Deco

Simplicity and harmony were hallmarks of California's early 20th-century Arts and Crafts style. Influenced by both Japanese design principles and England's Arts and Crafts movement, its woodwork and handmade touches marked a deliberate departure from the industrial revolution's mechanization. Bernard Maybeck and Julia Morgan in Northern California, and SoCal architects Charles and Henry Greene, popularized the versatile one-story bungalow. Today you'll spot them in Berkeley and Pasadena with their overhanging eaves, airy terraces and sleeping porches harmonizing warm, livable interiors with the natural environment outdoors.

California was cosmopolitan from the start, and couldn't be limited to any one set of international influences. In the 1920s, the international art deco style took elements from the ancient world – Mayan glyphs, Egyptian pillars, Babylonian ziggurats – and flattened them into modern motifs to cap stark facades and outline streamlined skyscrapers in Oakland, San Francisco and LA. Streamline moderne kept decoration to a minimum, and mimicked the aerodynamic look of ocean liners and airplanes.

Post-Modern Evolutions

True to its mythic nature, California couldn't help wanting to embellish the facts a little, veering away from strict high modernism to add unlikely postmodern shapes to the local landscape.

In 1997 Richard Meier made his mark on West LA with the Getty Center, a cresting white wave of a building on a sunburned hilltop. Canadian-born Frank Gehry relocated to Santa

Monica, and his billowing, sculptural style for LA's Walt Disney Concert Hall winks cheekily at shipshape streamline moderne. Also in Downtown LA, the Cathedral of Our Lady of the Angels, designed by Spanish architect Rafael Moneo, echoes the grand churches of Mexico and Europe from a controversial deconstructivist angle. Renzo Piano's signature inside-out industrial style can be glimpsed in the sawtooth roof and red-steel veins of the Broad in Los Angeles.

The Bay Area's iconic postmodern building is the San Francisco Museum of Modern Art, which Swiss architect Mario Botta capped with a black-and-white striped, marble-clad atrium in 1995 and Snøhetta architects expanded with wings shaped like ship sails in 2016. Lately SF has championed a brand of postmodernism by Pritzker Prize–winning architects that magnify and mimic the great outdoors, especially in Golden Gate Park. Swiss architects Herzog & de Meuron clad the MH de Young Memorial Museum in copper, which promises to oxidize green to match its park setting. Nearby, Renzo Piano literally raised the roof on sustainable design at the LEED platinum-certified California Academy of Sciences, capped by a living-roof garden.

Visual Arts

Although the earliest European artists were trained cartographers accompanying Western explorers, their images of California as an island show more imagination than scientific rigor. This mythologizing tendency continued throughout the gold-rush era, as Western artists alternated between caricatures of Wild West debauchery and manifest-destiny propaganda urging pioneers to settle the golden West. The completion of the Transcontinental Railroad in 1869 brought an influx of romantic painters, who produced epic California wilderness landscapes. After the 20th century arrived, homegrown colonies of California impressionist plein-air painters emerged at Laguna Beach and Carmel-by-the-Sea.

With the invention of photography, the improbable truth of California's landscape and its inhabitants was revealed. Pirkle Jones saw expressive potential in California landscape photography after WWII, while San Francisco–born Ansel Adams's sublime photographs had already started doing justice to Yosemite. Adams founded Group f/64 with Edward Weston and Imogen Cunningham in San Francisco. Berkeley-based Dorothea Lange turned her unflinching lens on the plight of Californian migrant workers in the Great Depression and Japanese Americans forced to enter internment camps during WWII, producing poignant documentary photos.

As the postwar American West became crisscrossed with freeways and divided into planned communities, Californian painters captured the abstract forms of manufactured landscapes on canvas. In San Francisco, Richard Diebenkorn and David Park became leading proponents of Bay Area Figurative Art, while San Francisco–born sculptor Richard Serra captured urban aesthetics in massive, rusting monoliths resembling ship prows and industrial Stonehenges. Meanwhile pop artists captured the ethos of conspicuous consumerism, through Wayne Thiebaud's gumball machines, British émigré David Hockney's LA pools and, above all, Ed Ruscha's studies of SoCal pop culture.

Today's California contemporary-art scene brings all these influences together with muralist-led social commentary, an obsessive dedication to craft and a new-media milieu pierced by cutting-edge technology. LA's Museum of Contemporary Art puts on provocative and avant-garde shows, as does LACMA's Broad, San Francisco's Museum of Modern Art and the Museum of Contemporary Art San Diego, which specializes in post-1950s pop and conceptual art.

City Lights Books (p57), San Francisco

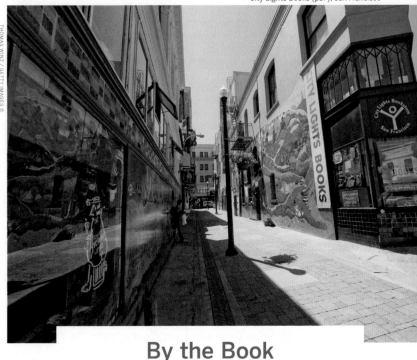

By the Book

Californians make up the largest market for books in the US, and read much more than the national average. Skewing the curve is bookish San Francisco, with more writers, playwrights and book purchases per capita than any other US city. The West Coast is a magnet for novelists, poets and storytellers, and California's multicultural literary community today is stronger than ever.

Early Voices of Social Realism

Arguably the most influential author to emerge from California was John Steinbeck, born in Salinas in 1902 in the heart of Central Valley farm country. He explored the lives and struggles of diverse California communities: Mexican American WWI vets adjusting to civilian life in *Tortilla Flat,* flat-broke wharf characters attempting to throw a party in *Cannery Row,* and migrant farm workers just trying to survive the Great Depression in his Pulitzer Prize–winning book *The Grapes of Wrath.* Acclaimed social realist Eugene O'Neill took his 1936 Nobel Prize money and transplanted himself near San Francisco, where he wrote the autobiographical play *Long Day's Journey into Night.*

Novelists took on the myth of California's self-made millionaires, exposing the tarnish on the Gold State. Classics in this vein include Upton Sinclair's *Oil!,* revealing the schemes of real-life LA oil tycoon Edward Mahoney that resulted in the Teapot Dome Scandal.

California became synonymous with adventure through the talents of early chroniclers such as Mark Twain and Bret Harte. Professional hell-raiser Jack London was a wild child from the Oakland docks who traveled the world with little more than his wits. He became the world's most successful adventurer and travel writer, sailing the seven seas, getting swept up in the Klondike gold rush, and dictating stories of his adventures on his pioneering permaculture ranch in Sonoma onto an early recording device.

Driving Tales

Road-trip through California with local storytellers as your copilots in *My California: Journeys by Great Writers*. Alternatively, get a slice of the state's heartland in *Highway 99: A Literary Journey Through California's Great Central Valley*, edited by Oakland-based writer Stan Yogi. It's full of multicultural perspectives, from early European settlers to 20th-century Mexican and Asian immigrant farmers.

Pulp Noir & Science Fiction

With mysterious fog and neon signs to set the mood, San Francisco and Los Angeles became crime-drama pulp-fiction capitals and the setting of choice for film noir movies. Dashiell Hammett *(The Maltese Falcon)* made a cynical San Francisco private eye into a modern antihero, while hard-boiled crime writer Raymond Chandler set the scene for murder and double-crossing dames in Santa Monica. The masterminds behind California's 1990s neo-noir crime fiction renaissance were James Ellroy *(LA Confidential)*, the late Elmore Leonard *(Get Shorty)* and Walter Mosley *(Devil in a Blue Dress)*, whose Easy Rawlins detective novels are set in South Central LA.

California technology has long inspired science fiction. Raised in Berkeley, Philip K Dick imagined dystopian futures, including a Los Angeles ruled by artificial intelligence in *Do Androids Dream of Electric Sheep?* It was adapted into the 1982 sci-fi movie classic *Blade Runner*. Berkeley-born Ursula K Le Guin *(The Left Hand of Darkness, A Wizard of Earthsea)* brings feminism to the genre of fantasy, imagining parallel realities where heroines confront forces of darkness.

Social Movers & Shakers

After surviving WWII, the Beat Generation refused to fall in line with 1950s conformity, defying McCarthyism with poignant, poetic truths. San Francisco Beat scene luminaries included Jack Kerouac *(On the Road)*, Allen Ginsberg *(Howl)* and Lawrence Ferlinghetti, the Beats' patron publisher who co-founded City Lights Bookstore. Censors called *Howl* obscene, and Ferlinghetti was arrested for publishing it – but he won the trial in a landmark decision for free speech.

But no author has captured California culture with such unflinching clarity as Joan Didion, whose prose burns through the page like sun on a misty California morning. Her collection of literary nonfiction essays *Slouching Towards Bethlehem* captures 1960s flower power at the exact moment it blooms and wilts. Didion pioneered immersive first-person New Journalism with fellow '60s California chroniclers Hunter S Thompson *(Hells Angels: A Strange and Terrible Saga)* and Tom Wolfe *(The Electric Kool-Aid Acid Test)*.

In the 1970s, Charles Bukowski's semiautobiographical novel *Post Office* captured down-and-out Downtown LA, while Richard Vasquez' *Chicano* took a dramatic look at LA's Latino barrio. Bret Easton Ellis followed the short lives and fast times of coked-up Beverly Hills teenagers in *Less Than Zero*, the definitive chronicle of 1980s excess.

Diving with jellyfish

The Land & Wildlife

You'll never have to leave California for a change of scenery: from snowy peaks to scorching deserts it's the most biodiverse state in the US. Species that are rare elsewhere thrive in this balmy climate, with its dry summers and wet winters. California's population puts a huge strain on natural resources, but for more than 150 years conservation-minded Californians have worked hard to protect the environment.

Lay of the Land

California is the third-biggest US state after Alaska and Texas, covering more than 155,000 sq miles – that's larger than 85 of the world's smallest nations. It shares borders with Oregon to the north, Mexico to the south, Nevada and Arizona to the east, and has 840 miles of glorious Pacific shoreline to the west.

Geology & Earthquakes

California is a complex geologic landscape formed from fragments of rock and earth crust squeezed together as the North American continent drifted westward over hundreds of millions of years. Crumpled coastal ranges, fault lines rippling through the Central Valley and jagged, still-rising Sierra Nevada mountains all reveal gigantic forces at work, as the continental and ocean plates crush together.

Everything changed about 25 million years ago, when the ocean plates stopped colliding and instead started sliding against each other, creating the massive San Andreas Fault. This contact zone catches and slips, rattling California with an ongoing succession of tremors and earthquakes.

In 1906 the state's most famous earthquake measured 7.8 on the Richter scale and demolished San Francisco, leaving more than 3000 people dead. The Bay Area was again badly shaken in 1989, when the Loma Prieta earthquake (6.9) caused a section of the Bay Bridge to collapse. In Los Angeles the last 'big one' was in 1994, when the Northridge quake (6.7) caused parts of the Santa Monica Fwy to fall down, resulting in damage that made it the most costly quake in US history.

California: Almost an Island

Cut off from the rest of North America by the soaring peaks of the Sierra Nevada, California is as biologically distinct as an island. Under these biologically isolated conditions, evolution and local adaptation have yielded unique plants and animals ranging from bristlecone pines in the north to Joshua trees in the south. California ranks first in the nation for its number of endemic plants, amphibians, reptiles, freshwater fish and mammals. In fact, 30% of all plant species, 50% of all bird species and 50% of all mammal species in the USA can be found here.

The Coast to the Central Valley

Rugged mountains take the brunt of winter storms along California's coast, leaving inland areas more protected. San Francisco marks the midpoint of the Coast Ranges, with fog swirling along the sparsely populated North Coast. To the south, beach communities enjoy balmier climates along the Central and Southern California coasts.

The northernmost reaches of the Coast Ranges get 120in of rain in a typical year, and persistent summer fog contributes another 12in of precipitation in some spots. This may not sound like the best climate for beach-going, but California's northern coastal lowlands are sublime for coastal wine tasting. Nutrient-rich soils and abundant moisture foster stands of towering coast redwoods, growing as far south as Big Sur and all the way north to Oregon.

On their eastern flanks, the Coast Ranges taper into gently rolling hills that slide into the sprawling Central Valley. Once an inland sea, this flat basin is now an agricultural powerhouse producing about half of America's fruits, nuts and vegetables. Stretching about 450 miles long and 50 miles wide, the valley sees about as much rainfall as a desert, but gets huge volumes of water runoff from the Sierra Nevada.

Before the arrival of Europeans, the Central Valley was a natural wonderland – vast marshes with flocks of geese that blackened the sky, grasslands carpeted with flowers sniffed by millions of antelopes, elk and grizzly bears. Virtually this entire landscape has been plowed under and replaced with non-native plants (including agricultural crops and vineyards) and livestock ranches. So when you savor your next great California meal, raise a glass to the flora and fauna that came before you.

Mountain Ranges

On the eastern side of the Central Valley looms California's most prominent topographic feature: the Sierra Nevada, nicknamed the 'Range of Light' by conservationist John Muir. At 400 miles long and 70 miles wide, this is one of the world's largest mountain ranges, punctuated with 13 peaks over 14,000ft high. The vast wilderness of the High Sierra (mostly above 9000ft) is an astounding landscape of shrinking glaciers, sculpted granite peaks and remote canyons. This landscape is beautiful to look at but difficult to access, and it was one of the greatest challenges for 19th-century settlers attempting to reach California.

The soaring Sierra Nevada captures storm systems and drains them of their water, with most of the precipitation above 3000ft turning to snow, creating a premier winter-sports destination. Melting snow flows down into a half-dozen major river systems on the range's western and eastern slopes, providing the vast majority of water needed for agriculture in the Central Valley and for the metro areas of San Francisco and LA.

At its northern end, the Sierra Nevada merges imperceptibly into the volcanic Cascade Mountains, which continue north into Oregon and Washington. At its southern end, the Sierra Nevada makes a funny westward hook and connects via the Transverse Ranges (one of the USA's few east–west mountain ranges) to the southern Coast Ranges.

The Deserts & Beyond

With the west slope of the Sierra Nevada capturing most of the precipitation, lands east of the Sierra crest are dry and desertlike, receiving less than 10in of rain a year. Some valleys at the eastern foot of the Sierra Nevada, however, are well watered by creeks, so that they're able to support livestock and agriculture.

At the western edge of the Great Basin, the elevated Modoc Plateau in far northeastern California is a cold desert blanketed by hardy sagebrush shrubs and juniper trees. Temperatures increase as you head south, with a prominent transition on the descent from Mono Lake into the Owens Valley east of the Sierra Nevada. This southern hot desert (part of the Mojave Desert) includes Death Valley, one of the hottest places on the planet. Further south the Mojave Desert morphs into the Colorado Desert (part of Mexico's greater Sonoran Desert) around the Salton Sea.

California's Flora & Fauna

Although the staggering numbers of animals that greeted the first foreign settlers are now distant memories, you can still easily spot wildlife thriving in California. Some are only shadow populations, and some are actually endangered – all the more reason to take the opportunity to stop by California's designated wildlife areas to appreciate their presence and support their conservation.

Marine Mammals

Spend even one day along California's coast and you may spot pods of bottle-nosed dolphins and porpoises swimming, canoodling and cavorting in the ocean. Playful sea otters and harbor seals typically stick closer to shore, especially around public piers and protected bays. Since the 1989 earthquake, sea lions have taken to sunbathing on San Francisco's Pier 39, where delighted tourists watch the city's resident beach bums nap, goof off and recover from their seafood dinners. To see more wild pinnipeds, visit Point Lobos State Natural Reserve near Monterey, or Channel Islands National Park in Southern California.

Once threatened by extinction, gray whales now migrate in growing numbers along California's coast between December and April. Adult whales live up to 60 years, grow longer than a city bus and can weigh up to 40 tons, making quite a splash when they leap out of the water. Every year they travel from summertime feeding grounds in the arctic Bering Sea, down to southern breeding grounds off Baja California then all the way back up again, making a 6000-mile round trip.

Also almost hunted to extinction by the late 19th century for their oil-rich blubber, northern elephant seals have made a remarkable comeback along California's coast. North of Santa Cruz, Año Nuevo State Reserve is a major breeding ground for northern elephant seals. California's biggest elephant seal colony is found at Piedras Blancas, south of Big Sur. There's a smaller rookery at Point Reyes National Seashore in Marin County.

Land Mammals

Lumbering across California's flag is the state mascot: the grizzly bear. Grizzlies once roamed California's beaches and grasslands in large numbers, eating everything from acorns to whale carcasses. Grizzlies were particularly abundant in the Central Valley, but retreated upslope into the Sierra Nevada as they were hunted to extinction in the 1920s.

California's mountain forests are still home to an estimated 25,000 to 30,000 black bears, the grizzlies' smaller cousins. Despite their name, their fur ranges in color from black to dark brown, auburn or even blond. These burly omnivores feed on berries, nuts, roots, grasses, insects, eggs, small mammals and fish, but can become a nuisance around campgrounds and cabins where food and trash are not secured.

As settlers moved into California in the 19th century, many other large mammals fared almost as poorly as grizzlies. Immense herds of tule elk and antelope in the Central Valley were particularly hard hit, with antelope retreating in small numbers to the northeastern corner of the state, and tule elk hunted into near-extinction. A small remnant herd was moved to Point Reyes, where it has since rebounded.

Mountain lions (also called cougars) hunt throughout California's mountains and forests, especially in areas teeming with deer. Solitary lions can grow 8ft in length and weigh 175lb, and are formidable predators. Few attacks on humans have occurred, happening mostly where suburbs have encroached on the lions' wilderness hunting grounds.

Birds & Butterflies

You might think this picture-postcard state is made for tourists, but California is totally for the birds. California is an essential stop on the migratory Pacific Flyway between Alaska and Mexico. Almost half the bird species in North America use the state's wildlife refuges and nature preserves for rest and refueling. Migration peaks during the wetter winter season starting in October/November, when two million fowl gather at the Klamath Basin National Wildlife Refuges for the world's biggest game of duck, duck, goose.

Year-round you can see birds dotting California's beaches, estuaries and bays, where herons, cormorants, shorebirds and gulls gather. Point Reyes National Seashore and the Channel Islands are prime year-round bird-watching spots.

Desert Critters

California's deserts are far from deserted, but most animals are too smart to hang out in the daytime heat. Most come out only in the cool of the night, as bats do. Roadrunners (black-and-white mottled ground cuckoos) can often be spotted on roadsides – you'll recognize them from their long tails and punk-style Mohawks. Other desert inhabitants include burrowing kit foxes, tree-climbing gray foxes, hopping jackrabbits, kangaroo rats, slow-moving (and endangered) desert tortoises and a variety of snakes, lizards and spiders. Desert bighorn sheep and migrating birds flock to watering holes, often around seasonal springs and native fan-palm oases – look for them in Joshua Tree National Park and Anza-Borrego Desert State Park.

Joshua Tree National Park (p184)

MATTEO COLOMBO / GETTY IMAGES ©

As you drive along the Big Sur coastline, look skyward to spot endangered California condors. You may also spot condors inland, soaring over Pinnacles National Park and the Los Padres National Forest.

Monarch butterflies are glorious orange creatures that take epic long-distance journeys in search of milkweed, their only source of food. They winter in California by the tens of thousands, clustering along the Central Coast at Santa Cruz, Pacific Grove, Pismo Beach and Santa Barbara County.

Wildflowers & Trees

Like human Californians, California's 6000 kinds of plants are by turns shy and flamboyant. Many species are so obscure and similar that only a dedicated botanist could tell them apart, but in the spring they merge into shimmering carpets of wildflowers that will take your breath away. The state flower is the native California poppy, which shyly closes at night and unfolds by day in a shocking display of golden orange.

California is also a region of superlative trees: the oldest (bristlecone pines of the White Mountains live to nearly 5000 years old), the tallest (coast redwoods reach 380ft) and the largest (giant sequoias of the Sierra Nevada exceed 36ft across). Sequoias are unique to California, adapted to survive in isolated groves on the Sierra Nevada's western slopes in Yosemite, Sequoia and Kings Canyon National Parks.

An astounding 20 native species of oak grow in California, including live (evergreen) oaks with holly-like leaves and scaly acorns. Other common trees include the aromatic California bay laurel, whose long slender leaves turn purple. Rare native trees include Monterey pines and Torrey pines, gnarly species that have adapted to harsh coastal conditions such as high winds, sparse rainfall and sandy, stony soils. Torrey pines only grow at Torrey Pines State Reserve near San Diego and in the Channel Islands, California's hot spot for endemic plant species.

Heading inland, the Sierra Nevada has three distinct eco-zones: the dry western foothills covered with oak and chaparral; conifer forests starting from an elevation of 2000ft; and an alpine zone above 8000ft. Almost two dozen species of conifer grow in the Sierra Nevada, with mid-elevation forests home to massive Douglas firs, ponderosa pines and, biggest of all, the giant sequoia. Deciduous trees include the quaking aspen, a white-trunked tree with shimmering leaves that turn pale yellow in the fall, helping the Golden State live up to its name in the Eastern Sierra.

Cacti & Other Desert Flora

In Southern California's deserts, cacti and other plants have adapted to the arid climate with thin, spiny leaves that resist moisture loss (and deter grazing animals). Their seed and flowering mechanisms kick into high gear during brief winter rains. Desert flora can bloom spectacularly in spring, carpeting valleys and drawing thousands of onlookers and shutterbugs.

One of the most common species is cholla, which looks so furry that it's nicknamed 'teddy-bear cactus,' but don't be fooled by its cuddly appearance. Cholla will bury extremely sharp, barbed spines in your skin at the slightest touch. Also watch out for the aptly named catclaw acacia, nicknamed 'wait-a-minute bush' because its small, sharp, hooked thorny spikes will try to grab your clothing or skin as you brush past.

> ### John Muir's Sierra Club
>
> Cofounded by naturalist John Muir in 1892, the Sierra Club (www.sierraclub. org) was the USA's first conservation group. It remains the nation's most active, offering educational programs, group hikes, organized trips and volunteer vacations.

You may also recognize prickly pear, a flat, fleshy-padded cacti whose juice is traditionally used as medicine by Native Americans. You can hardly miss spiky ocotillo, which grows up to 20ft tall and has canelike branches that sprout blood-red flowers in spring. Creosote may look like a cactus, but it's actually a small evergreen bush with a distinctive smell.

With gangly arms and puffy green sleeves, Joshua trees look like Dr Seuss characters from afar, but up close you can see they're actually a type of yucca. In spring they burst into blossom with greenish-white flowers. According to local legend, they were named by Mormons who thought their crooked branches resembled the outstretched arms of a biblical prophet.

California's National & State Parks

Most Californians rate outdoor recreation as vital to their quality of life, and the amount of preserved public lands has steadily grown since the 1960s with support from key legislation. The landmark 1976 California Coastal Act saved the coastline from further development, while the controversial 1994 California Desert Protection Act passed over the objections of ranchers, miners and off-highway vehicle (OHV) enthusiasts.

Today, California State Parks (www.parks.ca.gov) protect nearly a third of the state's coastline, along with redwood forests, mountain lakes, desert canyons, waterfalls, wildlife preserves and historical sites. In recent decades, state budget shortfalls and chronic underfunding of California's parks have contributed to closures, limited visitor services and increased park entry and outdoor-recreation fees. But with state revenues from recreational tourism consistently outpacing resource-extraction industries such as mining, California has a considerable vested interest in protecting its wilderness tracts.

While you could be disappointed to find a park closed or full, bear in mind that some limits to public access are necessary to prevent California's parklands from being loved to death. Too many visitors can stress the natural environment. To avoid the crowds and glimpse wilderness at its most untrammeled, plan to visit popular parks such as Yosemite outside of peak season. Alternatively, less-famous natural areas managed by the National Park Service (www.nps.gov/state/CA) often receive fewer visitors, which means you won't have to reserve permits, campsites or lodging many months in advance.

There are 18 national forests in California managed by the US Forest Service (USFS; www.fs.usda.gov/r5), comprising lands around Mt Whitney, Mt Shasta, Lake Tahoe, Big Bear Lake and Big Sur. Beloved by birders, national wildlife refuges (NWR), including the Salton Sea and Klamath Basin, are managed by the US Fish & Wildlife Service (USFWS; www.fws.gov/refuges). More wilderness tracts in California, including the Lost Coast and Carrizo Plain, are overseen by the Bureau of Land Management (BLM; www.blm.gov/ca/st/en.html).

Death Valley (p176)

KAVRAM / SHUTTERSTOCK ©

Survival Guide

Directory A–Z

Accommodations

California dreaming comes easy at a range of local accommodations, from scenic campsites and lighthouse hostels to sleek Hollywood hotels and deluxe wine-country resorts. The sooner you book, the better – especially June to August.

Campgrounds Not just a cheap sleep, but the best way to experience California's great outdoors by the beach, under the redwoods or nestled in desert dunes.

Hostels Budget-friendly dorm stays in key locations, including coastal parks and city centers.

B&Bs Home-style inns range from romantic vineyard

Book Your Stay Online

For more accommodations reviews by Lonely Planet authors, check out http://hotels.lonelyplanet.com/california. You'll find independent reviews, as well as recommendations on the best places to stay. Best of all, you can book online.

cottages to historic Victorian mansions.

Motels Handy for road-trippers and less expensive than hotels; some have swimming pools.

Hotels & Resorts Upscale options come with prime locations, views and deluxe amenities.

Amenities

○ Facilities in hostels typically include mixed dorms, semiprivate rooms with shared bathrooms, communal kitchens, lockers, internet access, coin-op laundry and TV lounges. Dorms in HI (Hostelling International; www.hiusa.org) hostels are typically gender-segregated.

○ B&B rates often include breakfast, but occasionally don't – never mind what the name 'B&B' suggests. Amenities vary widely, but rooms with TV and telephone are the exception; the cheapest units may share bathrooms.

○ At midrange motels and hotels, expect clean, comfortable and decent-sized rooms with at least a private bathroom, and standard amenities such as cable TV, direct-dial telephone, a coffeemaker, and perhaps a microwave and mini-fridge.

○ Top-end lodgings offer top-notch amenities and perhaps a scenic location, high design or historical ambience. Pools, fitness rooms, business centers, full-service restaurants and bars and other convenient facilities are often included.

○ In Southern California, nearly all lodgings have air-conditioning, but in perpetually cool Northern California, most don't. In coastal areas as far south as Santa Barbara, only fans may be provided.

○ There may be a fee at lodgings for wireless internet, especially for in-room access. Look for free wi-fi hot spots in hotel public areas such as the lobby or poolside.

○ Many lodgings are now exclusively nonsmoking. Where they still exist, smoking rooms are often left unrenovated and in less desirable locations. Expect a hefty 'cleaning fee' ($100 or more) if you light up in designated nonsmoking rooms.

Rates & Reservations

○ Generally midweek rates are lower, except at urban hotels geared toward business travelers. Hotels in Silicon Valley, downtown San Francisco, LA and San Diego may lure leisure travelers with weekend deals.

○ Hotel rooms are often priced by the size and number of beds, rather than the number of occupants. A room with one double or queen-size bed usually costs the same for one or two people, while a room with a king-size bed or two double beds costs more.

○ Discount membership cards , such as American Automobile Association

(AAA) and AARP, may get you about 10% off standard rates at participating hotels and motels.

○ Look for freebie-ad magazines packed with hotel and motel discount coupons at gas stations, highway rest areas, tourist offices and online at HotelCoupons (www. hotelcoupons.com).

○ High season is from June to August everywhere, except the deserts and mountain ski areas, where December through April are the busiest months.

○ Demand and prices spike around major holidays and for festivals, when some properties may impose multiday minimum stays.

○ Reservations are recommended for weekend and holiday travel year-round, and every day of the week during high season.

○ Bargaining may be possible for walk-in guests without reservations, especially at off-peak times.

○ The state park system has a variety of campgrounds. To reserve, check out www. reservecalifornia.com.

Customs Regulations

Currently, non-US citizens and permanent residents may import the following:

○ 1L of alcohol (if you're over 21 years of age)

○ 200 cigarettes (one carton) or 100 cigars (if you're over 18 years)

○ $100 worth of gifts Amounts higher than $10,000 in cash, traveler's checks, money orders and other cash equivalents must be declared. Don't even think about bringing in illegal drugs.

For more complete, up-to-date information, check the **US Customs and Border Protection website** (www. cbp.gov).

Electricity

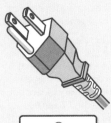

Type B
120V/60Hz

Food

○ Lunch is generally served between 11:30am and 2:30pm, and dinner between 5pm and 9pm daily, though some restaurants stay open later, especially on Friday and Saturday nights.

○ If breakfast is served, it's usually between 7:30am and 11am. Some diners and cafes keep serving breakfast into the afternoon, or all day. Weekend brunch is a laid-back meal, usually available from 11am until 3pm on Saturdays and Sundays.

○ Californian restaurant etiquette tends to be informal. Only a handful of restaurants require more than a dressy shirt, slacks and shoes that aren't flip-flops. At other places, T-shirts, shorts and sandals are fine.

○ Tipping 18% to 20% is expected anywhere you receive table service.

○ Smoking is illegal indoors. Some restaurants have patios or sidewalk tables where smoking is tolerated (ask first, or look around for ashtrays), but don't expect your neighbors to be happy about secondhand smoke.

○ You can bring your own wine to most restaurants; a 'corkage' fee of $15 to $30 usually applies. Lunches rarely include booze, though a glass of wine or beer is socially acceptable.

○ If you ask the kitchen to divide a plate between two (or more) people, there may be a small split-plate surcharge.

○ Vegetarians, vegans and travelers with food allergies or dietary restrictions are in luck – many restaurants are used to catering to specific dietary needs.

GLBTIQ Travelers

California is a magnet for GLBTIQ travelers. Hot spots include the Castro in San Francisco, West Hollywood (WeHo), Silver Lake and Long Beach in LA, San Diego's Hillcrest neighborhood, the desert resort of Palm Springs, Guerneville in the Russian River Valley and Calistoga in Napa Valley.

Same-sex marriage is legal in California. Despite widespread tolerance, homophobic bigotry still exists. In small towns, especially away from the coast, tolerance often comes down to a 'don't ask, don't tell' policy.

Helpful Resources

Advocate (www.advocate.com/travel) Online news, gay travel features and destination guides.

Damron (www.damron.com) Classic, advertiser-driven gay travel guides and 'Gay Scout' mobile app.

LGBT National Hotline (☏888-843-4564; www.glbthotline.org) For counseling and referrals of any kind.

Out Traveler (www.outtraveler.com) Free online magazine articles with travel tips, destination guides and hotel reviews.

Purple Roofs (www.purpleroofs.com) Online directory of LGBTQ-friendly accommodations.

Health

Health Care & Insurance

◉ Medical treatment in the USA is of the highest caliber, but the expense could kill you. Many health-care professionals demand payment at the time of service, especially from out-of-towners or international visitors.

◉ Except for medical emergencies (in which case call ☏911 or go to the nearest 24-hour hospital emergency room, or ER), phone around to find a doctor who will accept your insurance.

◉ Keep all medical receipts and documentation for billing and insurance claims and reimbursement later.

◉ Some health-insurance policies require you to get pre-authorization over the phone for medical treatment before seeking help.

◉ Overseas visitors with travel-health-insurance policies may need to contact a call center for an assessment by phone before getting medical treatment.

Insurance

Getting travel insurance to cover theft, loss and medical problems is highly recommended. Some

policies do not cover 'risky' activities such as scuba diving, motorcycling and skiing, so read the fine print. Make sure the policy at least covers hospital stays and an emergency flight home.

Paying for your airline ticket or rental car with a credit card may provide limited travel accident insurance. If you already have private health insurance or a homeowner's or renter's policy, find out what those policies cover and only get supplemental insurance. If you have prepaid a large portion of your vacation, trip-cancellation insurance may be a worthwhile expense.

Worldwide travel insurance is available at www.lonelyplanet.com/travel-insurance. You can buy, extend and claim online anytime – even if you're already on the road.

Internet Access

● Free or fee-based wi-fi hot spots can be found at major airports, many hotels, motels and coffee shops (eg Starbucks) and some tourist information centers, campgrounds (eg KOA), stores (eg Apple), bars and restaurants (including fast-food chains such as McDonald's).

● Free public wi-fi is proliferating and even some of California's state parks are now wi-fi enabled (get details at www.parks.ca.gov).

● Public libraries have internet terminals (online time may be limited, advance sign-up required and a nominal fee charged for out-of-network visitors) and, increasingly, free wi-fi.

Legal Matters

Drugs & Alcohol

● Possession of up to 1oz of marijuana (if you are 21 years or older) for recreational use is no longer a crime in California, but it is still illegal to use marijuana in public (subject to fines of up to $250, as well as mandatory community-service hours and drug-education classes).

● Possession of any other drug or more than 1oz of marijuana is a felony punishable by lengthy jail time. For foreigners, conviction of any drug offense is grounds for deportation.

● Police can give roadside sobriety checks to assess if you've been drinking or using drugs. If you fail, they'll require you to take a breath, urine or blood test to determine if your blood alcohol is over the legal limit (0.08%). Refusing to be tested is treated the same as if you had taken and failed the test.

● Penalties for driving under the influence (DUI) of drugs or alcohol range from license suspension and fines to jail time. It's illegal to carry open containers of alcohol inside a vehicle, even if they're empty. Unless they're full and still sealed, store them in the trunk.

● Consuming alcohol anywhere other than at a private residence or licensed premises is a no-no, which puts most parks and beaches off-limits (although many campgrounds legally allow it).

● Bars, clubs and liquor stores often ask for photo ID to prove you are of legal drinking age (21 years). Being 'carded' is standard practice, so don't take it personally.

Police & Security

● For police, fire and ambulance emergencies, dial ☏911. For nonemergency police assistance, contact the nearest local police station (dial ☏411 for directory assistance).

● If you are stopped by the police, be courteous. Don't get out of the car unless asked. Keep your hands where the officer can see them (eg on the steering wheel) at all times.

● There is no system of paying fines on the spot. Attempting to pay the fine to the officer may lead to a charge of attempted bribery.

● For traffic violations, the ticketing officer will explain your options. There is usually a 30-day period to pay a fine; most matters can be handled by mail or online.

● If you are arrested, you have the right to remain silent and are presumed innocent until proven guilty. Everyone has the right to make one phone call. If you don't have a lawyer, one will be appointed to you free of charge. Foreign travelers who don't have a lawyer, friends or family to help should call their embassy or consulate; the police can provide the number upon request.

● Due to security concerns about terrorism, never leave your bags unattended, especially at airports or bus and train stations.

Money

ATMs

● ATMs are available 24/7 at most banks, shopping

malls, airports and grocery and convenience stores.

◦ Expect a minimum surcharge of around $3 per transaction, in addition to any fees charged by your home bank.

◦ Most ATMs are connected to international networks and offer decent foreign-exchange rates.

◦ Withdrawing cash from an ATM using a credit card usually incurs a hefty fee and high interest rates; contact your credit-card company for details and a PIN number.

Cash

Most people don't carry large amounts of cash for everyday use, relying instead on credit and debit cards. Some businesses refuse to accept bills over $20.

Credit Cards

◦ Major credit cards are almost universally accepted. In fact, it's almost impossible to rent a car, book a hotel room or buy tickets over the phone without one. A credit card may also be vital in emergencies.

◦ Visa, MasterCard and American Express are the most widely accepted credit cards.

Moneychangers

◦ You can exchange money at major airports, bigger banks and currency-exchange offices such as American Express (www.

americanexpress.com) or Travelex (www.travelex.com). Always enquire about rates and fees.

◦ Outside big cities, exchanging money may be a problem, so make sure you have a credit card and sufficient cash on hand.

Taxes

◦ California state sales tax (7.5%) is added to the retail price of most goods and services (gasoline and groceries are exceptions). Local and city sales taxes may tack on up to 2.5%.

◦ Tourist lodging taxes vary statewide, but average 10.5% to 15.5% in major cities.

◦ No refunds of sales or lodging taxes are available for visitors.

Tipping

Tipping is not optional. Only withhold tips in cases of outrageously bad service.

Airport skycaps & hotel bellhops $2 or $3 per bag, minimum $5 per cart.

Bartenders 15% to 20% per round, minimum $1 per drink.

Concierges Nothing for simple information, up to $20 for securing last-minute restaurant reservations, sold-out show tickets etc.

Housekeeping staff $2 to $4 daily, left under the card provided; more if you're messy.

Parking valets At least $2 when handed back your car keys.

Restaurant servers & room service 18% to 20%, unless a gratuity is already charged (common for groups of six or more).

Taxi drivers 10% to 15% of metered fare, rounded up to the next dollar.

Opening Hours

Businesses, restaurants and shops may close earlier and on additional days during the winter off-season (November to March). Otherwise, standard opening hours are as follows:

Banks 9am–6pm Monday to Friday, some 9am–1pm or later Saturday

Bars 5pm–2am daily

Business hours (general) 9am–5pm Monday to Friday

Nightclubs 10pm–4am Thursday to Saturday

Post offices 8:30am–5pm Monday to Friday, some 8:30am–noon or later Saturday

Restaurants 7:30am–10am, 11:30am–2pm and 5pm–9pm daily, some open later Friday and Saturday

Practicalities

DVDs Coded for region 1 (USA and Canada only)

Newspapers *Los Angeles Times* (www.latimes.com), *San Francisco Chronicle* (www.sfchronicle.com), *Mercury News* (www.mercurynews.com), *Sacramento Bee* (www.sacbee.com)

Radio National Public Radio (NPR), lower end of FM dial

Smoking Smoking is generally prohibited inside all public buildings, including airports, shopping malls and train and bus stations. In some cities and towns, smoking outdoors within a certain distance of any public business is illegal.

TV PBS (public broadcasting); cable: CNN (news), ESPN (sports), HBO (movies), Weather Channel

Weights & Measures Imperial (except 1 US gallon equals 0.83 imperial gallons)

Shops 10am–6pm Monday to Saturday, noon–5pm Sunday (malls open later)

Supermarkets 8am–9pm or 10pm daily, some 24 hours

Public Holidays

On the following national holidays, banks, schools and government offices (including post offices) are closed, and transportation, museums and other services operate on a Sunday schedule. Holidays falling on a weekend are usually observed the following Monday.

New Year's Day January 1

Martin Luther King Jr Day Third Monday in January

Presidents' Day Third Monday in February

Good Friday Friday before Easter in March/April

Memorial Day Last Monday in May

Independence Day July 4

Labor Day First Monday in September

Columbus Day Second Monday in October

Veterans Day November 11

Thanksgiving Day Fourth Thursday in November

Christmas Day December 25

Safe Travel

Despite its seemingly apocalyptic list of dangers – guns, violent crime, riots, earthquakes – California is a reasonably safe place to visit. The greatest danger is posed by car accidents (buckle up – it's the law), while the biggest annoyances are metro-area traffic and crowds. Wildlife poses some small threats, and of course there is the dramatic, albeit unlikely, possibility of a natural disaster.

Earthquakes

Earthquakes happen all the time, but most are so tiny they are detectable only by sensitive seismological instruments. If you're caught in a serious shaker, take precautions:

○ If indoors, get under a desk or table or stand in a doorway.

○ Protect your head and stay clear of windows, mirrors or anything that might fall.

○ Don't head for elevators or go running into the street.

○ If you're in a shopping mall or large public building, expect the alarm and/or sprinkler systems to come on.

○ If outdoors, get away from buildings, trees and power lines.

○ If you're driving, pull over to the side of the road away from bridges, overpasses and power lines. Stay inside the car until the shaking stops.

○ If you're on a sidewalk near buildings, duck into a doorway to protect yourself from falling bricks, glass and debris.

○ Prepare for aftershocks.

○ Turn on the radio and listen for bulletins.

○ Use the telephone only if absolutely necessary.

Wildlife

• Never feed or approach any wild animal, not even harmless-looking critters – it causes them to lose their innate fear of humans, which in turn makes them dangerously aggressive. Many birds and mammals, including deer and rodents such as squirrels, carry serious diseases that can be transmitted to humans through a bite.

• Disturbing or harassing specially protected species, including many marine mammals such as whales, dolphins and seals, is a crime, subject to enormous fines.

• Black bears are often attracted to campgrounds, where they may find food, trash and any other scented items left out on picnic tables or stashed in tents and cars. Always use bear-proof containers where they are provided. For more bear-country travel tips, visit the SierraWild website (http://sierrawild.gov/bears).

• If you encounter a black bear in the wild, don't run. Stay together, keeping small children next to you and picking up little ones. Keep back at least 100yd. If the bear starts moving toward you, back away slowly off-trail and let it pass by, being careful not to block any of the bear's escape routes or get caught between a mother and her cubs. Sometimes a black bear will 'bluff

charge' to test your dominance. Stand your ground by making yourself look as big as possible (eg waving your arms above your head) and shouting menacingly.

• Mountain lion attacks on humans are rare, but can be deadly. If you encounter a mountain lion, stay calm, pick up small children, face the animal and retreat slowly. Make yourself appear larger by raising your arms or grabbing a stick. If the lion becomes menacing, shout or throw rocks at it. If attacked, fight back aggressively.

• Snakes and spiders are common throughout California, not just in wilderness areas. Always look inside your shoes before putting them back on outdoors, especially when camping. Snake bites are rare, but occur most often when a snake is stepped on or provoked (eg picked up or poked with a stick). Anti-venom is available at most hospitals.

Telephone

Cell Phones

• You'll need a multiband GSM phone to make calls in the USA. Popping in a US prepaid rechargeable SIM card is usually cheaper than using your network.

• SIM cards are sold at telecommunications and

electronics stores. These stores also sell inexpensive prepaid phones, including some airtime.

• You can rent a cell phone at San Francisco (SFO) International Airport from **TripTel** (www.triptel.com); pricing plans vary, but typically are expensive.

Dialing Codes

• US phone numbers consist of a three-digit area code followed by a seven-digit local number.

• When dialing a number within the same area code, use the seven-digit number (if that doesn't work, try all 10 digits).

• For long-distance calls, dial ☏1 plus the area code plus the local number.

• Toll-free numbers (eg beginning with ☏800, ☏855, ☏866, ☏877 or ☏888) must be preceded by ☏1.

• For direct international calls, dial ☏011 plus the country code plus the area code (usually without the initial '0') plus the local phone number.

• If you're calling from abroad, the country code for the US is ☏1 (the same as Canada, but international rates apply between the two countries).

Payphones & Phonecards

• Where payphones still exist, they're usually coin-operated, though some may only accept credit cards (eg in state or national parks). Local calls cost 50¢ minimum.

○ For long-distance and international calls, prepaid phonecards are sold at convenience stores, supermarkets, newsstands and electronics and convenience stores.

Tourist Information

○ For pretrip planning, peruse the information-packed website of the **California Travel & Tourism Commission** (Visit California; ☎877-225-4367, 916-444-4429; www.visitcalifornia.com).

○ The same government agency operates more than a dozen statewide California Welcome Centers (www.visitcwc.com), where staff dispense maps and brochures and may be able to help find accommodations.

○ Almost every city and town has a local visitor center or a chamber of commerce where you can pick up maps, brochures and information.

Travelers with Disabilities

More-populated areas of coastal California are reasonably well-equipped

for travelers with disabilities, but facilities in smaller towns and rural areas may be limited.

Download Lonely Planet's free Accessible Travel guide from http://lptravel.to/AccessibleTravel.

Accessibility

○ Most traffic intersections have dropped curbs and sometimes audible crossing signals.

○ The Americans with Disabilities Act (ADA) requires public buildings built after 1993 to be wheelchair-accessible, including restrooms.

○ Motels and hotels built after 1993 must have at least one ADA–compliant accessible room; state your specific needs when making reservations.

○ For nonpublic buildings built prior to 1993, including hotels, restaurants, museums and theaters, there are no accessibility guarantees; call ahead to find out what to expect.

○ Most national and many state parks and some other outdoor recreation areas offer paved or boardwalk nature trails that are graded and accessible by wheelchair.

○ Many theme parks go out of their way to be accessible to wheelchairs and guests with mobility limitations and other disabilities.

○ US citizens and permanent residents with a

permanent disability quality for a free lifetime 'America the Beautiful' Access Pass (http://store.usgs.gov/pass/access.html), which waives entry fees to all national parks and federal recreational lands and offers 50% discounts on some recreation fees (eg camping).

○ California State Parks' disabled discount pass ($3.50) entitles people with permanent disabilities to 50% off day-use parking and camping fees; for an application, click to www.parks.ca.gov.

Communications

○ Telephone companies provide relay operators (dial ☎711) for the hearing impaired.

○ Many banks provide ATM instructions in Braille.

Helpful Resources

A Wheelchair Rider's Guide to the California Coast (www.wheelingcalscoast.org) Free accessibility information covering beaches, parks and trails, plus downloadable PDF guides to the San Francisco Bay Area and Los Angeles and Orange County coasts.

Access Northern California (www.accessnca.org) Extensive links to accessible-travel resources, including outdoor recreation opportunities, lodgings, tours and transportation.

Access San Francisco Guide (www.sftravel.com) Search the city's official tourism site for this free, downloadable PDF guide – dated, but useful.

Access Santa Cruz County (www.scaccessguide.com) Free online accessible-travel guide for visiting Santa Cruz and around, including restaurants, lodging, beaches, parks and outdoor recreation.

California State Parks (http://access.parks.ca.gov) Searchable online map and database of accessible features at state parks.

Disabled Sports Eastern Sierra (http://disabledsports easternsierra.org) Offers summer and winter outdoor-activity programs around Mammoth Lakes.

Achieve Tahoe (http://achieve tahoe.org) Organizes summer and winter sports, 4WD adventures and adaptive-ski rental around Lake Tahoe in the Sierra Nevada (annual membership $50).

Flying Wheels Travel (507-451-5005; www.flyingwheels travel.com) Full-service travel agency for travelers with disabilities, mobility issues and chronic illnesses.

Los Angeles for Disabled Visitors (www.discoverlos angeles.com/search/site/disabled) Tips for accessible sightseeing, entertainment, museums and transportation.

Yosemite National Park Accessibility (www.nps.gov/yose/planyourvisit/accessibility.htm) Detailed, downloadable accessibility information for Yosemite National Park, including services for deaf visitors.

Wheelchair Traveling (www.wheelchairtraveling.com) Travel articles, lodging and helpful California destination info.

Transportation

○ All major airlines, Greyhound buses and Amtrak trains can accommodate people with disabilities, usually with 48 hours of advance notice required.

○ Major car-rental agencies offer hand-controlled vehicles and vans with wheelchair lifts at no extra charge, but you must reserve these well in advance.

○ For wheelchair-accessible van rentals, also try **Wheelchair Getaways** (800-642-2042; www.wheelchairgetaways.com) in LA and San Francisco, or **Mobility Works** (877-275-4915; www.mobility works.com) in LA, San Diego, San Francisco, Oakland and San Jose.

○ Local buses, trains and subway lines usually have wheelchair lifts.

○ Seeing-eye dogs are permitted to accompany passengers on public transportation.

○ Taxi companies have at least one wheelchair-accessible van, but you'll usually need to call and then wait for one.

Visas

○ Visa information is highly subject to change. Depending on your country of origin, the rules for entering the USA keep changing. Double-check current visa requirements before coming to the USA.

○ Currently, under the US Visa Waiver Program (VWP), visas are not required for citizens of 38 countries for stays up to 90 days (no extensions) as long as you have a machine-readable passport that meets current US standards and is valid for six months beyond your intended stay.

○ Citizens of VWP countries must still register with the Electronic System for Travel Authorization (ESTA; https://esta.cbp.dhs.gov) at least 72 hours before travel. Once approved, ESTA registration ($14) is valid for up to two years or until your passport expires, whichever comes first.

○ For most Canadian citizens traveling with Canadian passports that meet current US standards, a visa for short-term visits (usually up to six months) and ESTA registration aren't required.

○ Citizens from all other countries, or whose passports don't meet US standards, need to apply for a visa in their home country. The process has a nonrefundable fee (minimum $160), involves a personal interview and can take several weeks, so apply as early as possible.

○ For up-to-date information about entry requirements and eligibility, check the visa section of the US Department of State website (http://travel.state.

gov), or contact the nearest USA embassy or consulate in your home country (for a complete list, visit www. usembassy.gov).

Transport

Getting There & Away

Getting to California by air or overland by car, train or bus is easy, although it's not always cheap. Flights, cars and tours can be booked online at www.lonelyplanet. com/bookings.

Entering the Region

Under the US Department of Homeland Security's Orwellian-sounding Office of Biometric Identity Management, almost all visitors to the USA (excluding, for now, many Canadians, some Mexican citizens, children under the age of 14 and seniors over the age of 79) will be digitally photographed and have their electronic (inkless) fingerprints scanned upon arrival.

Regardless of your visa status, immigration officers have absolute authority to refuse entry to the USA. They may ask about your plans and whether you have sufficient funds; it's a good idea to list an itinerary,

produce an onward or round-trip ticket and have at least one major credit card. Don't make too much of having friends, relatives or business contacts in the US, because officers may think this makes you more likely to overstay. For more information, visit the US Customs and Border Protection website (www. cbp.gov).

California is an important agricultural state. To prevent the spread of pests and diseases, certain food items (including meats, fresh fruit and vegetables) may not be brought into the state. Bakery items, chocolates and hard-cured cheeses are admissible. If you drive into California from Mexico, or from the neighboring states of Oregon, Nevada or Arizona, you may have to stop for a quick questioning and inspection by California Department of Food and Agriculture (www.cdfa. ca.gov) agents.

Air

o To get through airport security checkpoints (30- to 45-minute wait times are standard), you'll need a boarding pass and photo ID.

o Some travelers may be required to undergo a secondary screening, involving hand pat downs and carry-on-bag searches.

o Airport security measures restrict many common items (eg pocket knives, scissors) from being carried on planes. Check current restrictions with the Transportation Security Administration (TSA; www. tsa.gov).

o Currently TSA requires that all carry-on liquids and gels be stored in 3oz or smaller bottles placed inside a quart-sized clear plastic zip-top bag. Exceptions, which must be declared to checkpoint security officers, include medications.

Climate Change & Travel

Every form of transport that relies on carbon-based fuel generates CO_2, the main cause of human-induced climate change. Modern travel is dependent on airplanes, which might use less fuel per kilometre per person than most cars but travel much greater distances. The altitude at which aircraft emit gases (including CO_2) and particles also contributes to their climate change impact. Many websites offer 'carbon calculators' that allow people to estimate the carbon emissions generated by their journey and, for those who wish to do so, to offset the impact of the greenhouse gases emitted with contributions to portfolios of climate-friendly initiatives throughout the world. Lonely Planet offsets the carbon footprint of all staff and author travel.

o All checked luggage is screened for explosives. TSA may open your suitcase for visual confirmation, breaking the lock if necessary. Leave your bags unlocked or use a TSA-approved lock.

Airports

California's major international airports are **Los Angeles International Airport** (LAX; www.lawa.org/welcomeLAX.aspx; 1 World Way) in Southern California and **San Francisco International Airport** (SFO; www.flysfo.com; S McDonnell Rd) in Northern California. Smaller regional airports throughout the state are mainly served by domestic US airlines. Many domestic and international air carriers offer direct flights to and from California.

Land

Bus

Greyhound (www.greyhound.com) is the major long-distance bus company, with routes throughout the USA, including to/from California. Routes trace major highways and may stop only at larger population centers, with services to many small towns having been cut.

Train

Amtrak (www.amtrak.com) operates a fairly extensive rail system throughout the USA. Trains are comfortable, if a bit slow, and are equipped with dining and lounge cars and sometimes wi-fi on long-distance routes. Fares vary according to the type of train and seating (eg coach or business class, sleeping compartments).

Amtrak's major long-distance services to/from California:

California Zephyr Daily service between Chicago and Emeryville (from $136, 52 hours), near San Francisco, via Denver, Salt Lake City, Reno, Truckee and Sacramento.

Coast Starlight Travels the West Coast daily from Seattle to LA (from $97, 35½ hours) via Portland, Sacramento, Oakland, San Jose, San Luis Obispo and Santa Barbara.

Southwest Chief Daily departures from Chicago and LA (from $141, 43 hours) via Kansas City, Albuquerque, Flagstaff and Barstow.

Sunset Limited Thrice-weekly service between New Orleans and LA (from $136, 46½ hours) via Houston, San Antonio, El Paso, Tucson and Palm Springs.

Getting Around

Most people drive themselves around California. You can also fly (it's expensive) or take cheaper long-distance buses or scenic trains. In cities, when distances are too far to walk, hop aboard buses, trains, streetcars, cable cars or trolleys, or grab a taxi.

Air

Several major US carriers fly within California. Flights are often operated by their regional subsidiaries, such as American Eagle, Delta Connection and United Express. Alaska Airlines/Virgin America, Frontier Airlines, Horizon Air and JetBlue serve many regional airports, as do low-cost airlines Southwest and Spirit.

Bicycle

Although cycling around California is a nonpolluting 'green' way to travel, the distances involved demand a high level of fitness and make it hard to cover much ground. Forget about the deserts in summer and the mountains in winter.

California Bicycle Coalition (http://calbike.org) has links to cycling route maps, events, safety tips, laws, bike-sharing programs and community nonprofit bicycle shops.

Rental

o You can rent bikes by the hour, day or week in most cities and tourist towns.

o Rentals start at around $10 per day for beach cruisers, and up to $45 or more for mountain bikes; ask about multiday and weekly discounts.

o Most rental companies require a large security deposit using a credit card.

Road Rules

o Cycling is allowed on all roads and highways – even along freeways if there's no suitable alternative, such as a smaller parallel frontage road; all mandatory exits are marked.

o Some cities have designated bicycle lanes, but make sure you have your wits about you in traffic.

o Cyclists must follow the same rules of the road as vehicles. Don't expect drivers to always respect your right of way.

o Wearing a bicycle helmet is mandatory for riders under 18 years of age.

o Ensure you have proper lights and reflective gear, especially if you're pedaling at night or in fog.

Bus

Greyhound buses are an economical way to travel between major cities and to points along the coast, but won't get you off the beaten path or to national parks or small towns. Frequency of service varies from rarely to constantly, but the main routes have service several times daily.

Greyhound buses are usually clean, comfortable and reliable. The best seats are typically near the front, away from the bathroom. Limited on-board amenities include freezing air-con (bring a sweater) and slightly reclining seats, and select buses have electrical outlets and wi-fi. Smoking on board is prohibited. Long-distance buses stop for meal breaks and driver changes.

Bus stations are typically dreary, and often in dodgy areas – if you arrive at night, take a taxi into town or to your lodgings. In small towns where there is no bus station, know exactly where and when the bus arrives, be obvious as you flag it down and pay the driver with exact change.

Car, Motorcycle & Recreational Vehicle

California's love affair with cars runs deep for at least one practical reason: the state is so big, public transportation can't cover it. For flexibility and convenience, you'll probably want a car, but rental rates and gas prices can eat up a good chunk of your trip budget.

Driver's Licenses

o Visitors may legally drive a car in California for up to 12 months with their home driver's license.

o If you're from overseas, an International Driving Permit (IDP) will have more credibility with traffic police and simplify the car-rental process, especially if your license doesn't have a photo or isn't written in English.

o To ride a motorcycle, you'll need a valid US state motorcycle license, or a specially endorsed IDP.

o International automobile associations can issue IDPs, valid for one year, for a fee. Always carry your home license together with the IDP.

Fuel

o Gas stations in California, nearly all of which are self-service, are ubiquitous, except in national and state parks and some sparsely populated desert and mountain areas.

o Gas is sold in gallons (one US gallon equals 3.78L). At the time of writing, the average cost for mid-grade fuel was around $3 a gallon.

Insurance

California law requires liability insurance for all vehicles. When renting a car, check your auto-insurance policy from home or your travel insurance policy to see if you're already covered. If not, expect to pay about $20 per day.

Insurance against damage to the car itself, called Collision Damage Waiver (CDW) or Loss Damage Waiver (LDW), costs another $10 to $20 or more per day. The deductible may require you to pay the first $100 to $500 for any repairs.

Some credit cards cover CDW/LDW, provided you charge the entire cost of the car rental to the card. Check with your credit-card issuer first to determine the extent of coverage and policy exclusions. If there's an

Road Distances (Miles)

	Anaheim	Arcata	Bakersfield	Death Valley	Las Vegas	Los Angeles	Monterey	Napa	Palm Springs	Redding	Sacramento	San Diego	San Francisco	San Luis Obispo	Santa Barbara	Sth Lake Tahoe
Arcata	680															
Bakersfield	135	555														
Death Valley	285	705	235													
Las Vegas	265	840	285	140												
Los Angeles	25	650	110	290	270											
Monterey	370	395	250	495	535	345										
Napa	425	265	300	545	590	400	150									
Palm Springs	95	760	220	300	280	110	450	505								
Redding	570	140	440	565	725	545	315	190	650							
Sacramento	410	300	280	435	565	385	185	60	490	160						
San Diego	95	770	230	350	330	120	465	520	140	665	505					
San Francisco	405	280	285	530	570	380	120	50	490	215	85	500				
San Luis Obispo	225	505	120	365	405	200	145	265	310	430	290	320	230			
Santa Barbara	120	610	145	350	360	95	250	370	205	535	395	215	335	105		
Sth Lake Tahoe	505	400	375	345	460	480	285	160	485	260	100	600	185	390	495	
Yosemite	335	465	200	300	415	310	200	190	415	325	160	430	190	230	345	190

accident, you may have to pay the rental-car company first, then seek reimbursement from the credit-card company.

Parking

○ Parking is usually plentiful and free in small towns and rural areas, but often scarce and/or expensive in cities.

○ When parking on the street, read all posted regulations and restrictions (eg street-cleaning hours, permit-only residential areas) and pay attention to colored curbs, or you may be ticketed and towed.

○ You can pay municipal parking meters and sidewalk pay stations with coins (eg quarters) and sometimes credit or debit cards.

○ Expect to pay $30 to $50 for overnight parking in a city lot or garage.

○ Flat-fee valet parking at hotels, restaurants, nightclubs etc is common in major cities, especially Los Angeles and Las Vegas, NV.

Rental

Cars

To rent your own wheels, you'll typically need to be at least 25 years old, hold a valid driver's license and have a major credit card, not a check or debit card. A few companies may rent to drivers under 25 years, but over 21 for a hefty surcharge. If you don't have a credit card, large cash deposits are infrequently accepted.

With advance reservations, you can often get an economy-size vehicle with unlimited mileage from around $30 per day, plus insurance, taxes and fees. Weekend and weekly rates are usually the most economical. Airport locations may have cheaper rates, but higher add-on fees; if you get a fly-drive package, local taxes may be extra when you pick up the car. City-center branches sometimes offer free pickups and drop-offs.

Rates generally include unlimited mileage, but expect surcharges for additional drivers and one-way rentals. Child or infant safety seats are legally required; reserve them when booking for $10 to $15 per day.

If you'd like to minimize your carbon footprint, some major car-rental companies offer 'green' fleets of hybrid or biofueled rental cars, but these fuel-efficient models are in short supply. Reserve them well in advance and expect to pay significantly higher rates.

All of the major car-rental companies are represented in California. To find and compare independent car-rental companies, try Car Rental Express (www.carrentalexpress.com).

Motorcycles

Motorcycle rentals and insurance are not cheap, especially if you've got your eye on a Harley. Depending on the model, renting a motorcycle costs $100 to $250 per day plus taxes and fees, including helmets, unlimited miles and liability insurance; one-way rentals and collision insurance (CDW) cost extra. Discounts may be available for multiday and weekly rentals. Security deposits

range up to $2000 (credit card required).

California Motorcycle Adventures (800-601-5370, 650-969-6198; www.california motorcycleadventures.com; 2554 W Middlefield Rd, Mountain View) Harley-Davidson and BMW rentals in Silicon Valley.

Dubbelju (415-495-2774, 866-495-2774; www.dubbelju. com; 274 Shotwell St; per day from $99; 9am-6pm Mon-Sat) Rents Harley-Davidson, Japanese and European imported motorcycles, as well as scooters.

Eagle Rider (888-900-9901, 310-321-3180; www.eaglerider. com) Nationwide company with 11 locations in California, as well as Las Vegas, NV.

Recreational Vehicles

Gas-guzzling recreational vehicles (RVs) remain popular despite fuel prices and being cumbersome to drive. That said, they do solve transportation, accommodation and cooking needs in one fell swoop. It's easy to find RV campgrounds with electricity and water hookups, yet there are many places in national and state parks and in the mountains they can't go. In cities RVs are a nuisance, because there are few places to park or plug them in.

Book RVs as far in advance as possible. Rental costs vary by size and model, but you can expect to pay more than $100 per day. Rates often don't include mileage, bedding or kitchen kits, vehicle-prep

fees or taxes. If pets are allowed, a surcharge may apply.

Camper USA (310-929-5666; www.camperusa.com) Campervan rentals in the San Francisco Bay Area, LA and Las Vegas, NV.

Cruise America (480-464-7300, 800-671-8042; www. cruiseamerica.com) Nationwide RV-rental company with 20 locations statewide.

El Monte (562-483-4985, 888-337-2214; www.elmonterv. com) With over a dozen locations in California, this national RV-rental agency offers AAA discounts.

Escape Campervans (877-270-8267, 310-672-9909; www. escapecampervans.com) Awesomely painted campervans at economical rates in the San Francisco Bay Area, LA and Las Vegas, NV.

Jucy Rentals (800-650-4180; www.jucyrentals.com) Campervan rentals in the San Francisco Bay Area, LA and Las Vegas, NV.

Road Bear (866-491-9853, 818-865-2925; www.roadbearrv. com) RV rentals in the San Francisco Bay Area and LA.

Vintage Surfari Wagons (714-585-7565; www.vwsurf ari.com) VW campervan rentals in Orange County.

Road Conditions & Hazards

For up-to-date highway conditions, including road closures and construction updates, check with the **California Department of Transportation** (CalTrans; 800-427-7623; www.dot.

ca.gov). For Nevada highways, call ☏877-687-6237 or check www.nvroads.com.

In places where winter driving is an issue, snow tires and tire chains may be required in mountain areas. Ideally, carry your own chains and learn how to use them before you hit the road. Otherwise, chains can usually be bought or rented (but not cheaply) on the highway, at gas stations or in the nearest town. Most car-rental companies don't permit the use of chains and also prohibit driving off-road or on dirt roads.

In rural areas, livestock sometimes graze next to unfenced roads. These areas are typically signed as 'Open Range,' with the silhouette of a steer. Where deer and other wild animals frequently appear roadside, you'll see signs with the silhouette of a leaping deer. Take these signs seriously, particularly at night.

In coastal areas thick fog may impede driving – slow down and if it's too soupy, get off the road. Along coastal cliffs and in the mountains, watch out for falling rocks, mudslides and avalanches that could damage or disable your car if struck.

Road Rules

• Drive on the right-hand side of the road.

• Talking, texting or otherwise using a cell (mobile) phone or other mobile electronic device without hands-free technology while driving is illegal.

• The driver and all passengers must use seat belts in a private vehicle. In a taxi or limo, back-seat passengers are not required to buckle up.

• Infant and child safety seats are required for children under eight years of age, or who are less than 4ft 9in tall.

• All motorcyclists must wear a helmet. Scooters are not allowed on freeways.

• High-occupancy (HOV) lanes marked with a diamond symbol are reserved for cars with multiple occupants, sometimes only during signposted hours.

• Unless otherwise posted, the speed limit is 65mph on freeways, 55mph on two-lane undivided highways, 35mph on major city streets and 25mph in business and residential districts and near schools.

• Except where indicated, turning right at a red stoplight after coming to a full stop is permitted, although intersecting traffic still has the right of way.

• At four-way stop signs, cars proceed in the order in which they arrived. If two cars arrive simultaneously, the one on the right has the right of way. When in doubt, politely wave the other driver ahead.

• When emergency vehicles (ie police, fire or ambulance) approach from either direction, carefully pull over to the side of the road.

• Driving under the influence of alcohol or drugs is illegal. It's also illegal to carry open containers of alcohol, even empty ones, inside a vehicle. Store them in the trunk.

Local Transportation

Except in cities, public transit is rarely the most convenient option, and coverage to outlying towns and suburbs can be sparse. However, it's usually cheap, safe and reliable.

Bicycle

• Cycling is a feasible way of getting around smaller cities and towns, but it's not much fun in traffic-dense areas such as LA.

• San Francisco, Napa, Arcata, South Lake Tahoe, West Sacramento, Chico and Santa Monica are among California's most bike-friendly communities, as rated by the League of American Bicyclists (www.bikeleague.org).

• Bicycles may be transported on many local buses and trains, sometimes during off-peak, non-commuter hours only.

Bus, Cable Car, Streetcar & Trolley

• Almost all cities and larger towns have reliable local bus systems (average $1 to $3 per ride). Outside of major metro areas, they may provide only limited evening and weekend service.

○ San Francisco's extensive Municipal Railway (MUNI) network includes not only buses and trains, but also historic streetcars and those famous cable cars.

○ San Diego runs trolleys around some neighborhoods and to the Mexican border.

Train

○ LA Metro is a combined, ever-expanding network of subway and light-rail trains around Los Angeles. Metrolink commuter trains connect LA with surrounding counties.

○ San Diego's Coaster commuter trains run from downtown and Old Town to Carlsbad, Encinitas, Solana Beach and Oceanside in the North County.

○ To get around the San Francisco Bay Area, hop aboard Bay Area Rapid Transit (BART) or Caltrain.

Taxi

○ Taxis are metered, with flag-fall fees of $2.50 to $3.50 to start, plus around $2 to $3 per mile. Credit cards may be accepted, but bring cash just in case.

○ Taxis may charge extra for baggage and airport pickups.

○ Drivers expect a 10% to 15% tip, rounded up to the next dollar.

○ Taxis cruise the streets of the busiest areas in large cities, but elsewhere you may need to call for one.

Train

Amtrak runs comfortable, if occasionally tardy, trains to major California cities and some towns. Amtrak's Thruway buses provide onward connections from many train stations. Smoking is prohibited aboard trains and buses.

Behind the Scenes

Acknowledgements

Climate map data adapted from Peel MC, Finlayson BL & McMahon TA (2007) 'Updated World Map of the Köppen-Geiger Climate Classification', Hydrology and Earth System Sciences, 11, 163344.
Illustration pp44–45 by Michael Weldon.

This Book

This guidebook was curated by Nate Cavalieri, and researched and written by Brett Atkinson, Andrew Bender, Sara Benson, Alison Bing, Cristian Bonetto, Jade Bremner, Michael Grosberg, Ashley Harrell, Josephine Quintero, Andrea Schulte-Peevers, Helena Smith, John A Vlahides and Clifton Wilkinson. This guidebook was produced by the following:

Destination Editors Clifton Wilkinson, Sarah Stocking

Product Editors Will Allen, Rachel Rawling

Senior Cartographer Alison Lyall

Book Designer Nicholas Colicchia

Assisting Editors Sarah Bailey, Andrew Bain, Judith Bamber, Andrea Dobbin, Carly Hall, Victoria Harrison, Kellie Langdon, Jodie Martire, Saralinda Turner

Assisting Cartographer Corey Hutchison

Cover Researcher Brendan Dempsey-Spencer

Thanks to Sasha Drew, Filomena Losi, Kate Mathews, Lyahna Spencer, Tony Wheeler

Send Us Your Feedback

We love to hear from travelers – your comments keep us on our toes and help make our books better. Our well-traveled team reads every word on what you loved or loathed about this book. Although we cannot reply individually to postal submissions, we always guarantee that your feedback goes straight to the appropriate authors, in time for the next edition. Each person who sends us information is thanked in the next edition, the most useful submissions are rewarded with a selection of digital PDF chapters.

Visit lonelyplanet.com/contact to submit your updates and suggestions or to ask for help. Our award-winning website also features inspirational travel stories, news and discussions.

Note: We may edit, reproduce and incorporate your comments in Lonely Planet products such as guidebooks, websites and digital products, so let us know if you don't want your comments reproduced or your name acknowledged. For a copy of our privacy policy visit lonelyplanet.com/privacy.

A – Z

Index

000 Map pages

Symbols & Map Key

Look for these symbols to quickly identify listings:

- ⊚ Sights
- ⊕ Activities
- ⊖ Courses
- ⊙ Tours
- ⊛ Festivals & Events
- ⊗ Eating
- ⊖ Drinking
- ⊛ Entertainment
- ⊖ Shopping
- ⊕ Information & Transport

These symbols and abbreviations give vital information for each listing:

- ⊘ Sustainable or green recommendation
- **FREE** No payment required

- ☏ Telephone number
- ⊙ Opening hours
- P Parking
- ⊖ Nonsmoking
- ✳ Air-conditioning
- @ Internet access
- ⊚ Wi-fi access
- ⊠ Swimming pool
- ⊡ Bus
- ⊡ Ferry
- ⊡ Tram
- ⊡ Train
- ⊡ English-language menu
- ⊘ Vegetarian selection
- ⊞ Family-friendly

Find your best experiences with these Great For... icons.

- Art & Culture
- Beaches
- Budget
- Cafe/Coffee
- Cycling
- Detour
- Drinking
- Entertainment
- Events
- Family Travel
- Food & Drink
- History
- Local Life
- Nature & Wildlife
- Photo Op
- Scenery
- Shopping
- Short Trip
- Sport
- Walking
- Winter Travel

Sights

- ⊚ Beach
- ⊚ Bird Sanctuary
- ⊚ Buddhist
- ⊚ Castle/Palace
- ⊚ Christian
- ⊚ Confucian
- ⊚ Hindu
- ⊚ Islamic
- ⊚ Jain
- ⊚ Jewish
- ⊚ Monument
- ⊚ Museum/Gallery/ Historic Building
- ⊚ Ruin
- ⊚ Shinto
- ⊚ Sikh
- ⊚ Taoist
- ⊚ Winery/Vineyard
- ⊚ Zoo/Wildlife Sanctuary
- ⊚ Other Sight

Points of Interest

- ⊚ Bodysurfing
- ⊚ Camping
- ⊚ Cafe
- ⊚ Canoeing/Kayaking
- • Course/Tour
- ⊚ Diving
- ⊚ Drinking & Nightlife
- ⊗ Eating
- ⊚ Entertainment
- ⊚ Sento Hot Baths/ Onsen
- ⊚ Shopping
- ⊚ Skiing
- ⊚ Sleeping
- ⊚ Snorkelling
- ⊚ Surfing
- ⊚ Swimming/Pool
- ⊚ Walking
- ⊚ Windsurfing
- ⊚ Other Activity

Information

- ⊚ Bank
- ⊚ Embassy/Consulate
- ⊚ Hospital/Medical
- @ Internet
- ⊚ Police
- ⊚ Post Office
- ⊚ Telephone
- ⊚ Toilet
- ⊕ Tourist Information
- • Other Information

Geographic

- ⊚ Beach
- ⊷ Gate
- ⊚ Hut/Shelter
- ⊚ Lighthouse
- ⊚ Lookout
- ▲ Mountain/Volcano
- ⊚ Oasis
- ⊕ Park
-)(Pass
- ⊚ Picnic Area
- ⊚ Waterfall

Transport

- ⊚ Airport
- ⊚ BART station
- ⊚ Border crossing
- ⊚ Boston T station
- ⊚ Bus
- ⊹⊚⊹ Cable car/Funicular
- ⊶⊚ Cycling
- ⊖ Ferry
- ⊚ Metro/MRT station
- ⊶⊚⊷ Monorail
- P Parking
- ⊚ Petrol station
- ⊚ Subway/S-Bahn/ Skytrain station
- ⊚ Taxi
- ⊹⊚⊹ Train station/Railway
- ⋈⋈⋈⋈ Tram
- ⊚ Tube Station
- ⊚ Underground/ U-Bahn station
- • Other Transport

Sara Benson

Survival Guide After graduating from college in Chicago, Sara jumped on a plane to California with one suitcase and just $100 in her pocket. Today she makes her home in Oakland. The author of more than 70 travel and non-fiction books, she has written for Lonely Planet guides covering Peru, Japan, Malaysia, Las Vegas, California, Southwest USA, Canada, Australia and Hawaii.

Alison Bing

San Francisco Over 10 guidebooks and 20 years in San Francisco, author Alison has spent more time on Alcatraz than some inmates, become an aficionado of drag and burritos, and willfully ignored Muni signs warning that safety requires avoiding unnecessary conversation. Alison also contributed to the Plan Your Trip and In Focus sections.

Cristian Bonetto

Los Angeles Cristian has contributed to over 30 Lonely Planet guides to date, covering New York City, Italy, Venice and the Veneto, Naples and the Amalfi Coast, Denmark, Copenhagen, Sweden and Singapore. His writing has appeared in numerous publications around the world, including the *Telegraph* (UK) and *Corriere del Mezzogiorno* (Italy). He lives in Melbourne, Australia.

Jade Bremner

San Diego Jade has been a journalist for more than a decade. Wherever she goes she finds action sports to try – the weirder the better – and it's no coincidence many of her favorite places have some of the best waves in the world. Jade has edited travel magazines and sections for *Time Out* and *Radio Times* and has been a correspondent for the *Times, CNN* and the *Independent*.

Michael Grosberg

Yosemite National Park Michael has worked on over 45 Lonely Planet guidebooks, from Myanmar to New Jersey. Other work has included development on the island of Rota in the western Pacific, writing about political violence in South Africa and teaching in Ecuador. He has a Masters in Comparative Literature, and taught literature and writing as an adjunct professor at several New York colleges.

Ashley Harrell

Sonoma Valley After a brief stint selling day-spa coupons door-to-door in South Florida, Ashley decided she'd rather be a writer. She has traveled widely and moved often, from a tiny NYC apartment to a vast California ranch to a jungle cabin in Costa Rica,

where she started writing for Lonely Planet. Her travels since became more exotic and farther-flung, and she still laughs when paychecks arrive.

Josephine Quintero

Redwood Forests; Coastal Highway 1 Josephine began her journalism career with a Napa Valley wine-and-lifestyle magazine. This was followed, ironically, with a move to 'dry' Kuwait, where she was editor of the *Kuwaiti Digest* for six years until August 1, 1990 – the day Iraq invaded. After six weeks as a hostage and escape to Turkey, Josephine moved to Andalucia, where she mainly earned a crust as a ghostwriter.

Andrea Schulte-Peevers

Palm Springs Andrea has traveled the distance to the moon and back in her visits to some 75 countries. Born and raised in Germany and educated in London and at UCLA, she has earned her living as a professional travel writer for over two decades and authored or contributed to nearly 100 Lonely Planet titles, as well as to newspapers, magazines and websites around the world. She also works as a travel consultant, translator and editor.

Helena Smith

Lake Tahoe Helena is an award-winning writer and photographer, and has written guidebooks on destinations from Fiji to Norway. Helena is from Scotland but was partly brought up in Malawi, so Africa always feels like home. She also enjoys her multicultural home area of Hackney and wrote, photographed and published *Inside Hackney*, the first guide to the borough (https://insidehackney.com).

John A Vlahides

San Francisco John has been a cook in a Parisian bordello, a luxury-hotel concierge, a television host, a safety monitor in a sex club and a French–English interpreter, and he is one of Lonely Planet's most experienced guidebook authors. A native New Yorker living in San Francisco, John has contributed to about 20 Lonely Planet guidebooks since 2003. He also cohosted the TV series Lonely Planet: Roads Less Travelled.

Clifton Wilkinson

Santa Barbara Christmases spent near Sacramento, bike rides across the Golden Gate Bridge and hiking in Yosemite National Park have all reinforced Clifton's opinion that the Golden State is the best state in the whole US, and Santa Barbara is one of its most beautiful corners. Having worked for Lonely Planet for more than 11 years, he's now based in the London office.

Our Story

A beat-up old car, a few dollars in the pocket and a sense of adventure. In 1972 that's all Tony and Maureen Wheeler needed for the trip of a lifetime – across Europe and Asia overland to Australia. It took several months, and at the end – broke but inspired – they sat at their kitchen table writing and stapling together their first travel guide, *Across Asia on the Cheap*. Within a week they'd sold 1500 copies. Lonely Planet was born.

Today, Lonely Planet has offices in Franklin, London, Melbourne, Oakland, Dublin, Beijing, and Delhi, with more than 600 staff and writers. We share Tony's belief that 'a great guidebook should do three things: inform, educate and amuse'.

Our Writers

Nate Cavalieri

Curator Nate is a writer and musician based in Oakland, California, and has authored over a dozen titles for Lonely Planet including guides to California, the Caribbean and Latin America, and *Epic Bike Rides of the World*. He's cycled across China and Southern Africa as a guide with Tour d'Afrique, played third chair percussion in an Orlando theme park and accompanied modern dance classes.

Brett Atkinson

Big Sur Brett is based in Auckland, New Zealand, but is frequently on the road for Lonely Planet. He's a full-time travel and food writer, and is featured regularly on the Lonely Planet website and in newspapers, magazines and websites across New Zealand and Australia. Since becoming a Lonely Planet author in 2005, Brett has covered areas as diverse as Vietnam, Sri Lanka, the Czech Republic, New Zealand, Morocco, California and the South Pacific.

Andrew Bender

Los Angeles; Orange County An award-winning travel and food writer, Andrew has written three dozen Lonely Planet guidebooks, plus numerous articles for lonelyplanet.com. Outside of Lonely Planet, he writes the Seat 1A travel site for Forbes.com and is a frequent contributor to the *Los Angeles Times*, in-flight magazines and more. Andrew has lived in Japan, France and the Netherlands; a native New Englander, he now lives in the Los Angeles area.

More Writers

STAY IN TOUCH LONELYPLANET.COM/CONTACT

AUSTRALIA The Malt Store, Level 3, 551 Swanston St, Carlton, Victoria 3053
☎03 8379 8000,
fax 03 8379 8111

IRELAND Digital Depot, Roe Lane (off Thomas St), Digital Hub, Dublin 8, D08 TCV4, Ireland

USA 124 Linden Street, Oakland, CA 94607
☎510 250 6400,
toll free 800 275 8555,
fax 510 893 8572

UK 240 Blackfriars Road, London SE1 8NW
☎020 3771 5100,
fax 020 3771 5101

 twitter.com/lonelyplanet

 facebook.com/lonelyplanet

 instagram.com/lonelyplanet

 youtube.com/lonelyplanet

 lonelyplanet.com/newsletter